MADMAN

The Incredible True Story of John Calvin "Rastus" Russell,
the Heinous Crime, and Sensational Manhunt that
Terrified Central Florida in 1949

M.F. Gross

MINDSTIR MEDIA

Published by MindStir Media, LLC
45 Lafayette Rd | Suite 181 | North Hampton, NH 03862 | USA
1.800.767.0531 | www.mindstirmedia.com

Printed in the United States of America.
ISBN: 978-1-967458-52-3 (Paperback)
       978-1-967458-53-0 (Hardcover)

Dedication

*T*his book is dedicated to the hard-working men and women of Pinellas and Hillsborough County, Florida Law Enforcement, past and present. Your job gets harder every day. Yet you do it with integrity and professionalism.

Introduction

While I have authored non-fiction books before, I have never authored a historical true crime book.

In fact, I never planned, nor set out to become a "true crime" author. Rather, I came across a true story so mesmerizing, so unbelievable, and at the same time so utterly chilling that it ate at me for years until I finally decided to dive in and discover the real story for myself.

You see, I have been told that the best way to become an expert on a topic is to write a book about it. I so desperately wanted to learn what really happened, I decided to write a book for myself.

You, the reader, will be the beneficiary of my own selfish project of discovering the true story of what was, until now, a local legend in my hometown.

I lived in Crystal Beach, Florida, for twelve years, moving just outside the tiny community in 2019. I still visit often.

Sometime in 2017, I picked up a copy of a local book called *Crystal Beach Shangri-La*. It was a collection of stories from old-time residents, telling tales of their pasts and memories of growing up in this charming little beach community on the Gulf Coast of Florida.

Amidst the fond memories of swimming in the tropical waters, teenage hijinks, and community picnics, I stumbled across a story of a more macabre nature.

It was the story of a horrific and bloody murder that rocked the tiny village in 1949, and the incredible manhunts that followed. The suspect was a former convict and asylum patient. Captured, escaped, and on the run again, the fear of him terrified the entire county for nearly a month.

What really sucked me in, however, was the description by long-time Crystal Beach resident Linda Henry. Ms. Henry penned a short piece in the book about her memory of the bloody murder near her childhood home. Henry was six years old when the murder took place.

"As a small child, I can remember looking into the house, seeing all of the blood through the bedroom window," she recalls in the piece. *"...Plus, out in the detached garage where Mr. Browne was taken, there was a lot of blood. To this day, I can go down into that area of Crystal Beach, and there is a smell that comes over me that triggers that incident."*

"Oh wow," I thought, "That is REALLY creepy."

Later, when researching the story, I came across a police officer's description of the smell of blood that permeated the house in the summer heat. Could that be the smell to which she is referring?

Even creepier.

I had the privilege of corresponding with Ms. Henry for this book and her consultation has been most invaluable.

Imagine my surprise to learn, through her and others, that the house in which this unsettling crime occurred stood on a spot only 100 yards from my former home. The location was a place I crossed nearly every day while walking my dog, clueless as to the carnage that had stained its history.

Perhaps it was psychological, but now I got a strange feeling every time I passed it.

My interest was rekindled when, earlier this year, a site near this murder house once stood was being excavated. A new owner was building a house on the site that had remained vacant and wooded for so many years.

I did some initial research and learned the story was not only a local legend but that nearly every old-time resident either remembered or participated in it. Not only that, but the *real* story ran much, much deeper than the local legends.

I was hooked. My first thought was, "My God, this is a movie!"

But let's start with a book.

This is the story of Rastus Russell, a thirty-four-year-old criminal and former mental patient, and his day-long torture of

---

* *Crystal Beach: Gulf Coast Shangri-la and Other Nearby Places,* by Francine Larson and William A. Wisner, 2018

seventy-five-year-old Norman Y. Browne and his wife, Anne. Three other innocents were then unknowingly drawn into the carnage.

The year was 1949. The month was August. Television is in its infancy, and most homes still rely on radio for news and entertainment. Doris Day, Mel Torme, and Bing Crosby soothe the nation through songs on the airwaves. Minimum wage has just been raised to a lofty 75 cents an hour. Gasoline is 17 cents per gallon.

Crime fighting, while less advanced than today, was also more straightforward. The country had just emerged from World War II. Optimism reigned. Crystal Beach, Florida, was a tiny, beachside utopia consisting of close-knit residents, many of whom considered each other family. Crime was virtually nonexistent in the community. Kids played outdoors all summer, all day. They often ate dinner at whoever's house they happened to be when the hour struck. Doors and windows were left unlocked all night, with never a thought given.

The stark contrast between this shocking event and this tropical Eden made it all the more horrifying to those who experienced it.

But the crime, horrific as it was, is only the beginning of this incredible and, at times, almost unbelievable story. In it, we see heroic lawmen, struggling with the limitations of their tools of the time, driving themselves to near exhaustion to catch the killer. We find a murderer who has a complicated and mysterious past, who not only manages to stay one step ahead of his pursuers but seems to have a guardian angel watching over him, either spiritual or a living, breathing person or people. We discover a frightened and yet determined public, taking to the streets and woods with weapons to track down the heinous criminal. And it's all wrapped in a strange and twisted love story, the depths of which we may never know.

The case of Rastus Russell was the biggest, most sensational murder and manhunt ever to occur on Florida's West Coast up to 1949, and maybe even through today. Of all the residents I have interviewed who lived here at the time, there was not a single one who did not remember the event. It was etched in their memories like a rock carving.

Through these tales, there was one word that kept coming up each time the story was retold from their childhood memories:

Terrified.

My goal in this book is to not only untangle these legends and tell the true story of their childhood Freddy Kruger. My goal is to introduce this story to a worldwide audience.

It really is that good.

After reading it, I think you will agree that truth is stranger than fiction. Neither I nor any other author could ever make this up.

Enjoy.

-M.F. Gross
January 2025
Dunedin, FL

1

August 7, 1949
5:45 a.m.
Crystal Beach, FL

W hen Norman Young Browne awakens on this steamy Florida morning, he has no idea he has just done so for the last time.

At seventy-four, Browne lives a quiet life in a quiet place. The retired Edison Power Company inspector is a first-generation immigrant to the United States. As a young boy in the early 1880s, Browne moved to the Bronx, New York City, with his parents and siblings from Scotland. Only two years earlier, he and his wife Anne, sixty, remarried after being divorced for several years.

Norman and Anne first married in New York City in 1905. Their marriage produces a daughter, Elizabeth Marie Browne. Several years later, the Brownes divorce.

Norman then married Grace Lane in New Jersey.

In October 1946, the two moved to a home in the tiny seaside enclave of Crystal Beach, Florida, to enjoy retirement.

However, on April 9, 1947, only seven months after moving to Florida, Grace Lane Browne died. Her obituary states only that she died in a nursing home near Crystal Beach. She is sixty-two.

Shortly thereafter, Norman Browne returned to New York City, where he reconnected with his first wife, Anne. Seventy-seven days after his second wife's death, Norman Browne remarried Anne in New York City.

Born Anna Elizabeth Costello, the retired machine operator, agreed to move back to Florida with her former and present husband. The couple's daughter, twenty-eight-year-old Elizabeth "Betty" Browne, remained in New York.

Nestled within sprawling seas of orange groves and cattle pastures on Florida's Gulf Coast, Crystal Beach seemed like the perfect place for the Brownes to spend their golden years. Located in the heart of Florida's citrus belt, Pinellas County, the community is bordered on one side by St. Joseph's Sound, an inlet of the Gulf of Mexico, and Tampa Bay, seventeen miles to its southeast.

The Brownes have many friends in a community made up of friends. Most everyone knows and socializes with one another. Crime is virtually unheard of. Doors are left unlocked and windows open, even at night, and especially during the hot summer months. In 1949, the sea breeze from the nearby sound is the only air conditioning in Crystal Beach. While the main roads are paved, most streets are made of sand, some topped with a layer of crushed seashells, the most economical gravel at the time.

In addition to socializing, entertainment often comes from the clean, clear waters surrounding the community. The fertile grass beds of the flats team with mollusks, mullet, snook, redfish, and sea trout.

Scalloping is a favorite pastime of many locals. When the tide recedes, residents don bathing suits and wade through the ankle-deep muck into the grass beds of St. Joseph's Sound. There, standing in the knee-to-waist-deep water, they can reach down into clearings of seagrass and pluck a virtually unlimited supply of succulent scallops. The mollusks are tossed into a floating washtub pulled behind the scalloper with a rope tied to his or her waist. A couple of scallopers can fill a washtub in a few hours. The tiny animals are deshelled later and either canned in glass jars or enjoyed fresh – sometimes roasted over an open fire.

Whether scalloping, fishing, snorkeling, boating, swimming, or spearfishing, Crystal Beach residents have an ample source of food and enjoyment only feet from their front doors. In addition to the readily available seafood, local produce is widely available. Orange, grapefruit, lemon, and lime trees grow on nearly every square mile in North Pinellas County. Wild mulberries and blueberries are available by the bucketful in surrounding swamps and cattle pastures for anyone willing to harvest them.

Crystal Beach is surrounded by the unincorporated community of Palm Harbor and the towns of Dunedin and Tarpon Springs. A slightly larger Clearwater is a short drive south. While the tight-knit community is comprised of many full-time families, it shares its paradise with a seasonal influx of affluent "snowbirds." These seasonal residents flock to their seaside winter homes from cold, northern climates.

Norman and Anne Browne live on the isolated edge of this idyllic beach village with their two cats, "Fluffy" and "Kippy." Their old, two-story, wood-frame house sits down a dusty sand path called "Rattlesnake Road."

The Brownes are people of limited means, living off of Norman's fixed retirement pension. They do not own a car. Should they need supplies, they walk the approximate half mile north to Crum's Store. The store is Crystal Beach's only source of sundries, owned by their friends, Miles and Thelma Crum.

For a wider selection of groceries, they can walk further into Palm Harbor to Adair's Grocery Store, the all-purpose general store of the area in 1949. Here, they can buy a dozen eggs for 55 cents or a pound of bacon for 57 cents.

Yet the Brownes may have miscalculated their retirement needs and are struggling financially. As such, Anne Browne has decided to go back to work to help with the bills. She has just arranged a job interview with a business in St. Petersburg.

The couple's faded white house sports batten red accents. It stands amongst tree-filled thickets of moss-draped Oaks, towering Longleaf Pines, Palmetto Palms, twisted vines, thorns, and various brush, homing a variety of local wildlife. The home is known to old timers as "the old Allen house," an apparent reference to the age of the house and its previous owners.

The blue waters of St. Joseph's Sound lie only two blocks away. From their front porch, the Brownes enjoy an inspiring view of Honeymoon Island, a sandy enclave that separates the Gulf of Mexico from the calmer and shallow Sound. Only fifty yards directly in front of the Brownes' home is a saltwater pond where woodland ducks, White Ibis, and red-tailed hawks all mine food from and around its fertile waters.

A small garage, made of the same old wood as the house, sits steps behind the house. Norman Browne has filled it with tools, boxes, lawn equipment, and various other items one might find in a rural home's shed.

Despite the couple's satisfaction with the neighborhood, Norman Browne has pounded a "For Sale" sign into his front yard. There it has remained for the last several months. For unknown reasons, perhaps financial, the couple has decided to sell.

At 6:15 a.m. on this Sunday morning, the Brownes have just finished eating breakfast. The summer sun rose fifteen minutes earlier. Its early morning rays are already pushing through the oak leaves, mangroves, and palm fronds that surround their home. From their open windows, the couple can hear the morning cries of mockingbirds, the coos of mourning doves, and the occasional squawk of a crow.

They are blissfully unaware that their day is about to turn very, very bad.

As Mrs. Brown clears the breakfast table and walks into her kitchen, she pauses to watch a Black 1946 Ford creep past their home towards the nearby bayou.

Anne Browne recognizes the driver.

While she does not remember his name, the homemaker recalls the man stopping by her home about three months prior.[*] He had initially asked for some water to put in his car. Mrs. Browne had taken him to the back of the house where the well pump was located. When the pump didn't work, the man had offered to help Norman Browne repair it. While there, he had inquired about their home for sale.

He told the couple he had a "policeman friend coming down soon" and that the friend might be interested in buying a house.

"I'm looking for a nice, quiet place for me and my friends to stay awhile," he told Mrs. Browne.[**]

When the two could not get the pump to work, Mrs. Browne had directed the stranger to a neighbor's house, where she said he could get water. He left without incident.

---

[*] *At least that is a composite of Mrs. Browne's version of events. In different interviews with both police and newspapers later, Anne Browne changes her story several times as to the reasons why the man visited months earlier and how the couple knew him.*

[**] *The Evening Independent, August 8, 1949*

Browne wonders if the man has come back to arrange a meeting for his friend. She returns to her morning routine.

Fifteen minutes later, the black Ford returns and rolls up into the Brownes' front yard.

From behind the wheel steps one John Calvin "Rastus" Russell.

* * *

With a thick head of bushy black hair, a muscular physique, and striking good looks, the 165-pound Russell has the physical appearance of a movie star or magazine model. But his appearance is a stark contrast to what lurks deep inside.

At thirty-four-years old, Russell is known to many locals and law enforcement officers as a *ne'r do well* and the "bad boy" of Palm Harbor. He is described by some as "slow" and "not very bright." Russell is feared on the streets of Palm Harbor. Many a local will cross to the other side of the street to avoid the man with a reputation for violence.

John Calvin "Rastus" Russell has a long history of trouble with the law. Possibly because of this, he also uses the aliases of James Russell and Jim Sullivan.

In 1925, Russell moved to Palm Harbor at the age of ten with his mother, Claude Estelle Baker Russell. Ms. Russell, a single mother, is a talented artist and painter and a member of the prominent Baker family of Thonotosassa, a farming community east of Tampa. She is familiar with Palm Harbor from her time spent as an art instructor at nearby Southern College years earlier.

Young John quickly develops a reputation as a problem child, getting into fights and other malfeasance, such as torturing small animals. Some begin to suspect that Russell is mentally challenged. Shortly after arriving in Palm Harbor in 1925, he was sent to the state home for the feeble-minded in Gainesville, FL.

It is around this time that Russell is given the nickname that will stick with him for the rest of his days:

"RASTUS."

How or why he acquired the moniker is debatable.

Several old-timers claim Russell escaped from this institution, making it his first escape. While that seems unlikely given the boy's young age, how or why he left the group home is unknown. Regardless, Russell returned to his mother's home in Palm Harbor. Here, he spends his teen years, becoming known to many locals—but not for upstanding reasons.

Thomas T. "T.B." Barlow, Palm Harbor filling station operator and civic leader of the time remembers the young Russell: "He was always into some mean stuff, such as stealing things or beating some other boy."*

John's chiseled physique in later life is not part of his teenage appearance. Russell is remembered as a heavy eater and obesely overweight. One acquaintance estimates the boy weighed as much as 300 pounds in his mid-teens.

He would win bets with other boys by eating up to a dozen hamburgers in one sitting. Another time, he downs twenty half pints of milk in succession. One local resident describes him as being "as broad as he was tall."

Doctors attribute Russell's freakish size to a "glandular imbalance."

In his twenties, Russell grows out of his teenage obesity and into his statuesque appearance. But the childhood ridicule he endures leaves a scar on the boy's mind. As a young man, he does not turn his physical advantages into positive pursuits such as baseball, boxing, or military training.

He occasionally works as a "farm hand," likely in the plentiful orange groves around Palm Harbor. This physically demanding work may have contributed to his weight loss and chiseled physique. He is also known to occasionally work as a mechanic.

As a young man, Russell turns to petty crime. He is known by locals to cross the street from his apartment upstairs at Adairs Grocery Store in Palm Harbor to Stansel's service station, where he steals bottles of cold Yoo-Hoo from the cooler.

Rumors swirl that Russell is responsible for several Model A car thefts in the area. Some claim he took one for a joy ride and then dumped it in "Blue Sink," a local spring hole and favorite swimming spot that is thought to be several hundred feet deep.

---

* *The Tampa Tribune, August 10, 1949.*

Another local story says Russell regularly stands outside his apartment building and stares menacingly at passers-by to goad them into conflict with himself.

Whether the local legends are true or not, Russell is already well known in the Palm Harbor community by the time he is arrested on a breaking and entering charge in 1934.

To this, Russell pleads insanity.

He is examined by a medical committee and declared insane with "hallucinations tending to cruelty." The committee goes as far as to say mechanical restraint is needed to keep Russell from injuring others.

Russell is sent to the state insane hospital in Chattahoochee, FL.[*]

On May 10, 1935, Russell escapes from Chattahoochee and returns to Palm Harbor. For whatever reason, he is not recaptured and sent back.

In 1938, he was arrested for stealing a car in Tampa. Again, Russell pleads insanity. But a jury convicts him, and he is sent to the Florida state prison in Raiford.

In 1939, Raiford sent him back to Chattahoochee for a sanity check. Doctors there decide Russell is "not insane" and "without psychosis." However, they add the caveat that Russell could suffer from a "psychotic personality." At the time, Dr. J.H. Therrell, superintendent of the hospital, explained that Russell could have a "Jekyll and Hyde" personality. This means that Russell could be sane most of the time but with "brief periods of insanity."

Nonetheless, they send him back to Raiford. He does his time and is released.

In the summer of 1941, Russell is involved in an assault and attempted murder of eighty-two-year-old Warren Newbern in Palm Harbor. In an apparent robbery attempt, Russell savagely attacks the old man with a bottle.

Responding to the police call is one constable Rufus Carey.

Constable Carey arrives on scene and confronts Russell. As Carey attempts to arrest him, Russell turns on the constable. A vicious

---

[*] *Chattahoochee later becomes infamous for its cruel and unusual treatment of patients. An investigation into the facility uncovers widespread abuse and leads to nationwide reform in the oversight of mental hospitals. A 1989 movie starring Gary Oldman and Dennis Hopper explores the abuses and investigation that led to the reforms.*

fight ensues between the two in which they roll down a flight of stairs, brawling all the way.

Battered and bruised, Carey eventually subdues Russell. Russell is arrested and charged with attempted murder of Newbern.

Rufus Carey will die six months later.

After being held for nearly three months in county jail, Russell is supposedly called to appear before Judge John U. Bird for a hearing (Bird claims Russell requested a special hearing.) At the hearing, Russell supposedly requests his own release so that he can visit his sick mother in Illinois. Why or if his mother is in Illinois, we do not know. Yet Bird agrees to release the attempted murder suspect on the condition that he pay $107 in court costs and that he leaves the state. He is ordered to report back to the court in December of 1941.

The court provides Russell with a one-way ticket to Akron, Ohio.

The man charged with attempted murder is then released.

Obeying his exit order, Russell departs for Ohio. After a short stay, he ends up in Chicago. He does not report back to the court in December.

In 1942, he was arrested in West Memphis, Arkansas, for auto theft in Chicago. While awaiting trial, he escapes the jail and flees back to Palm Harbor. FBI agents track him and re-arrest him in Pinellas County. Russell is returned to Illinois, convicted, and sentenced to serve one to twenty years in state prison.[*]

While doing his time in Illinois, he is again sent to a mental hospital. In 1949, he was again released.

Russell returns home to Palm Harbor in early 1949. A few months later, he makes his first visit to the Browne's house.

The Brownes, allegedly, have no inkling of Russell's colorful past.

And on this early, muggy August morning, Rastus Russell is once again standing in the driveway of Norman and Anne Browne, admiring their old, wooden house with the well pump out back.

---

[*]   *The Tampa Tribune, August 10, 1949, page 5*

2

Seeing the familiar man in their driveway, Anne Browne asks her husband to go out to see what he wants. Perhaps he is ready to make an offer on the house?

Norman Browne complies.

After exchanging pleasantries, Russell informs Browne that his "police friend" will be arriving on Tuesday or Thursday and would like to see the house.

Browne is delighted. His house has languished on the market for several months.

Mrs. Browne joins the two men.

The morning sun already hints at the brutal heat ahead. The forecast calls for a high of 90 degrees, oppressive humidity, with a good chance of passing thundershowers. Gulf Coast August days are often carbon copies of one another. Today's forecast is the standard. It is uncomfortable standing outdoors.

The Brownes invite Russell inside for a cup of coffee.

As the two men enjoy coffee at the dining room table, Anne Browne busies herself with morning housework. Anne eventually joins them, and the three sit and talk for some time about "all manner of things."

It must be some conversation, for Russell spends over three hours conversing at the Brownes' home.[*]

It is during this time that the local milk delivery man arrives at the Browne residence on his morning route. As he leaves the fresh milk near the Brownes' front door, the man notices Russell at the

---

[*] *Some accounts say Russell tells the couple his friend is coming today, and he is awaiting his friend's arrival.*

house. He remembers seeing Russell near the entrance of Crystal Beach earlier that morning. Something about the stranger's manner disturbs the milkman. He jots down the black Ford's license plate and hurriedly departs.

After coffee, Browne says he'd like to go get a morning paper. Russell offers to drive him in his car. Browne accepts, and the two depart in the Ford.

When the two return, Russell invites Mrs. Browne back to the driveway to have a look at his "new" car.

It is at this time that Anne Browne begins to suspect there is something wrong with Rastus Russell. While Russell stands only 5'9", he carries a menacing air about him. Browne notes a "glassy" look in his eyes that leads her to believe he is "hopped up" on something.*

More alarmingly, Russell then produces a .12-gauge shotgun from the vehicle and hands it to the Brownes to inspect. The weapon has had both the wooden stock and the barrel sawed off, reducing it to nearly half the size of a normal shotgun.

"We had a lot of trouble with him," Mrs. Browne tells authorities the next day from her hospital bed.

The three return to the wood frame house. Russell then asks the Brownes if he can use their bathroom to "wash up."

It is approximately 10:00 am. Rastus Russell has been visiting with Norman and Anne Browne for over three hours. Now, he is back inside their home.

This time, he's not leaving.

* * *

Rattlesnake Road has not been named arbitrarily.

---

*   *The Evening Independent, August 9, 1949. It is not known if Mrs. Browne was referring to the attack in general with this comment or if Russell had become disruptive or belligerent prior to the attack.*

The climate and landscape of Florida's Gulf Coast offers ideal living conditions for the venomous reptiles. The animals thrive in the area's warm, subtropical environment and diverse ecosystem. The abundant availability of prey and variety of ample hiding spots makes Norman Browne's backyard – and, in fact, most of Pinellas County, a prime habitat for rattlesnakes to call home.

For residents of Crystal Beach in 1949, this most often means Eastern Diamondback Rattlesnakes or the tiny but potent Pygmy Rattlesnake. The former is the largest venomous snake in North America, with specimens in the South often reaching six feet or longer. While residents rarely see the slithering reptiles, a thriving population infests the wooded area around Norman Brown's secluded home. Also inhabiting the woods around Crystal Beach are ample populations of raccoons, opossums, and coyotes.

As such, Norman keeps two shotguns on hand for encounters with unwelcome wildlife on his property. In fact, the retiree recently killed a six-foot Diamondback not far from the house. Inside the female snake, he found twenty-two eggs[*]

On this day, one of the weapons leans innocuously in a corner of the Brownes' bathroom.

Rastus Russell has just disappeared behind the bathroom door.

When he emerges, the visitor is gripping Browne's loaded .12 gauge shotgun in his rugged, farm worker hands.

And he's not examining it for purchase.

He raises the weapon and points it at Norman Browne's chest.

"What's the idea?" Browne demands, seated at the dining room table.

Irritated, Russell smashes the coffee cup and saucer out of Browne's hands with the butt of the weapon. The cup crashes to the table, breaking off a piece of porcelain and staining Mrs. Browne's white tablecloth with hot, dark coffee.

"I'm a desperate man!" he tells Browne as he explains his situation.

---

[*] *An interview with Mrs. Anne Browne, Dunedin Register, September 9, 1949*

He tells the terrified couple that he is connected to a Chicago drug smuggling gang looking for a hideout. He threatens that if anything happens to him, his gangster pals will "take care of it."

He then demands to know where the Brownes keep their money. When the Brownes state they have no money, Russell becomes agitated. He continues to argue with the couple, repeatedly asking about the money. The Brownes try to convince Russell they are telling the truth.

Rastus Russell isn't buying it.

He tells Mr. and Mrs. Browne he is going to tie them up while he looks for it. He asks if they prefer to be tied up in the bedroom or their garage.

Apparently making the decision himself, the lifelong criminal marches the couple out to the back porch, down the steps, and takes them on the short walk through the yard to the garage. The Brownes obediently comply – the powerful weapon pointed at their backs.

Inside the tiny, wooden, dirt floor structure, the Brownes breathe the trapped, familiar air smelling of earth, mildew, and mouse droppings. The intruder finds some spare rope. Between old cardboard Crisco boxes, light wood bushel baskets, and Norman Browne's push-powered grass cutter, Rastus Russell binds the couple by the hands and feet. He then tosses the rope over the wooden beam in the ceiling, pulling the couple's hands over their heads, then tying the rope tight.

Leaving the Brownes restrained in the garage, Russell closes the dual, barn-like doors and locks them with the outside deadbolt, securing a steel hasp.

He vanishes into the house. Norman and Anne Browne hear their captor rustling through their home, searching for money he is convinced is inside.

After a short time, Rastus Russell exits the house and, unexplainedly, climbs back into the Ford and drives away.

Traumatized but relieved, the Brownes believe their ordeal is over.

3

Rastus Russell has just pulled out of the yard of Norman and Anne Browne. Believing the couple is securely tied and locked in their own garage, Russell drives his black V-8 Ford back down Rattlesnake Road, back onto the streets of Crystal Beach, and back out to the highway of Old US 19.

From there, he drives approximately forty-five minutes east to his Aunt Maud's house on Louisiana Avenue in Tampa. Why Russell drives all the way to his aunt's house with the Brownes locked in their garage is unclear.

When he arrives at his aunt's home at approximately 11:15 a.m., Maud McCord questions Russell about his whereabouts. She was expecting him earlier in the morning. In addition, her nephew is driving a car she does not recognize.

Russell crafts an excuse, then explains the 1946 black Ford is "borrowed."

The convict does not stay long. He tells his aunt he has "another little job" in Pinellas County. He then departs again in the black Ford.

Russell arrives back at the Brownes' residence in Crystal Beach around noon. When he does, Norman Browne is kicking furiously at the garage door in a desperate effort to escape.

This makes Rastus Russell very unhappy.

* * *

As Norman Browne listens to the murmur of Rastus Russell's Ford retreat down Rattlesnake Road, he struggles to free himself.

Despite his traumatic experience, he is clear enough of mind to focus on one, clear goal.

Escape.

Browne wriggles, pulls, turns, and twists until finally, after several minutes, manages to free his hands. He unties the rope, struggling to his feet, and immediately turns to Anne Browne.

Once he unties his wife, Browne finds the garage doors have been locked from the outside.

He turns and begins ruffling through the garage until he finds the tool he seeks: a steel blade hacksaw.

By now, it is late morning.

Wedging the blade of the saw through the crack between the doors, Browne begins furiously sawing at the metal hasp that keeps the couple imprisoned. The seventy-five-year-old man sweats and strains as he works in the rising tropical heat.

Despite Brownes' efforts, the hasp is not giving much ground.

While her husband labors, Anne Browne has a startling moment of clarity. While being marched to the garage, the astute woman observed the Pinellas County license plate on her kidnapper's car. She uses a nail to scrawl the memorized plate number on a piece of wood.

Outside the Brownes' enclosure, it is just another normal morning in Crystal Beach. Ospreys soar overhead with keen eyes for schools of mullet. Great Blue Herons stalk too-slow geckos in the sprawling, green mangroves. White Egrets wade through the warm, sandy shallows of St. Joseph Sound. All are routinely pursuing their morning breakfasts.

Inside the tiny garage, the morning has become anything but routine.

It is now nearly 11:45 a.m. Russell has been gone for approximately 90 minutes. As Norman Browne continues to struggle with the door lock, the Brownes believe they have been robbed. But they have not been physically harmed. The robber left some time ago, apparently with something from their home. The only danger they believe themselves in is the heat inside their garage.

But as Browne files away at the stubborn hasp, his wife hears a terrifying sound.

It's the motor of the black Ford, growling back up Rattlesnake Road.

Anne Browne presses her eye to the crack between the doors.

"My God!" she whispers to her husband, "He's coming back, Norman!"*

Rastus Russell is arriving at the Brownes' home for the third time today. This time, the lifelong criminal pulls the Ford discreetly behind the Brownes' home, lest the odd traveler down the dirt path notice a stranger at the house.

He strides over to the little whitewashed structure that cages the Brownes. In a frantic last effort to escape, Norman Browne begins violently kicking at the door, trying to break the weakened lock before the kidnapper can reach them.

Hearing the loud pounding, Russell realizes his captives are trying to escape.

Lifting the lock, he flings open the garage doors. The intruder no longer holds Mr. Browne's full size shotgun, but the smaller, sawed-off version he had shown the Browne's earlier.

Enraged, Russell draws back and slugs Norman Browne in the head with the hardwood stock of the weapon.

Browne collapses to the floor. Anne Browne screams and rushes to his aide.

As she tends to her husband, she begs Russell to allow her to tend to her husband's injury. She asks Russell to go inside and bring her first aid supplies from the bathroom cabinet.

Oddly enough, Russell complies.

She also asks Russell to bring her a bottle of whiskey from her cabinet.

"I already drank all that," Russell replies.

It is now that Anne Browne suspects that Russell is under the influence of at least alcohol.**

---

*   *The Evening Independent, August 10, 1949*

**   *If this quote from Anne Browne is indeed correct, Russell is apparently lying. Investigators find the bottle of liquor later at the scene, about one-third of its contents still in the bottle.*

After allowing Mrs. Browne to treat her husband, the kidnapper orders the couple back into the house.

En route to the house, Russell, for whatever reason, momentarily disappears out of sight.

Norman Browne sees his opportunity. In a mad dash, the old man bolts into the yard.

But Browne is woozy and confused from the blow he has taken to his head. Instead of running towards the road and freedom, he runs into the enclosed, fenced yard.

Hearing the second escape attempt, Russell races out of the house after Browne. Upon catching him at the barbed wire fence, a furious Russell begins savagely beating and kicking Browne in a profanity-laced tirade.

Standing in the doorway of her home, Mrs. Browne has a spontaneous thought. Lying close to her, she spies a giant iron plumbing wrench belonging to Norman's tool collection. In an ordeal-ending scene she plays out in her head, she seizes the wrench and smashes Russell in the face with it, blinding him and allowing the couple to escape.

As Russell drags the wounded Norman back toward the house, Anne makes her move and reaches for the makeshift weapon.

But it is not to be. In the tussle with the intruder, her hand has become injured. She cannot grip the wrench tight enough. The size and weight of the wrench would have made it difficult for the sixty-year-old to lift it under normal circumstances. Now, her damaged hand makes it impossible.

Anne releases the wrench and rushes to her injured partner.

* * *

As Anne approaches the two men, Russell levels the shotgun, this time pointing it at her. He instructs the distraught woman to return to the yard and fetch him some rope from the clothesline. She obeys.

As the three again march into the house, Norman Browne is becoming belligerent. Injured, likely concussed, possibly delirious, and certainly angry, Browne begins growling insults at his captor.

Anne Browne, alarmed, tries to calm her husband.

"Stay calm," she warns him, "Or you'll only make it worse!"*

But Norman Browne is far from calm at this point. In a fit of fury, he turns and fists flying, tears into Russell, beating him about the head and torso.

Russell is initially taken aback. However, with his muscular frame, the young man easily throws off the older Browne.

But Rastus Russell is through playing nice.

The kidnapper again flies into a rage and again begins savagely beating Browne with kicks, punches, and the hardwood butt of the shotgun. As Browne moans helplessly on the floor, his wife screams in terror. Russell spins and smashes the rifle butt into her head, sending the former New Yorker sprawling to the floor.

* * *

John Calvin Russell, born February 15, 1915, near Dade City, Florida, grew up without a father. Perhaps to compensate, he became very close to his mother.

According to some, Claude Estelle Baker, age twenty-eight, married her first husband in 1914. Little is known about her first marriage, if it even existed. A scant paper trail suggests her husband may have been the troubled boy's father was from Kentucky and carried the last name of Russell (which Claude took at marriage). If he existed, he apparently died while John Calvin was young. In a 1930 census, Claude Estelle Baker lists her last name as "Russell" and categorizes herself as "widowed."

However, there is no concrete evidence that Claude Estelle Baker was married prior to her son's birth. There is also no record of where the name Russell originated.

Rumors later circulate in Palm Harbor that Russell is the illegitimate child of a high-ranking judge.

Also of interest is Rastus Russell's skin tone. He is described as having darker or olive skin, thick black hair, and a "Latin type." The infamous name he is later given, "Rastus," is a stereotypical, derogatory name for black men in the United States in the first half of the 20th century.

---

*   *Clearwater Sun, August 10, 1949*

The reference originates from Joel Chandler Harris's character, Brer Rastus, from his 1881 book *Uncle Remus*, a collection of African American folktales. As such, Rastus becomes a familiar name in minstrel shows, films, fiction, and songs. Notably, Rastus is also the name of the popular African American character featured on Cream of Wheat packages through the 1920's, the same time Russell acquired the nickname. It does not seem unreasonable to suspect that Russell could have been given the name by his white childhood peers because of certain non-white traits he possessed in his appearance.

Rastus, however, is also a Greek name. Russell's olive skin and dark hair could also have been indicative of a Greek father.

As Claude Estelle Baker is white, it seems plausible to draw one of three alternate conclusions.

One, that Rastus Russell's father and Claude Estelle's first husband was possibly of African American, Hispanic, or Greek descent.

Two, that Russell's father was not the man Claude was married to in 1914 and that Russell's birth was the result of an affair outside of the marriage (judge or otherwise.)

Or, three, that Claude Estelle was never married and Rastus Russell was the result of an out-of-wedlock relationship.

In my interview with the one living man I could find who actually met Rastus Russell, I was told that if he had to guess, he would guess Russell was of Greek descent.

It is interesting to note that at the time of Rastus Russell's conception, Claude Estelle Baker was working as a teacher at Sutherland College in Palm Harbor. Tarpon Springs, the next town over, boasts a large Greek community.

While some records list Claude marrying in 1914, no marriage certificate can be found. Regardless, any of the above would have been considered scandalous in 1915 and could explain Claude raising the child alone inside her mother's home and later moving away from the family.

If any of the above were true, it would make perfect sense, given the social stigma at the time, for Claude to avoid the whole topic and call herself a "widow."

The exact truth may never be known. The only fact that is certain is that Russell's father was absent, either from birth or very early childhood.

Until age ten, Russell lived with his grandmother, his mother, her sister, and four brothers at their family home in Thonotosassa, Florida. Russell's grandfather, Dr. Thomas Baker, a prominent dentist, citizen, and Mason in Thonotosassa, was alive while Russell lived there. Strangely, he does not appear as a member of the household on a 1920 census when Russell was four years old.

In 1925, Claude Estelle Baker Russell moved from her childhood home to Palm Harbor, Florida, with young John (Rastus). There, she ran a boarding house for some time. In 1931, at age forty-four, she married Chauncey Gates McCoy, forty-two. McCoy listed himself as a "private tutor."

In the 1930 census, Mr. McCoy listed himself as a "roomer" at Claude's boarding house and, interestingly, also listed himself as "married" a year before he married Claude.

It is unknown what kind of relationship McCoy had with John. However, the boy was sixteen at the time of the couple's wedding and already had a long list of run-ins with the law.

Young John Calvin Russell worshiped his mother. She was described as educated and gentle. She tried her best to softly discipline the young Russell when he began demonstrating disturbing behaviors, such as pulling the heads off chickens or cutting the tails off cats with sharp-bladed knives. Russell sulked for long periods after his mother's corrections. Psychiatrists later speculate that these gentle remonstrations may have made Russell feel "rejected."

Indeed, Russell later reflects with a girlfriend that his mother never had time for him as a child, making him feel neglected and alone.

Regardless, the boy remained close to his mother, even as his criminal career took flight. While Russell was awaiting trial in the Pinellas County Jail in 1941 for the attempted murder of Walter Newbern, Mrs. McCoy brought food to Russell every day.

But shortly afterward, on July 21, 1942, at the age of fifty-six, Claude Estelle Baker McCoy died.

Twenty-six-year-old Rastus Russell was jailed in Illinois at the time. It is unknown if this is the impetus for Russell's escape from there or not.

However, when Russell returned to Palm Harbor on the run from authorities, he attempted to break into a local store one night. In the midst of the crime, he was confronted by one Dewey Adair. Acting as special deputy, Adair arrests Russell.

The good-natured Adair was a pioneer resident of Palm Harbor, a well-esteemed citizen, and the owner of Adairs Grocery Store. Active in the community, Adair was a prominent member of the local Masonic Lodge. He is known to extend generous credit to customers of his store.

Adair and Russell have known each other since they were ten years old. The nature or depth of their relationship is unclear. However, it is rumored that Russell briefly lived in one of the apartments upstairs of Adair's establishment.[*]

Russell asked Adair about his (Russell's) mother. Adair broke the news of her death to Russell.

Russell was devastated.

"I don't know what I will do without her," he wept, "I always had her to fall back on."[**]

In this strange interaction, it is possible that this was Dewey Adair's store that Russell was attempting to rob. On the run, Russell was likely desperate, hungry, and in need of money. Adair's store was certainly a familiar haunt.

This was about the time that Russell was on the run from the FBI after escaping jail in Illinois. It is likely this is how Russell was captured, turned over to the FBI, and returned to prison in Illinois.

* * *

As Norman Browne lay moaning on the floor, Rastus Russell has run out of patience. He came for money today, and he wants it now.

---

[*]   *From personal interview.*

[**]   *The Evening Independent, August 11, 1949*

Anne Browne, remembering Russell's apparent act of sympathy in the garage, calls on the madman's better nature again and pleads for mercy.

Russell is not in the mood this time.

He hoists the ailing man to his feet and drags him into the bedroom.

"I'll fix you so you won't bother anybody!" Russell fumes at the old man.[*]

The couple's twin beds sit aligned parallel inside, a wooden nightstand separating the two. Still steaming from Browne's attack, Russell launches the dazed senior into the bed nearest the door. He throws Browne so hard that Browne's head goes completely over and then under the bed while his feet remain atop the mattress.

As Norman lays atop the sheets, Russell hauls Mrs. Browne into the room, tossing her into the adjacent bed on the further side of the tiny, square bedroom. The bed in which Anne lands sits on the far side of the room. It sports bedposts on both the headboard and footboard. In this way, it differs from the one in which Norman Browne lays.

The former asylum patient momentarily disappears into the kitchen, then returns wielding a long blade butcher knife.

Russell begins slashing pieces of sash cord from the clothesline Mrs. Browne fetched for him earlier. He uses pieces of the cord to tie Norman Browne, spread eagle, to the footboard and headboard of the dark, wood-framed bed.

He runs out of sash cord before he finishes tying Norman Browne.

Russell looks around the room for another makeshift restraint. Atop the thin, rectangular, dark wood nightstand between the Brownes' twin beds is a wooden box supporting an electric radio.

Standing between the two beds, Russell rips the plug to the device out of the bedroom socket, then slices the power cord with the razor-sharp blade.

Anne Browne resists, but she is no match for the powerful Russell. He yanks her wrists up to the headboard bedpost and ties her to the bed in the same fashion he did her husband. He restrains her wrists and feet with cut pieces of the electrical cord.

---

[*]   *Tarpon Springs Leader, August 11, 1949*

"He tied us to the pair of twin beds," Anne Browne tells police later. "One to one bed, the other to the other. He tied our arms to the heads of the beds and our feet to the end posts, using wires ripped from the radio."

As Russell ties Mrs. Brown to her bedposts, Norman remains defiant from the other bed.

"I'll keep the son of a bitch quiet!" he roars.[*]

Enraged, Russell again hoists the shotgun and bashes the male Browne in the head several more times. Then he finishes tying the semi-conscious man.

Using pieces of white cloth possibly cut from the Brownes' bedsheets, Russell ties gags around both of their mouths.

The Brownes are now subdued and helpless.

* * *

Convinced there is cash in the house, the agitated Russell again demands to know where the Brownes are keeping "the money."

When Norman Browne again tells Russell there is no money, Russell plunges the knife into Browne's lower body.

Browne screams in pain. Russell continues to use the sharp instrument to cut and stab Browne, non-fatally, at different points of his body, demanding to know where Browne keeps the money.

With Browne still unable to give a location of hidden cash, Russell storms out of the bedroom.

As the Brownes lay bleeding and bruised, they hear the violent smashing of drawers, slamming of furniture being overturned, and shattering glass as Russell rummages through their homestead like a badger.

Having turned over the kitchen, Rastus Russell has still not found what he's looking for. As a consolation prize, he begins loading food, flour, sugar, and other groceries from the Browne's pantry into his car outside.

Back in the bedroom, the Brownes believe they are going to die. They pray together and then say their goodbyes to each other.

"At least we'll go together," Anne Browne consoles her husband.[**]

---

[*]   *The Evening Independent, August 9, 1949*

[**]   *Clearwater Sun, August 10, 1949*

4

A s it often does in Florida summer, an afternoon thunderstorm has erupted in the skies over Crystal Beach. A geyser of driving rain hammers the rooftop of the Brownes' house.

Through the occasional flashes of daytime lightning and the gentle rumble of overhead thunder, Rastus Russell ominously reappears in the Brownes' bedroom doorway.

The Brownes are horrified.

His prize still not located, Russell changes tactics. He turns his attention to Mrs. Browne.

The farm worker threatens to rape her.

"Do your worst!" Anne Browne defiantly shouts back at him.*

She then adds a scathing remark about Russell's lack of "manhood."

Russell, either humiliated or simply changing his mind, doesn't act on his threat. Instead, he throws a sheet over Anne Browne, covering her from head to toe.

He then covers Norman Browne with a second sheet. An eerie moment of silence follows.

Then Anne Browne hears her husband cry out a chilling call.

"Oh my God!" he screams, "he's cut my wrists!"*

Norman Young Browne is already poked full of stab wounds on various parts of his body. Dark crimson blood stains the sheets, pillow, and mattress of Browne's bed.

---

*   *Clearwater Sun, August 10, 1949*

Sweat runs down Rastus Russell's neck and back from underneath his thick, black hair. It's 90 degrees outside and the humidity has now reached excruciating levels in and outside of the aged house.

Then, standing between the twin beds and facing south, Russell raises the butcher knife above his head and plunges it violently into Norman Browne's torso, the young man's powerful arms driving the blade through Browne's seventy-four-year-old flesh, bones, and vital organs. By most accounts, he does this several times, any one of which could have been fatal. However, the most lethal is a deep stab wound that enters the side of Browne, just under his left arm, penetrating his heart.

The fatal heart wound is almost certainly delivered by Russell holding the knife above Browne with both hands, driving down and pulling back into Browne's opposite (left) side, facing the wall. The blade enters at an angle perpendicular to Browne's ribs. The attack is so savage that Russell breaks off the tip of the knife inside Browne's body.[*]

"Mr. Browne didn't talk after that." Anne Browne recalls later.

As her husband screams and gasps, Anne Browne cries out in horror.

As she does, Russell spins with the broken knife and turns it on the terrified woman.

But Anne Browne has a surprise of her own.

When the killer was tying her hands, the crafty housewife had drawn up. When she relaxed afterward, the bounds were slightly looser.

She had used this same tactic when Russell had gagged her. It was because of this that the gag in her mouth hung looser, allowing her to speak to her husband and Russell. But unbeknownst to Russell, it has also now allowed her to free her left hand.

---

[*] *United Press, August 8, 1949. The exact details of how and when Norman Browne's lethal knife wounds were administered are varied and, at times, contradictory – the only witness being a semi-delirious Anne Browne. Great effort has been made to get the event as close to the actual order as possible. In describing this incident, we've made the best interpretation we can based on police reports and Mrs. Browne's own, sometimes inconsistent, recounting of the event*

As Russell drives the knife at her, Browne raises up her hand to block the thrust. The knife, missing its tip, slices her pinky finger. Russell draws back and plunges the steel blade again, this time driving the broken point deep into her left wrist, slashing arteries, severing tendons, and exposing the bone.

Her wrist immediately goes numb. Then Anne Browne feels warm blood spewing down her arm.

Frustrated, Russell drops the broken knife onto the nightstand and snatches up the modified .12 gauge he has used to terrorize the Brownes all day. He draws it back and slams the butt of the weapon into Anne Browne's head several times.

At some point immediately before or after this action, another odd conversation occurs between the semi-conscious Mrs. Browne and her captor.

"What time is it?" she asks Russell in shocked resignation.

"It's shortly after one o'clock," he replies honestly.[*]

For whatever reason, he spares Anne Browne's life. But he leaves her with an ominous warning.

"You better keep your damn mouth shut about this!" he growls. "If you go running to the newspaper, I'll come back here and kill you too!"[**]

But Rastus Russell isn't finished yet.

---

[*]   *St. Petersburg Times, August 19, 1949*
[**]   *The Evening Independent, page 2, August 8, 1949*

Note to readers: The description of the murderous rampage of Rastus Russell is almost entirely Anne Browne's version of events, taken from direct interviews with both media and police. As Browne is the only living witness to the crime other than Russell himself, it is all we have to go on. If Browne had anything to hide, however, this testimony could very well be slanted to obscure or muddy the facts.

5

Sunday, August 7, 1949
1:30 p.m.
Crystal Beach, FL
Crum's Grocery Store

A s Rastus Russell is bringing his Sunday visit to the Browne's to
its violent climax, thirty-one-year-old Miles Crum is preparing
for an enjoyable family day at the beach.

Crum owns Crum's Store, a local landmark in Crystal Beach that
sells a variety of sundries. The store occupies the bottom floor of a
two-story wooden building that stands prominently on the main entry
road to Crystal Beach. Crum owns the store with his 29-year-old wife,
Thelma. The couple live in the apartment on the building's second floor
with their eight-month-old daughter, Judy.

Crum is a World War II era army veteran who bought the store
shortly after the couple married in 1948 and moved to Crystal Beach
from Clarion, PA. He is known as good-natured and gregarious. Miles
Crum is 5'6", slim but wiry, and has brown hair. Friends describe him as
entertaining and rhythmic, with a voice resembling the 1960s cartoon
character Dudley Do-Right.

Thelma Crum is a soft-spoken woman of slight stature. The
dark-haired Thelma wears glasses and stands about the same height
as her husband.

In addition to selling candy, fishing gear, and groceries, Crum's
store offers a soda fountain bar and serves as Crystal Beach's unofficial
gathering place. Here, locals can enjoy a cool drink on a hot day, share
local news, and catch up on the latest gossip.

With the store closed on the Sabbath, the Crum's often enjoy a
swim on Sundays. The warm, tropical waters surrounding Crystal Beach,

Palm Harbor, and nearby Clearwater offer almost unlimited opportunities for locals to do so.

The Crum's have delayed their swimming excursion today because of the thunderstorm. But now the clouds are clearing, and the fiery sun is again lighting the sky. Miles Crum throws a few items into his Jeep while Mrs. Crum readies little Judy for a day away from home. The swimming trip will happen after all.

Because almost everyone in the enclave has visited the store, the Crum's have many friends in Crystal Beach and the surrounding Palm Harbor community.

One such couple is Norman and Anne Browne. Despite their age difference, the couples enjoy a close friendship. They are so close, in fact, that the Browne's often babysit little Judy when Miles and Thelma have other matters to attend to.

Today, Anne Browne has agreed to look after Judy while the Crum's go swimming.*

With Thelma and Judy secure, Miles Crum fires the Jeep's ignition and starts up nearby Vincent Street. The trip to the Browne's is only a half-mile drive.

As Crum drives the open jeep, the stifling air is sticky after the storm. Vincent is one of the few paved streets in Crystal Beach. Steam drifts up from the hot pavement in front of the Jeep as the sun evaporates the remnants of the storm's moisture. Crum reaches the end of Vincent, turns left onto Florida Avenue, and makes a right onto the dirt path known as Rattlesnake Road.

After a short crawl up the path, Crum pulls the Jeep up to his friend's house and shuts off the ignition. He climbs out of the vehicle and walks towards the Browne's front porch. Thelma follows him through the wet, sandy grass, baby Judy in her arms.

Upon approaching the porch, Crum immediately senses something is wrong. A strange man in a white shirt is standing inside the covered porch at the doorway. The man has dark, wavy hair, a mustache,

---

*   *Some accounts indicate the Brownes and Crums intended to go swimming together, others that they planned only a visit, and others still that the Crums were merely delivering groceries.*

and looks to be of Latin or Greek descent. Thick and muscular, the stranger has blood on his shirt and a menacing look on his face.

He is also holding a sawed-off shotgun.

Miles Crum has just met Rastus Russell.

* * *

Anne Browne is struggling to free herself.

For some reason, the man who killed her husband has remained on her property. Anne Browne does not know why. Is he going to continue searching for money? Is he waiting for somebody else? Is he going to kill her?

Russell, for his part, sits placidly on the steps of the Browne's front porch, accompanied by the sawed-off shotgun resting in his lap. It is now almost 2:00 p.m. Russell has remained at the Browne's house nearly an hour after killing Norman Browne.*

At this point in his life, Rastus Russell has been a well-rounded criminal. He has been a thief, a thug, a robber, a brutalizer, and has shown a reckless disregard for human life. One thing he has not yet been, at least regarding human beings, is a cold-blooded murderer. That has changed today.**

As the killer stares off into the mass of green trees and brush surrounding his crime scene, he hears an engine rumbling up Rattlesnake Road.

* * *

Anne Browne hears the engine, too. She knows it's Miles and Thelma Crum. She is expecting them and recognizes the whine in

---

*   *While many newspaper reports at the time state that the Crum's visit to the house "interrupted" the potential murder of Anne Browne, this is not the case, at least according to Anne Browne's account later.*

**   *At least as far as official accounts are concerned. We know little of Russell's activities in Chicago or the Midwest in the 1940s. He had claimed to have killed three police officers in Chicago and was suspected in the violent hold-up of W.J. Graham of Tampa. Graham later died of injuries sustained in the crime.*

Crum's jeep. As it has many times today, horror grips the restrained woman.

Turning her head just enough, she sees Miles and Thelma Crum pull up in their Jeep.

In an attempt to save her friends, Browne opens her mouth and screams at the top of her lungs – trying to warn the Crums of the menace inside.

But it is too late.

* * *

Miles Crum knows he is facing danger.

But while Russell poses an intimidating profile standing on the front porch, Miles Crum is no slouch himself. At three years Russell's junior, he is in fair shape, has military training, and the added incentive of a young family to protect – not to mention his friends inside.

Unintimidated, Crum proceeds to investigate.

As Browne screams from the bedroom, Crum is already on the porch. Whether he hears Anne Browne's initial screams is unclear. But he hears them now.

"What goes on here?!" Crum demands.

The killer steps forward, raises the sawed-off shotgun, and points it directly at Crum's head.

"Get inside," Russell orders. He tells Crum he "shot three policemen in Chicago," a claim he made two weeks earlier to Lester Lambert.[*]

Crum initially indicates compliance. But the mild-mannered grocer then decides he won't go quietly.

Crum strikes quickly, snagging the barrel of the gun, forcing it away from his head. The two men collapse onto the porch, locked in mortal combat, struggling for control of the weapon.

---

[*] *It is unclear as to what Russell is referring to here. No evidence of any police shootings attributed to Russell can be found. It is possible Russell believes the claim will strike enough fear into his victims to induce compliance. But it is also possible Russell is telling the truth.*

"I nearly got the gun away from him," Crum says later, "but he wrenched free."[*]

After a violent scruff, Russell pulls away from Crum with the gun still in his hands. He takes a few steps backward and drops to a one-kneed crouching position. Crum charges again. When he does, Russell fires a single blast directly into the lower right side of Crum's belly.

"As I charged him again, he fired, and the full charge caught me in the stomach," Crum reported.[*]

The force from the blast drives Crum backward. He grabs his gut, falls backward on the steps, and collapses in the yard.

There are several versions of what happened next. But the following is likely the most accurate. It was relayed by the incident's only coherent witness, Mrs. Thelma Crum. It is told by Mrs. J.B. Swan of Dunedin days after the attack, as told directly to her by Thelma Crum.

Holding young Judy in her arms, Thelma instinctively starts towards her stricken husband. As she does, the killer steps out into the yard and charges the terrified mother.

Only feet from her, he stops and raises the shotgun again. He points it directly at her face.

Preparing to die, the young mother instinctively pushes her baby away from her and raises her arms in front of her face. The baby lands on the sandy ground nearby.[**]

Rastus Russell squeezes the trigger.

But nothing happens. There is no cartridge in the gun.[***]

Undeterred, Russell changes his grip on the weapon, holding it like a baseball bat with both hands near the stock.

Thelma Crum turns and starts to run. But the killer is faster.

---

[*]   *The Evening Independent, August 10, 1949.*

[**] *Mrs. Swan sympathetically states that Crum "rolled" the baby into the sand. Anne Browne claims Crum "tossed" the baby into soft sand. But an interview with Michael Ramirez in 2024, a former friend of Miles Crum, reveals Crum told him Thelma "threw" the baby into the air in panic, the baby landing hard on the ground. Ramirez stated that Mrs. Crum "never got over" the guilt of what happened that day.*

[***] *This is according to Mrs. Swan's testimony. Whether she or Mrs. Crum assumed this or were told by police is unknown.*

Russell swings the weapon like an ax, the gun's hot, steel barrel crashing down from above. The vicious blow strikes Thelma Crum on top of the head, sending her collapsing to the ground, unconscious.

The force of the blow is so ferocious that the firing pin pops out of the weapon and lands on the ground nearby.[*] At the same time, a shard of the wooden gun butt breaks off and tumbles into the sandy grass.

The blow opens a wide gash near Thelma Crum's forehead, causing blood to stream down over her face and into the muddy ground.

It's approximately 2:00 p.m.

* * *

---

[*] *Some newspaper accounts claim the firing pin popped out during Russell's struggle with Miles Crum. But if this were the case, the gun would not have fired when Russell pointed it at Mr. Crum. This would seem to support Mrs. Swan's contention that the weapon contained only one shell. This, however, suggests Russell didn't think he would need more than one shell, didn't plan to use the shotgun, or was simply unprepared and careless. No official explanation was able to be located. Thus, we must rely on Mrs. Swan's account*

6

August 7, 1949
2:00 p.m.
Cotton House, Crystal Beach, FL

By early afternoon on this sweltering summer Sunday, Robert Cotton has already been fishing.

Cotton lives on Vincent Street with his wife, a first-grade teacher, and daughters. Their home sits roughly two blocks west and a block north of the Brownes' house.

Cotton is busy cleaning his daily catch in his backyard when he hears a booming explosion echo from the woods less than two blocks away. The blast is followed by a woman's voice screaming, "Oh my God!...Help, please!"

Alarmed, Cotton drops the freshly caught fish and bloody knife. Wiping his hands, he strides towards the woods near the southeast corner of his yard, still not sure of exactly what he just heard.

Listening intently for another few minutes, he hears nothing.

Suddenly, he hears the engine of a vehicle raging towards the front of his house. The horn is blaring urgently.

Bleep! Bleeep! Bleeeeeeeeep!

Cotton runs around his house to the front yard. There, he is stunned to see an open-top Jeep spin into his front yard. Slumped over the steering wheel is his friend, Miles Crum. Crum is still hammering on the horn.

Bright, fresh blood covers the grocery man's front, legs, and arms. As he runs toward the vehicle, Cotton can see Crum's intestines lying partially in his lap, his right hand trying to restrain them. Robert Cotton has just gone from one small-scale scene of blood and guts to another, more horrifying one.

33

"Get the doctor! Get the Police!" Crum begs through a hoarse voice. "I've been shot!"

He then collapses.

* * *

Five minutes earlier…

Incredibly, Miles Crum is still alive and conscious. There is a gaping hole in his abdomen, exposing the vital organs inside. Blood gushes from the wound. Along with the blood, bits of flesh and tiny pellets of buckshot stick to his skin, ripped shirt, and pants. But Crum still has some fight left in him. He simply has too much to lose.

Holding his intestines inside his body with one hand, Crum drags himself across the ground. As he does, he hears his baby, and then his wife let out horrific screams. He must experience a terrible sense of helplessness. Reaching the Jeep, he pulls himself up into the driver's seat.

As his head pops over the steering wheel, he cannot see his child or wife. What he does see is the sweaty, panting face of Rastus Russell standing directly in front of his Jeep. Fresh blood stains the convict's pants and shirt. He is still holding the sawed-off shotgun.

Crum has no idea that Russell's gun is empty. But Crum now has a weapon, too - nearly two tons worth. And he is sitting behind the wheel.

Weak and dazed, Crum cranks the engine and slams the vehicle into gear. With his attacker only feet away, the veteran stomps his foot on the gas and releases the clutch.

What he doesn't know is that his baby daughter, Judy Crum, is lying directly in front of the Jeep's right tire. The child landed there when pushed away by her mother.

Fortunately, in his haste, Crum has accidentally shifted the transmission into reverse.

The Jeep's tires peel backward, shooting up a splattering of mud and wet grass to the front and sides of the vehicle. The Jeep jolts violently backward, rumbling back through the yard, plowing over a section of Norman Browne's barbed wire fence. With only one hand available, Crum forces the transmission back into first gear, slams on the gas, and races away, moving his free, bloody hand up to grip the steering wheel.*

Retreating to the Brownes' front porch, Rastus Russell watches as Miles Crum tears out of the yard in the Jeep. With five victims now felled by his hand, the booming explosion of the shotgun charge likely alerting neighbors, and now this stranger escaping to spread the news, Russell knows it's time to go.

Leaving Thelma Crum and her baby lying in the front yard, Russell flees back through the house, past the bedroom containing a semi-conscious Anne Browne, and out the back door. He tosses the shotgun into the trunk, hops into the driver's side of his black Ford, and drives away.

* * *

Through the opaque walls of her unconsciousness, Thelma Crum hears the muffled screams of an older woman echoing through the darkness. As she opens her bleary eyes, she sees a sideways view of long grass, ferns, and overgrown palmetto brush. Her head is throbbing, and she feels warm liquid trickling down her forehead to her face.

The screams grow louder. Gradually, the horror of what has just happened comes flooding back to the young mother.

The wounded Crum staggers to her feet and rushes to her baby. She hoists young Judy into her arms, squeezing the child in panic, praying the infant has not been seriously injured. The baby is crying but shows no signs of life-threatening injury.

Only partially relieved, the young mother realizes the screams for help are coming from inside the house. It is the frantic voice of her

---

*   *In doing so, Crum leaves his injured wife and baby behind, potentially still in the presence of a killer with a loaded shotgun. While Crum later claims his thought was to go for help, it is possible he was in shock and simply reacting out of instinct. Writer Monte Gurwit, in his article for Official Detective Stories magazine, states that Crum thought his wife and baby were dead when he left the scene. But as writers of Gurwit's genre were known to sensationalize stories, there is no way of knowing if Gurwit got the information from a direct source or whether he simply supposed it.*

friend, Anne Browne. Thelma rushes into the Browne's home to find the semi-conscious Browne lying in a scene of blood and gore.

Nearly hysterical, Thelma lays the baby on the bloody bed near the tied feet of Mrs. Browne. She then works feverishly to untie the ropes binding the older woman. But Rastus Russell has strong hands. Crum is unable to free Mrs. Browne.

According to Mrs. Swan, who relayed Thelma Crum's story as told her by Mrs. Crum, Thelma then ran into the kitchen and found a knife lying on the kitchen counter. She takes the knife back into the room and cuts Mrs. Browne free. She then ties a tourniquet around her upper arm to stem the bleeding in Browne's slashed wrist.

Swan claims Crum did not know it at the time, but the knife she used was the very same knife Rastus Russell used to stab both Norman and Anne Browne. If this were the case, the knife would likely have been bloody and have the tip broken off. Swan claims Crum was "dazed" and did not realize it was the killer's weapon.[*]

Anne Browne also claims it was Thelma Crum who freed her from her bonds and tied her arm in a tourniquet, although she does not mention the knife story, claiming only that Crum "untied" her.[**]

Seriously injured herself and fretting for her baby, Thelma Crum tells Browne she's going for help. She grabs her infant and bolts out the front door.

Choosing to bypass the road, she takes a shortcut. Hoisting baby Judy in one arm, Crum stumbles into the six acres of Florida woods and scrub brush that separate the Brownes' house from the house of their nearest neighbor. She bolts through the brush towards the same house at which her wounded husband has just arrived.

Robert Cotton is unsure what has just happened. What he does know is that his friend, Miles Crum, is in dire circumstance. Fearing for his own family, Cotton dashes inside his house and orders his wife and children upstairs.

---

[*]   *Tampa Tribune, September 17, 1949.*
[**] *Dunedin Register, September 9, 1949.*

"I don't want you to see what has happened outside!" he tells them.*

In 1949, there was no 9-1-1 system in Pinellas County. Cotton called both the Clearwater and Tarpon Springs police departments, begging for an ambulance. From there, calls were relayed to Dunedin police, the Florida Highway Patrol, the Pinellas County Sheriff's office, and a local ambulance service.

A call also goes out to Constable Walter Carey of Tarpon Springs. Help is on the way.

But it may be too late for Miles Crum.

* * *

Cotton runs back to his ailing friend. Regaining consciousness, Crum tells Cotton of his violent encounter with the armed stranger.

As Crum relays his story, Cotton hears screams coming from the woods beside his house. Startled, he turns to see a bloody, hysterical Thelma Crum charging towards his yard, holding her baby in her arms.

Thelma's run through the swampy woods is a horrific jaunt. It is the heat of the afternoon, the temperature a sweltering 91 degrees. Today's afternoon thundershower has just ceased. The humidity has pushed the feel-like temperature to well over 100 degrees.

As Mrs. Crum struggles, stumbles, and scurries through the bushy, dripping palmetto brush, a deep layer of greenery hides the ground beneath her feet, concealing all manner of creatures that may lurk on the soggy woodland floor. Despite the afternoon sun, the mosquitos are thick and aggressive in the shade the forest's canopy provides.

The distance to the Cotton house is less than a quarter mile from the Brownes'. The journey takes approximately four minutes.** Yet to Thelma Crum, it must seem like light years. In addition to carrying the twenty-pound weight of her child, she almost certainly has a serious concussion. The adrenaline in her system coupled with the stress

---

*   *St. Petersburg Times, August 10, 1949.*

**   *As reenacted by the author at the actual site, carrying his twenty-three-pound Sheltie in place of the baby.*

of the run, has amped up her heart rate, forcing blood to flow more profusely from the swollen gash on the top of her head.

She arrives at the Cotton's drenched in sweat, panting profusely, blood covering her face and upper body, and now also, her baby. Her arms and legs burn from the journey. But these are all likely eclipsed by the shock she has just experienced.

Hearing the cries of the stricken mother, Mrs. Cotton hurries down the stairs of her home.* She meets the traumatized woman at her front door. Her face and body are covered in blood and sweat; Crum babbles incoherently to Mrs. Cotton.

Cotton pulls the injured woman and child inside.

*   *   *

After Miles Crum's incredulous story, Robert Cotton is taking no chances. With authorities on the way, Cotton runs next door and borrows a gun from his neighbor. He then returns to his home, keeping a wary eye should the madman come there.

Word spreads quickly through Crystal Beach. Stunned neighbors remain indoors, guarding their families. Is this really happening? This can't happen *here*, can it? Perhaps there has been some misunderstanding.

They wait anxiously for help to arrive.

It does.

An ambulance is first on scene.

The Cotton house is a scene of trauma and carnage. As she watches, the ambulance crew prepares a bloody Miles Crum for transport; a groggy Thelma Crum frets over both her husband and child. As the neighborhood women examine baby Judy and tend to Thelma's head,

---

* *Miles Crum drove on the road and then pulled into the front of the Cotton house. If Thelma came directly through the woods, she may have come out on the South side of the Cotton house. While the home has no upstairs windows facing the front, there is an upstairs window facing the South. Thus, it is possible that Mrs. Cotton saw Thelma Crum emerge from the woods on the side of the house. Although modernized and updated, the Cotton house remains intact today with much the same appearance it had in 1949.*

she rants wildly about the scene at the Brownes' home. Thelma tells the sinister tale of her and her husband's run-in with the armed intruder – urgently insisting the Brownes need immediate help.

Robert Cotton realizes there may not be time to wait for the police. He gathers a few of his male neighbors who have arrived and tells them to grab their guns. If the Brownes need help, they are the only ones who can provide it at this moment.

In the front yard, Miles Crum has been loaded into the back of the ambulance on a gurney. The white, station wagon-style ambulance pulls out of the Crum yard and heads North on Vincent Street, back towards the entrance to Crystal Beach. The single red cherry top light on top turns slowly as the dull drone of the siren fades from earshot.

With the ambulance gone, other than the Crum Jeep parked diagonally in the front yard and a handful of neighbors gathered outside, there is no sign of anything abnormal going on at Robert Cotton's house.

7

August 7, 1949
2:15 p.m.
Tarpon Springs, FL

Seven miles north of Crystal Beach, forty-seven-year-old Constable Walter Carey is enjoying a quiet Sunday afternoon at home in Tarpon Springs. Carey has been constable for Pinellas County's District 4, which includes Crystal Beach, for the last seven years.

A family man of old Irish stock, Carey lives in the Anclote area of Tarpon Springs with his wife and six children. He is respected in the community and known as an even-tempered and fair man. He is also popular, having already been reelected constable twice.

In this part of Pinellas County, Walter Carey is the law. If you have a problem, you either call Walter on the phone or you go to his house and get him. The stoic Carey does not take lightly his duty to protect his fellow citizens.

In 1949, constables were elected officials in Pinellas County with four-year terms. They operated independently (although often in cooperation with) other law enforcement agencies. They answered only to the governor.

The former fisherman and sponger does not work from a government office or drive a government-issued police car. He drives his own car and carries his own firearm. While he often checks in and handles business at the Tarpon Springs Police Department, his home serves as his office.

Tall and slender, Carey wears round, wire-rimmed glasses. With a chiseled, serious face, the constable resembles a 1940's version of actor Nick Nolte. He does not don a uniform. Trousers, a modest, button-down, short-sleeved shirt, and a Fedora do nicely most of the time. Those who encounter him on the street typically do not know he is a law enforcement officer. He is, in fact, more of a peacekeeper. Carey is not one to harass the locals for no good reason, especially when those locals are voters.

That being said, Walter Carey is no empty badge. He is a serious lawman and is not to be trifled with. Although violent crime is not the norm in his little corner of Pinellas County, it is not unheard of either. In 1949, Pinellas County was made up of rugged farm workers, cattle ranchers, fisherman, and hog hunters. The rural environment is stocked full of rough and tumble, independent frontier types. World War II has just ended, and many, if not most, young men of the era are veterans. Guns are a common household item. Most men, boys, and even some women are comfortable handling them.

There is still a considerable military presence in the area as well, mixing with this eclectic blend of cowboys and farmhands. Nowhere is this truer than on the sponge docks of Tarpon Springs. The long, boardwalk-style strip sits at the point where the Anclote River meets the waters of St. Joseph Sound. All manner of fishermen, spongers, and military personnel dock here to unload catches, embark and depart, and most importantly, enjoy the dock's plethora of bars and other entertainment preferred by virile young men. Thus, in 1949, the Sponge Docks were known as a tough part of town.

Walter Carey is the man primarily in charge of policing this adult carnival. Few have any doubt he is the man for the job.

A former military man himself, Carey prefers to handle conflicts between government personnel and locals personally, rather than involve the shore patrol and potentially expose the men to military discipline.

While Carey walks with a gun strapped to his side, he prefers to handle conflict diplomatically if possible.

"The key to being a good police officer," he tells his grandson, "is not how many fights you get in, it's how many you can stay out of."

That does not mean Carey shies away from using force when necessary. Quite the contrary. Carey's grandson, Rick Carey, shared with me a story that paints a portrait of his grandfather's character.

One night, Carey is called to the Sponge Docks to deal with a drunken sailor. Carey takes his fifteen-year-old son along, who witnesses the entire event.

When the two arrived, a large man was standing in the street, yelling and cursing, challenging all bystanders to fight. The constable pulled his car near the man, stepped out, and calmly opened the back door of the vehicle. He then approached the sailor.

"Look," said Carey, "What I'd like you to do right now is stop your yelling and go sit in the back of that car."

"Who are you?" asked the man.

"Well, I'm Walter Carey, and I'm the law in this town. Who are you?" Carey inquired.

"I'm a bad man," replied the sailor.

"Well, bad man," Carey answered unfazed, "Go sit in the back of that car."

What the drunk man does not know is that the leather strap around Carey's wrist is not a watch. It is what is known as a "slapstick." The leather bracelet is filled with lead.

When the sailor answers Carey's request by balling his fist and swinging at the constable, Carey slips the slapstick into his palm and cracks the man upside the head.

"All you really got to do is tap em'," Carey explained to his son later. "You try to pin the ear to the side of the head."

The musclebound sailor fell harmlessly into Carey's arms. Carey dragged the unconscious man to the back of the car and drove him to jail.

The next morning, the sailor awakened to the smell of breakfast cooking. He looks up to see none other than Walter Carey flipping eggs and bacon on a stove outside his cell – likely a holding pen in Tarpon Springs.

"Want some breakfast?" Carey asked nonchalantly.

"Well, I do," replied the prisoner, "but I sure am sorry about last night. I got out of hand."

Then he said thoughtfully, "Mister, have you ever boxed?"

"No," Carey replied.

"Well, you've got a hell of a right hand."

The man was released shortly afterward. Carey's grandson doubts Carey even filed a report on the man. Such was the nature of Walter Carey.

But Carey is known for more than just handling drunken sailors and fishermen. He has seen his share of gunplay. He is also recognized as one of the best detectives on the west coast of Florida.

* * *

Despite the roughneck sections of his patrol area, Sundays are often a calm time for the constable. He is expecting today to be the same.

Shortly after 2 p.m., Carey gets a call to respond to a shooting somewhere in Crystal Beach, seven miles south of his home in Tarpon Springs. Carey grabs his keys, straps on his weapon, and heads to his car. He is not overly concerned. Firearm infractions are not uncommon. Accidents or personal squabbles are always possible. But he also knows that even behind the most benign seeming situations, danger can lurk.

His older brother, Rufus Carey, knew this all too well.

Rufus was also a lawman. In fact, Rufus Carey served as constable of District 4 before Walter. His and Walter's families shared the same house in Tarpon Springs, a practice not uncommon in the 1940s. One night on the job, Rufus was severely injured in a scuffle with an assault suspect in Palm Harbor.

He seems to recover, but the thirty-eight-year-old Rufus suffers from Tuberculosis. In 1942, six months after the dust-up, Rufus is transporting a misdemeanor suspect to the county jail on Old US 19, just outside of Crystal Beach. Suddenly, while driving, he is overcome with a coughing fit.

The constable pulls the car over to the side of the road, his coughing becoming violent. He begins hemorrhaging blood out of his mouth. Rufus Carey dies on the side of the road, bleeding to death in the front seat of his vehicle.

The suspect, horrified at the bloody turn of events, reaches into the front seat and removes Carey's wallet from his pocket. Noting the constable's identification and address, the suspect drives the vehicle back to the Carey residence.

There, he meets Walter Carey by the front door.

"I'm sorry to do this," the man tells Carey, "but this man died in the front of the car. I am just bringing him home."

Carey approaches the car with the man and peers inside. He sees his brother's corpse lying in the passenger side of the front seat.

The suspect then looks at Carey.

"Well," he asks, "what do you want *me* to do?"

"I don't care what you do," says Carey, "I'm not the law."[*]

It is not known what, if any, role Rufus Carey's scuffle with the assault suspect played in his untimely death six months later.

What is known is the man who hurt Walter Carey's brother had somehow escaped much punishment for his crime. That suspect is well known to lawmen in Pinellas County as an unstable troublemaker.

That suspect's name is John Calvin Russell. Everyone called him "Rastus."

Walter Carey knows *damn* well who *he* is.

But Rastus Russell supposedly left the state years ago. He was ordered to do so by Judge John U. Bird in relation to the very case that injured Carey's brother, Rufus. The last Carey heard of Russell, he was being hauled back to Illinois by the FBI after escaping prison there.

On this sunny weekend afternoon, Rastus Russell is the last thing on Carey's mind. He has a potential shooting to investigate.

Carey hops in his car and heads south on two-lane Old US Highway 19 through orange groves and cattle pastures, towards Crystal Beach.

When he arrives in the small community, he drives up and down its tree-lined streets but can find no sign of disturbance.

Is it a false alarm? Perhaps a young man's jalopy backfired?

Driving past the post office, Carey decides to pull in and see if anyone knows anything.

Inside, he encounters Mrs. Lou Barnes. She tells Carey that an ambulance just drove down Vincent Street, red light flashing, siren howling.

Carey jumps back in his car and rushes back towards Old Highway 19. He catches the hospital wagon just as it is turning left out of Crystal Beach. It must be headed to Tarpon Springs, Carey figures. He speeds up on the vehicle and follows it the 3.6 miles to the Tarpon Springs Hospital. The ride takes about seven minutes.

As the ambulance crew wheels the gurney into the small facility, an impatient Carey catches up to the bloody victim. The man has a large gaping hole in his abdomen. But he is conscious.

He tells Carey his name is Miles Pershing Crum.

---

[*]	*From personal interview with Rick Carey, grandson of Walter Carey.*

* * *

Crum tells Carey there is a madman loose in Crystal Beach. He says he thinks the man killed the Brownes, and he believes the killer is still inside the house. His wife and child are injured, maybe even dead. He doesn't know. Through a raspy, whispering voice, he tells Carey the location.

Carey runs to his sedan and races back to Crystal Beach, radioing State Patrolman Carl Cassels.[*] Cassels rushes toward the Browne home to meet Carey. Unlike Carey, State Patrolman Cassels is a uniformed officer who drives a government-issued, marked police car, complete with a red light and siren. Cassels undoubtedly activates both en route to his destination.

On his way to the Browne house, Carey stops to pick up special deputy Dewey Adair and Adair's son, Harold. He also picks up Leonard Rogers.[**]

As the stiff rush of blazing air blows through the open windows into the men's faces, adrenaline must be surging through their bodies. They could be heading into a violent confrontation.[***]

Carey bypasses the Cotton house and heads straight to the wood frame, white house with red trim down the dirt path known as Rattlesnake Road – exactly to where Miles Crum directed them. The four men wheel into the Browne's house at approximately 2:40 p.m., about the same time Cassells arrives.

Carey wastes no time.

---

[*]   *Radios in police cars are a relatively new technology at the time. While Carey and Cassells have radios in their vehicles, Pinellas County Sheriff's deputies do not possess the devices in their cars yet.*

[**]   *Special deputies are volunteer citizen deputies that assist Carey on an as needed basis. As constable, Carey has the power to enlist special deputies at his discretion. It is likely, although not certain, that Harold Adair and Rogers are also volunteer special deputies. Note that Dewey Adair, who is known to have been a special deputy, is the same man who arrested Russell for robbing a store years earlier and has been an acquaintance of Russell since the age of 10. He has no idea the "madman" he is now after is Russell*

[***] *There was no air conditioning in vehicles in 1949. Car windows were rarely rolled up in the summer, except perhaps in rainstorms.*

Thinking the killer is still inside, Carey assigns Dewey and Harold Adair to guard both corners of the house. He places Rogers at the front door.

Then, weapons drawn, Carey and Patrolman Cassels storm through the front door of the Browne's home.

The first thing they notice is the house is a disaster. Broken glass and dishes cover the floor. Drawers are ripped out of their cabinets, overturned with contents spilled everywhere. Furniture is broken and upturned.[*]

A pool of fresh vomit lays stagnantly in front of the refrigerator.

But the house is strangely silent. The metallic scent of blood lingers in the sweaty air.

The two lawmen rush upstairs. They find no one.[**]

Climbing back down the stairs, the two notice a smeared trail of dark red leading from the back door, through the house, to the Northwest bedroom. The two follow the trail.

When they enter the bedroom, Carey and Cassels are greeted with a sickening scene of blood and carnage that makes even the seasoned lawmen recoil.

---

[*]   *From the account of Walter Carey, St. Petersburg Times, August 11, 1949.*
[**] *From Walter Carey's comments to The Tarpon Springs Leader, August 11, 1949, courtesy of Tarpon Springs Historical Society.*

8

August 7, 1949
6:00 a.m.
Barlow's Filling Station, Palm Harbor, FL

I t is seven hours before the murder of Norman Browne.
The sun has just begun to rise when Thomas T. "T.B." Barlow watches a late model, black Ford, pull up to his service station. Barlow's station sits in a prominent place in Palm Harbor – at the corner of Florida Avenue (Main Street) and Old US 19, the major highway through the area.

Barlow is a prominent member of the community and a World War II Veteran of the US Army. His service station is less than a block west of Dewey Adair's grocery store. Barlow knows Adair well, not only as another local merchant but as a fellow member of the Palm Harbor Masonic Lodge. He is also a member of the Florida Sheriffs Association.

Barlow knows, or at least knows of, Rastus Russell. But he has not seen Russell in seven years.

When the black Ford rolls to a stop, a young man steps out of the driver's side. The man stands about 5'9, 165 pounds, is wearing a white shirt along with a blue hat and has dark hair. He walks around back, unscrews the Hillsborough County license plate on the back of the vehicle, and replaces it with a Pinellas County tag.

He then crawls back in the vehicle and exits the service station, driving north towards Crystal Beach.

Barlow makes a mental note of the strange occurrence. He does not recognize the man as Rastus Russell. Russell's appearance has changed radically from the heavyweight teenager the locals remember. In addition, he now sports a mustache, further altering the appearance of his now slender face.

49

A few minutes later, the black Ford turns left off Old US 19 onto Crystal Beach Boulevard. It passes through two white stone pillars that announce to motorists the entry into the seaside community.

Somewhere around this entrance, Russell stops the vehicle again. Here, he is spotted by an early-morning milkman. The milkman drives the area almost every day and knows most of the people on his route. The black Ford seems strange and out of place. The milkman too, makes a mental note of the stranger, then carries on.

The stranger carries on, too, navigating the black Ford up Crystal Beach Avenue and into the sleepy little community that is just waking up.

9

Lying before Carey and Cassels are two single beds holding what appear to be two bloody corpses. One body is tied spread eagle on the bed, the hands and feet bound to the headboards and footboards with what looks like electrical and sash cord. A bloody gag is tied in the mouth of one victim.

The other body is on the right. It appears to be an older male with multiple stab wounds across his body. He is covered in a white bed sheet. His stomach is sliced open. Both wrists appear to be cut. Under his left arm, a wide gash is visible that has exposed part of the lungs. His head is badly bludgeoned. His torso is so damaged that the officers initially believe he is the victim of a shotgun blast.

The body on the left is female. Also covered with a sheet, she appears to have head and face wounds. A deep crimson stains the bedding around her. According to Constable Carey, her left hand appears to be free, but she is still tied to the bed by both her feet and her right hand. Carey's account contradicts both Anne Browne's and Thelma Crum's version, both who state that Thelma entered the house and untied the older Browne before running for help.*

---

*   It is here that a discrepancy appears between witnesses and lawmen. Both Anne Browne and Thelma Crum (through J.B. Swan) state that Thelma Crum ran into the house, untied Mrs. Browne, and tied a tourniquet around her left arm before running for help. However, Constable Carey states that both victims were still tied to the beds when he and Cassels entered the room. He makes no mention of a tourniquet. Carey has no reason to lie. It could be that Browne and/or Crum was concussed and didn't remember the events clearly. Perhaps one did not remember at all, taking the other's word for what happened. After reviewing the facts, I am inclined to believe Carey's version of events.

On the nightstand between the beds sits a crooked box radio with the cord cut. Also lying on the nightstand are two wallets, which appear to have been emptied, along with a bloody, long-blade butcher knife, the tip of which has been broken off.

Suddenly, the body on the left moans.

Anne Browne is still alive.

* * *

As the lawmen rush to assist her, blood still gushes from the deep wound on her wrist and from various gashes on her face and head.

"Mr. Browne won't answer me!" she cries, "He must be hurt!"[*]

As the officers try to calm the traumatized woman, law enforcement from various agencies begin arriving on scene. Pinellas County Deputy Sheriff Wilmer James, Highway Patrolman Gallop, and Clearwater Police Chief George McClomma first arrive at the Cotton House.

There, they discover that the actual crime scene is a quarter of a mile away, in the woods.

Tarpon Springs Police, Clearwater Police, Dunedin Police, Florida Highway Patrol, and deputies from both Hillsborough and Pinellas County Sheriff's offices begin arriving outside both the Browne and Cotton houses. Ambulances await outside.

Anne Browne regains consciousness enough to begin relaying her tale to the officers. Her description of the murderer as a dark-haired "Latin type" matches Crum's description given to Carey earlier. Crum described a curly-haired man in his early thirties, about 5' 9", 170 pounds, wearing a blue shirt.[**]

Anne Browne adds the details that the man had some front teeth missing, wore a mustache, and had done some "pump work" for the couple three months earlier.

As Mrs. Browne speaks to investigators, officers comb the inside and outside of the home for clues. County Patrol and Forensic Officer

---

[*]   *Clearwater Sun, August 9, 1949.*

[**] *While Crum describes the man as wearing a blue shirt, the bloodstained shirt found later that was supposedly worn during the crime is white. Russell was wearing a blue hat. It could be that Crum simply confused the two in his memory.*

JF Peacock arrives with his fingerprinting kit, and the gentle art of gathering evidence begins.

The electricity is not working. Officers look for a cause. But all fuses are in workable condition. The wires leading to the home have not been cut.

Inside, amidst the emptied drawers and broken furniture, investigators site a broken tea cup on the dining room table. They also find a two-thirds empty bottle of whiskey and a puddle of vomit on the kitchen floor.[*]

Combined with Mrs. Browne's testimony that Russell was "glassy-eyed" during the crime, these factors initially lead investigators to believe the suspect was intoxicated at the time of the kidnapping and murder.

Browne never mentions anyone vomiting in her testimony. This suggests to investigators that the puddle is from the suspect.

They also find a lockbox, dented with its lock damaged but left behind unopened.

In the front yard, they pick up a dark blue hat, size seven and one-eighth, with a piece of rolled Sunday comic strip inside the band.

They also find what appears to be a firing pin from a gun and a chip of wood that could be from the stock of a shotgun or rifle.

Behind the tiny garage in back, the men discover tire tracks leading out of the yard. Inside the wooden garage, they find pieces of rope hanging from the rafters and a bloody rag lying on the dirt floor.[**]

Then Anne Browne drops a bombshell.

She has the license plate of the black Ford.

As officers and ambulance personnel lift Mrs. Browne from her blood-soaked bed, the only other live witness to the scene, Fluffy, the Browne's gray cat, bolts from under her bed and scurries out the door.

---

[*] *Clearwater Sun, August 9, 1949.*

[**] *Investigators are initially baffled by the rag in the garage and suspect the killer stabbed one or both of the Brownes in the garage and then carried them to the bedroom. In all likelihood, the rag is what Mrs. Browne used to treat the head wound to Norman Browne in the garage.*

With a critically injured Anne Browne on her way to the hospital, Justice of the Peace J.S. Register of Tarpon Springs arrives at the murder scene. Inside, the body of Norman Browne remains morbidly bound to the wooden bed, his open eyes staring hauntingly at the ceiling, his teeth grotesquely clenching the blood-soaked, white rag stuffed in his mouth.

Register examines the body and officially pronounces Browne dead as a result of stabbing. Photographs are snapped of the crime scene. The gruesome work of removing Browne's butchered corpse can now begin.

* * *

As a despairing Anne Browne endures the six-and-a-half mile ambulance ride to Mease Dunedin Hospital, Walter Carey is already in pursuit mode. With a description of the suspect, the vehicle, and a plate number carved into the wood of the Browne's garage in hand, Carey, as lead investigator, consults with Pinellas County Sherrif Todd Tucker on the next move.

Tucker has just arrived on scene to assume command of the manhunt. Tucker is a fifty-year-old military veteran of World War I. Beginning his career as a St. Petersburg Police officer, Tucker was elected as Pinellas County Sheriff in 1941. His platform is a zealous fight against gambling. The Sheriff is so ardent about stamping out the practice that he outlaws gumball machines in the county, claiming they "lured pennies from children." Tucker and his force of deputies enforce the law throughout Pinellas County and are also responsible for the operation of the county jail in downtown Clearwater – the facility from where Tucker is headquartered.

The Sheriff lives on rural acreage in the nearby town of Largo with his wife, Nellie May. He is a member of the local Masonic Lodge and is known as a straight-shooting lawman.

Tucker has worked many cases with Walter Carey. Upon arrival, Tucker gets a full debriefing from his old friend.

Believing the killer can't be far, Tucker orders roadblocks set up around Pinellas County, including the Courtney Campbell Bridge that spans across Tampa Bay from Pinellas to Hillsborough County. An alert is issued to law enforcement agencies throughout the state of Florida, including the Hillsborough County Sheriff's office on the other side of Tampa Bay. Hillsborough Sheriff Hugh Culbreath orders roadblocks established on his side of the bay as well.

Meanwhile, back at the crime scene and around the Cotton house, a posse of restless locals is organizing to begin assisting law enforcement in the search. In rural Pinellas County in 1949, it was not uncommon for armed citizens to join law enforcement to aid in searches or criminal apprehensions.

With Crystal Beach citizens terrified, the turnout has been large. Men and boys carrying pistols, shotguns, and rifles stand ready for duty. Some without arms are provided them courtesy of the Sheriff's office, including .45 caliber Thompson submachine guns.

Locked and loaded, the citizen army joins the swarming contingent of law enforcement in combing the orange groves, neighborhoods, and wooded areas in and around Crystal Beach, south to Dunedin, and north to Tarpon Springs. Together, they wade through pine needle forests, vine-covered Sable Palms, and towering Bald cypresses, climb over tangled underbrush rattling bushes, and peering behind fallen logs. More often, they patrol row after orderly row of leafy, green, orange trees.

Some go knocking door to door, checking on the residents inside. Others man the roadblocks set up around the immediate area.

To many of the rattled and angry residents of Crystal Beach, capture is not the first thing on their minds. They want vengeance. Murmurs of "won't bring him back alive" are heard throughout the ranks of the armed militia. Others wonder what they will do if they do come across the killer.

Ninety-six-year-old Ralph Jones recounted his thoughts to me as a twenty-one-year-old member of the citizen posse:

"Well, it was mostly in the (orange) groves. We just picked up in an area to see if we could find some strange tracks, people tracks or men's tracks or something of that nature, and just tried to follow it through. The best I can remember, I saw some and I started following em.' They'd go down one row a little bit and then maybe go back over to another row and then make circles, like somebody was looking for somebody or trying to keep away from somebody.

I kept doing the best I could. It was no organized thing at all. Everybody was just so upset about it, so angry. It was a challenge to try to find that man that did such a horrible thing. I had a pistol. I don't know what I would have done with it. I was not in a killing feeling, if you know what I mean. Maybe I could have at least scared him or something like that. I had just gotten out of the Navy and I wasn't too concerned. But I don't think nobody was out there with this idea of shooting him. But we didn't know whether he had a gun. It was more a case of we want to find that son of a gun and put him where he needs to go – in jail."

At stop signs and intersections around the county, cars are stopped and searched.

Carey and Tucker are confident the killer is still in the area. Pinellas County comprises of a peninsula bordered by water on three sides. The only way out (by automobile) is across the recently completed Courtney Cambell Causeway bridge or by driving north off the peninsula. Tucker has all of those routes blocked. The two colleagues feel they have their killer contained. They just have to flush him out.

But then they get a tip that changes their thinking.

Hearing of the violence in Crystal Beach and possible involvement of a black Ford, T.B. Barlow arrives on scene. Barlow tells Carey of his strange encounter with the black Ford earlier that morning. He tells how a man driving a late model Ford stopped at his station and changed the tags, driving off in the direction of Crystal Beach. It was just after 6 a.m.

Carey and Tucker believe the man Barlow saw could be their suspect. Furthermore, they now suspect a Tampa connection. Based on their initial interviews with both Anne Browne and Miles Crum, the team also contemplates a Chicago link. An initial theory begins to take hold.

The killer may be part of a Chicago drug gang – known as the most violent and brutal of all criminal organizations. And while it's still only a theory, Tucker mentions to the press that the killer may have been intoxicated with marijuana at the time of the murder.

A rumor floats that a partially smoked marijuana cigarette was found at the murder scene.

---

*   *From 2024 interview with Mr. Ralph Jones.*

As the wilting heat of the Florida day gives way to the balmy calm of evening, the sensational rumor rages through Crystal Beach and Pinellas County, adding additional terror to an already horrific story. A drug-crazed lunatic is on the loose. No one is safe.

In 1949, the theory of a drug-crazed lunatic does not need much embellishment to take hold. It has only been a few years since a manic paranoia swept through the nation about the strange and mysterious drug known as marijuana.

And Rastus Russell has an odd link to one of its drivers.

10

October 16, 1933
Ybor City, Tampa, FL
Licata Residence
Early Morning

It is fifteen years and ten months before Norman Browne is murdered.

In the dark early morning, twenty-one-year-old Victor Licata rises from his bed in his family's Tampa home. The young Licata has been diagnosed with a mental illness. Measures are currently underway to have him institutionalized.

But on this quiet morning, in the bedrooms around him, his mother, father, two brothers, and one sister are deep in slumber. As Licata silently creeps down the hallway of his family home, he carries a long handle axe. Silently entering the room of his parents, the disturbed young man raises the axe high above his head and swings violently downward, splitting the skull of his father with the sharp blade of the tool. Quickly, he does the same to his mother.

He then systematically moves to the next bedroom and repeats the process. He goes about his work quietly and methodically until every one of his family members lies murdered in a pool of blood and brain matter.

The next morning, police find a confused and delirious Licata in a bedroom of the family home. He is wearing a clean, pressed shirt and trousers. Underneath the clean exterior, police find the man's skin and body smeared with blood.

Somewhere in the home, police alledgedly find a partially consumed marijuana cigarette.

In 1933, marijuana was not yet illegal, nor was it widely known. It was a "new" recreational substance that is draped in mystery.

The next day, Chief City Detective W.D. Bush claims he had investigated Licata prior to the crime and learned that the killer had been "addicted to smoking marijuana cigarettes for more than six months."

The media runs wild. They report the sensational murders as the work of an "axe-murdering marijuana addict."

The narrative proves to have legs and the national media eats it up. Soon, marijuana has not only become known to the public, its reputation has been forged.

The Tampa Tribune published an editorial four days later entitled "Stop this Murderous Smoke," in which it proclaimed "...*whether or not the poisonous mind-wrecking weed is mainly accountable for the tragedy, its sale should not be and should never have been permitted here or elsewhere.*"

Three years later, the 1936 film *Reifer Madness* makes its debut. While the film is part comedy, it contains a sinister message about the use of marijuana and its ability to cause severe psychosis and mental illness to its users. The film has a chilling effect on the public and forges the image of marijuana as a dangerous and potentially violence-inducing substance.

Licata is never prosecuted for the crime. He is examined by psychiatrists and is diagnosed with "dementia praecox with homicidal tendencies" that made him "overly psychotic." He is committed to the Florida Hospital for the Insane in Chattahoochee in 1933. His medical file never references marijuana usage.

One year later, in December of 1934, Licata is joined at Chattahoochee by a small-time car thief by the name of John Calvin Russell. Russell is known to the other patients as "Rastus."

It is unknown as to whether Russell and Licata ever met and if so, what type of relationship they may have had.

But six months later, Rastus Russell escapes from Chattahoochee.

Russell returns to Chattahoochee in 1939 for a brief stay. Does he talk with Victor Licata then? Does he share the details of his escape?

Whether inspired by Russell's escape years earlier or not, on October 15, 1945, Victor Licata and four other inmates stage their own escape from the hospital. All but one are quickly recaptured.

But Victor Licata gets away and is not seen or heard from for nearly five years.

In the fall of 1950, Licata is staying with a cousin in New Orleans. The cousin turns him in to the police, and Licata's life on the lamb comes to an end. He is sent to the Florida State Prison in Raiford – another institution to which Rastus Russell is intimately familiar.

It is there on December 4, 1950, that Victor Licata kills himself by hanging.[*]

But the fear and loathing of marijuana that he inspired will linger in the minds of the public and law enforcement for decades.

In 1949, that fear and loathing is still fresh in the minds of Walter Carey and Todd Tucker. According to an interview with Anne Browne by Deputy Sheriff Roy James, the killer openly told Mrs. Browne he was part of a narcotics gang from Chicago. He told Miles Crum he shot three policemen in Chicago. Anne Browne describes her attacker as being intoxicated on something and had "glassy eyes." Both Crum and Browne describe the perpetrator as a "Latin type." Is he a drug smuggler from South America?

The lawmen don't know. But they believe they have another drug-crazed lunatic on their hands, just like Victor Licata. And this time, he's on *their* side of the bay.

Operating on the theory that the killer has connections to a Tampa-Chicago gang of marijuana smugglers, Sherriff Tucker asks for assistance from the federal narcotics bureau. Tucker and Carey believe the crime follows the pattern of narcotics gangsters, known as the most brutal of all underworld mobsters.[**]

Constable Carey pulls no punches when talking to the press.

"I'm convinced the killer is a marijuana addict," he wearily announces the Monday after the crime. "The clues Deputy James got from Mrs. Browne bear out a hunch I've had from the start."[**]

For no apparent reason, Carey then reverses himself later in the day, telling reporter Bob Prichard of the Clearwater Sun that he no longer believes this (the killer was a marijuana addict) to be the case.

No marijuana is found at the scene.

---

[*]   *Wikipedia, Victor Licata.*
[**]   *The Tampa Tribune, August 8, 1949.*

Carey's suspicions are likely influenced by the popular villain of the times, marijuana, and Tampa Bay's original poster boy for murderous drug rampages – Victor Licata.

As it turns out, Rastus Russell is no Victor Licata. But he might be just as dangerous.

11

June 1949
Home of Maud A. (Baker) McCord
914 Louisiana Street, Tampa, FL

I t is two months prior to Norman Browne's murder.

Rastus Russell has a project today.

Since returning from incarceration in Illinois, the convict has found a temporary home with a sympathetic aunt. Mrs. Maud A. (Baker) McCord is the younger sister of Rastus Russell's deceased mother, Claude Estelle Baker.

McCord is recently widowed. Her husband, Cecil A. McCord, passed away only six months earlier. The two made the newspaper ten years earlier when they wed seated inside Cecil's car. Maud had two broken legs at the time, the result of an automobile accident, and could only be married sitting down. It was Cecil's second marriage, his first yielding several children. At fifty-six years old, it was Maud Baker's first. She had no children of her own. The couple lived together for ten years at 914 East Louisiana Avenue in Tampa before Cecil's passing.

Rastus Russell is the black sheep of the Baker family. His arrival in Tampa to stay with Maud shortly after her husband's passing may or may not be a coincidence. Russell's uncle, Paul O'Brien Baker, lives in Chicago, where Russell spent much of his time while out of Florida in the 1940s. It is possible he hears through Paul that "Uncle Cecil" passed away and arranges to come live with the lonely widow, who may or may not be happy for the company.

Or, Russell could have simply returned to Florida and shown up on her doorstep.

Regardless, we must assume that Maud was close with Claude Estelle to take in her troubled adult son.

Like many residents in 1940's Florida, Mrs. McCord keeps a weapon in the house. In her case, Aunt Maud owns a .12-gauge shotgun she keeps for personal protection. The sixty-six-year-old widow keeps it inside a cloth sack that hangs on the wall in her home.

Rastus Russell has found it. And unlike Aunt Maud, he has plans to put it to use.

Russell removes the weapon from its sleeve and replaces it with a "dummy" gun: a piece of wood fitted with a broomstick barrel that resembles a weapon the approximate size of the gun. From the outside, it appears as though the real gun is still inside the sleeve.

He then takes the shotgun to the garage and, with a hacksaw, proceeds to saw off the steel barrel and the back of the wooden butt. This has the effect of both making the weapon easier to carry and conceal but also allows the lethal pellets to spread wider in a shorter distance. A "sawed-off" shotgun is a devastating weapon in close quarters.

Russell does not discard the severed barrel or stock of the gun. Instead, he hides them in the garage.

The modified .12 gauge will be a favorite tool of Russell's through the summer of 1949.

Aunt Maud will never be the wiser.

12

July 24, 1949
Sunday Morning
7:00 a.m.
Dunedin, FL

Exactly two weeks prior to the murder of Norman Y. Browne in Crystal Beach, Lester Lambert was looking forward to a day with friends. Thirty minutes into his two-and-a-half-hour drive north to Ocala, FL, Lambert is enjoying a day off from his job as chief assistant to Pinellas County tax collector, M. Walter Lanier.

It seems like a good day for a drive, if one doesn't mind the heat. The temperature is 74 degrees on the way to a sweltering 94. While the skies are clear, the dew point hovers at 73.9, meaning the air virtually drips with moisture. As do most drivers in the 1940s Florida summer, Lambert has rolled down the windows of his 1939 gray Plymouth coupe to provide some comfort in the stifling humidity.

As he passes through Dunedin Isles on US 19 in Pinellas County, Lambert spots a young man in a khaki shirt and trousers on the side of the road. The man is waving at Lambert as though in distress.

The tax man slows to a stop as the stranger approaches, then leans into Lambert's passenger side window. He tells Lambert that his car won't start and asks for help. Behind him sits a new-looking sedan with two tires parked on the berm of the highway. Lambert pulls of the road and walks back to help.

The distressed motorist seems to be good-mannered and physically fit. Lambert makes him for a soldier, recently discharged from the service.

The two work for several minutes, attempting to diagnose the problem and start the engine. But they are unable to start the car.

The young man thanks Lambert profusely for his efforts. Lambert climbs back into his Plymouth and drives off.

Nearly ten minutes later, just south of Tarpon Springs, Lambert spots the late-model sedan again. This time, it is in his rear-view mirror. The vehicle is charging up behind him, zig-zagging wildly on US 19. The crazed car speeds up beside Lambert and forces him to the side of the road. Lambert skids to a stop.

As Lambert peers through the dust, the black barrel of a sawed-off shotgun pokes through his open, driver-side window. The sinister weapon is pointed at his face. It lies nestled in the hands of the young man in the khaki shirt whom Lambert had just assisted.

The man orders Lambert into the passenger seat, then jumps into the driver's side of Lambert's gray Plymouth coupe.

The two take a long drive. As they go, the man seems agitated and, at times, appears to be looking for someone. He also has a dazed look about him. Lambert later believes the man is under the influence of something, suspecting barbital tablets. During the drive, he tells Lambert he "can't make up his mind what to do."*

After taking a circuitous route, the driver turns down Curlew Creek Road just south of Palm Harbor. Pulling off onto a tiny dirt road, the young man orders Lambert out of the car.

As Lambert steps out of the vehicle, the man points the shotgun at him again.

"I shot three policemen in Chicago," he tells his frightened captive.

He threatens that if every command he gives is not followed, he will kill Lambert. He then orders Lambert to undress.

The terrified Lambert strips naked.

The captor then demands Lamberts's watch. Lambert complies.

Ordering Lambert to sit against a tree, the kidnapper ties Lambert to it using his own clothes, making sure to remove the naked man's wallet in the process. It contains $13 in cash.

He then speeds off in Lambert's coupe.

Lambert struggles for nearly thirty minutes before he breaks free. He walks to a local dairy, where he calls Pinellas County Sherriff

---

* *The Evening Independent, July 26, 1949.*

Todd Tucker. Tucker calls up a posse and his friend from Tarpon Springs, constable Walter Carey.

They find the young man's sedan back where Lambert was hijacked. The lawmen begin searching for Lambert's Plymouth. They have the license plate – 4-49.

Carey discovers the strange man's sedan was reported stolen in Tampa. He begins his investigation there. When the constable shows Lambert a series of mug shots later, Lambert identifies a man in one of the photos as the robber.

But when Carey hauls in twenty-six-year-old Edward Smith for the crime, Lambert can't identify him. Smith is cut loose. That is because Smith is not the perpetrator.

The glossy-eyed young man with the sawed-off shotgun, who seemed dazed and confessed he didn't know what to do next, the man who struck early on a Sunday morning exactly two weeks before Norman Browne's murder, is indeed *not* Edward Smith.

The young man is Rastus Russell.

13

August 6, 1949
Evening
Seminole Heights Neighborhood, Tampa, FL

It is approximately seventeen hours before Norman Browne is murdered.

Nadine Russell has just left her parent's house at 1214 New Orleans Avenue. Her father, H.L. Russell, a local floor resurfacer, knows his daughter is headed to the grocery store to pick up a few items.

Although they share a surname, the father and daughter are not related to, nor do they know Rastus Russell.

But they are about to be impacted by the man with the same last name.

Nadine pulls the black 1946 Ford Sedan with the V8 engine into a parking spot near Curtis Street and Nebraska Avenue in Seminole Heights.

She ambles into the grocery store across the street.

* * *

A short distance away at Maud McCord's house on Louisiana Avenue, Rastus Russell tells his aunt he is going "to a job" with a construction company. He says he will be back around 5 a.m. the following morning.

Russell leaves his aunt's house. His mode of transportation is unknown. It is believed that Dorothy Jean Crain was staying with Russell at the time. But her whereabouts are not known on Saturday night. She does not stay behind at Maud McCord's house. Mrs. McCord will not see Russell until 11 a.m. the next morning; when she does, he will be alone.

Shortly after leaving his aunt's house, Rastus Russell, a seasoned car thief, arrives in Seminole Heights. There, he comes across H.L. Russell's black 1946 Ford parked in the parking spot where Nadine Russell left it. It is unclear as to whether the keys are left inside or if the convict breaks into the car and starts it himself.

Regardless, within minutes, Russell is driving away in the black Ford.

Where Russell goes immediately after or who he is with is not known. What is clear is he arrives back at the home of Sam Crain shortly after midnight. When he arrives, he has Dorothy Jean Crain with him.

Back in Seminole Heights, H.L. Russell has notified Tampa Police that his car has been stolen.

In Hillsborough County at least, police are already on the lookout for a 1946 Black Ford Sedan.

But Rastus Russell is no longer in Hillsborough County.

14

Sunday, August 7, 1949
4:00 a.m.
Sam Crain House, Palm Harbor

It is 4:00 am, Sunday, August 7[th,] when Sam Crain hears Rastus Russell leaving his house. Russell had shown up at his home around 12:30 a.m. He did not sleep. He was now departing again.

The forty-one-year-old Crain is a Citrus plant worker at the nearby Pasco Citrus Plant. He lives in a wood frame, two-story house on Curlew Creek Road, about two miles south of Palm Harbor.* The home is an old-style Florida house with a wraparound porch, a fireplace, and a chimney. There is no electricity and no running water. It is cold in the winter and hot in the summer. But it is large enough to accommodate Crain's still-growing family.

Water comes from a hand pump in the back. Outside, a filled-in dirt circle is all the remains of a coy pond maintained by the previous residents. To the side sits a smokehouse where Sam Crain smokes meats for his family's enjoyment. The home lies in the vicinity of the Dunedin Isles Golf Course and the Atlantic Coastline Railroad. When the train comes, often transporting well-heeled visitors from out of town, Crain can clearly hear the long, hooting whistle of the airhorns, alerting residents of its approach.

Much like the Browne's home in Crystal Beach, the Crain house is surrounded by woods on three sides. Curlew Creek Road runs in front of the home. Across the road, down over an embankment, lies

---

*   *Crain does not own the home. It is owned by the Pasco Packing Plant and provided to him as an employment benefit.*

Curlew Creek. The creek is a regular source of adventure and activity for the Crain children and their dog, Smokey, a mix breed brindle.

Crain occupies the house with his wife, Flora, three sons (Wilbur Eugene, 12, Allen Garfield, 18, and Furrell Richard, 21) and three daughters (Emmie Lois, 2, Alma Inez, 4, and Dorothy Jean, 16.) Mrs. Crain is currently pregnant with the couple's eighth child. The Crain's eldest son, Charles Edward, twenty-three, is away serving in the military.

When Rastus Russell returns to Palm Harbor in 1949, many do not recognize him. He has been away for seven years. His body has transformed into a hardened statue. He sports a mustache, of which, according to Sam Crain, he is quite proud.

While Russell makes a temporary home at his Aunt Maud's house in Tampa, Russell's heart is in his old stomping ground of Palm Harbor, a place to which he often returns.

It is here that he meets Furrell Richard Crain and Allen Garfield Crain. The two Crain brothers, along with their father Sam, are no choir boys. While all three work hard at Pasco Citrus Plant, they are known to play hard as well. A Saturday night dust-up at a local tavern is never out of the question for the three men. Scrapes with local police happen occasionally. They are hellraisers, but not, at least as far as our research was concerned, criminals. At the same time, they are not to be trifled with.

As Wilburn Crain, son of Sam Crain, remembers:

"He (Sam Crain) was a scrapper. My brothers were scrappers too. They used to go and get tanked up and clean the clock at some of the bars around there. Garfield, I want to say he was the mean one, but he was the bad one. If you looked at him wrong, he'd knock you out. He didn't wait around for you to pull a gun or a knife or something. He'd just knock you out.

Furrell, he was something else. He was low-key, but he could be bad too. I remember the three of 'em used to go in, and the next thing you know, we'd hear about the law looking for 'em because they created such a disturbance at the bar and all. That was the gruesome threesome."

Somewhere in their Palm Harbor travels, Furrell and Allen (Garfield) meet Rastus Russell. They, as do the rest of the Crain family, know him as Jim Sullivan, an alias Russell uses. The brothers strike up

---

* *From author interview with Wilburn Crain, May 2024.*

a friendship with Russell. The three share an interest in cars. Russell becomes a regular visitor at the Crain house, often arriving in the same car as Furrell and Allen. The three pass many an hour working on automobiles in the Crain's front yard. Russell is a knowledgeable mechanic, and the Crain boys enjoy learning from the older man. [*]

It is through his sons that Sam Crain, also handy with an engine, comes to know Russell. While raised in Florida, Russell does not speak with a southern drawl. In a lower key, slightly raspy voice, Russell has what some would call a Midwest accent, or as some say, no accent at all. Around the Crain home, he is mild-mannered and polite. Perhaps because of this, Sam Crain initially has no problems with Russell and does in fact, even seem to like the young man they call "Jim." [*]

"He was just as nice as he could be as far as I can remember," says Wilburn Crain. "He was just nice." [*]

Crain relates an antidote that demonstrates the softer side of Rastus Russell. It was also, in hindsight, the side of Russell that the Crain's likely knew.

Crain spent many days in the woods across the road from his house. Through those woods and down an embankment was Curlew Creek, a brackish inlet that homed both freshwater and saltwater fish – a virtual playground for a twelve-year-old boy. Crain remembers redfish and large snook swimming through the sometimes deep and sometimes shallow water.

One afternoon, Crain is down at the creek with his dog, Smokey. Over the creek bank comes one Rastus Russell, or as Wilburn knows him, "Jim." Having grown up on the water, Russell is a strong swimmer. He is also a familiar face around the Crain home during this time. Wearing swim trunks, Russell wades into the creek and swims across.

Crain explains it from there:

"He went in the water and was swimming around. He asked me if I knew how to swim. I said I didn't. So he said, 'well, I'll try to teach you.' So over a period of time, he did teach me how to swim…At first he was just trying to teach me how to stay afloat in the water because he knew that sooner or later, if I got into deep water and didn't know how to swim, I'd be a goner. We went through the procedure of dog paddling. Then he'd teach me to

---

[*]   *From author interview with Wilburn Crain, May 2024.*

overhand and all that. I don't recall how many days we did that. But I got to be a good swimmer after all that. He didn't treat me like a twelve-year-old. He treated me like, older. Thats my memory of John Calvin Russell – of one on one with him."*

According to Sam Crain, on or about May 21, Crain rents a room in his home to the thirty-four-year-old Russell. While Sam Crain is not in the business of renting out rooms in his house, Russell wants a place to stay in Palm Harbor, and Crain has a big house and an empty bedroom. The two agree on a rent of $15 per week. But Russell doesn't pay and after a week, moves back in with his aunt in Tampa.

He does, however, become smitten with Crain's sixteen-year-old daughter, Dorothy Jean. During Russell's numerous visits and short stay, the teenager takes note of the older man's handsome looks and well-shaped physique. A flirtatious relationship develops between the two.**

"He was a pretty sharp-looking dude," says Wilburn Crain. *"I don't remember seeing any contact between them two, although there probably was on my sister's part because she's sixteen years old. She was fascinated by the guy."**

Dorothy Jean Crain is a good-natured, browned-eyed girl next door. With light, sandy hair that hangs to her shoulders, she often wears it in a pony tail. With her parents and older brothers working to support the family, the teen has recently dropped out of school and assumed the mantle of daytime home manager. She spends her days housecleaning, cooking meals, and tending to twelve-year-old Wilburn and her two and four-year-old sisters.

"She was really, really ... vibrant," remembers Wilburn. *"My mother and father and brothers would work. So there'd be nobody home but maybe Dorothy and me, and the girls. But we didn't call her Dorothy. We called her 'sister.' She was stern though. If she said do something, you better do it!"****

On June 4th, while the Crain parents are shopping in Clearwater, Rastus Russell returns to the house.

---

* *From author interview with Wilburn Crain, May 2024.*

** *To what extent this relationship progressed before or after Russell's stay at the house may never be 100% known, but in perspective, can certainly be guessed at.*

*** *From author personal interview with Wilburn Crain, May 2024.*

Whether Russell "takes" Dorothy Jean or she leaves willingly, the two depart in Russell's car and disappear.

While Sam and (later) Dorothy Crain both insist she was taken and kept against her will, it seems more likely she went willingly.

June 4th is a Saturday. We know it isn't a work day, because her parents are at the grocery store. Sam Crain's sons work with him at the citrus plant. If he is not working, they probably aren't either. Thus, it is possible, if not likely, that her older brothers are at home at the time.

It seems questionable that they would allow their friend to drag their sister out of the home kicking and screaming without putting up a fight. While Russell may be older and stronger, the Crain brothers are no choir boys. It is likely the two together could have fought off Russell (or at least put up a fight) had they chosen to, despite the massive Russell's size.

Wilburn Crain has no memory of Dorothy leaving with Russell. If the girl was home alone babysitting Wilburn, it would seem almost certain Wilburn would remember it, especially if she was taken by force.

Regardless, Sam Crain notifies authorities, reporting Dorothy missing to Clearwater Police. A search begins for the man known as "Jim Sullivan" and the girl. But the couple seems to have vanished without a trace.

On July 24th, nearly two months later, Rastus and Dorothy return home to the Crain house. Russell tells the Crain's that he and their daughter have been in California, and the couple were married in Baxley, Georgia, on June 6th, two days after leaving the Crain home. Rastus Russell now refers to the teenage Dorothy as his "wife."*

The couple stays for two hours. The family then watches as their daughter and new, apparent son-in-law climb back into a 1939 gray Plymouth coupe and drive away again.

Oddly, the Crains do not seem to challenge the situation. No mention or evidence of any further communication with law enforcement on the matter can be found.

---

* *The Evening Independent, August 19, 1949. Dorothy later denies this and claims Russell had threatened to kill her if she did not tell everyone they were married. No record of the marriage is ever located. However, Russell also goes by several aliases.*

* * *

As the couple pulls out of the Crain's driveway, Russell turns the car east towards Aunt Maud's in Tampa. Here the couple will live for the next two weeks.

As they ride to Tampa, Dorothy must know, or at least suspect, that the car they are riding in is stolen. For earlier in the day, Rastus Russell robbed Lester Lambert, took his watch and wallet, tied him to a tree naked, and stole his car – the car in which the couple are now driving to Tampa. After all, when the day began, Russell was driving a different car. And while Lambert does not mention a girl in the car during his ordeal, he does state that Russell seemed to be driving around looking for somebody.[*]

According to Sam Crain, he does not see his daughter and Russell again until that early morning of August 7th, when they return to the Crain home at 12:30 a.m. Whether Crain is aware of it or not, Russell arrives driving the black, V-8 Ford he stole in Seminole Heights only a few hours earlier.

Dorothy is with him.

It begs the question, was Dorothy with him when he stole the car? According to Maud McCord, Russell leaves the house around 7 p.m. on Saturday. She does not mention Dorothy or her whereabouts. The car is stolen around 8 p.m.

Regardless, when Russell departs the Crain's house at 4 a.m. Sunday, he leaves the girl behind.

At some point between 4 a.m. and 6 a.m. that morning, Rastus Russell steals a Pinellas County license plate. By 6 a.m., he'll be fastening it to his car at Barlow's Filling Station.

---

[*]   *St. Petersburg Times, July 26, 1949.*

15

August 7, 1949
2:00 p.m.
Browne House on Rattlesnake Road

Rastus Russell's white shirt and khaki trousers are stained in the blood of Norman and Anne Browne. The layer of sweat dripping from his body mixes with the crimson gore on his hands and arms. The blue hat he wore when he arrived at the Browne's is missing.

As a crumpled Thelma Crum lies unconscious in front of him, Rastus Russell runs back through the house to the rear of the Browne's property.

There awaits his black 1946 Ford. With the odor of discharged gunpowder still lingering in the hot, still air, Russell tosses the shotgun into the trunk of the vehicle and slams it shut. The killer hops into the driver's seat and fires the Ford's V8 engine.

Russell avoids the better-traveled Vincent Street and instead drives straight down the less-traveled but parallel Broadus Street. Somewhere past the Cotton house, he turns back onto Vincent and escapes Crystal Beach well before police arrive.[*]

Despite the trail of carnage left behind, Russell does not leave with what he came for. Instead, his take for the entire day is a trunk full of groceries, Norman Browne's .12 gauge shotgun, and a total of $30 he pilfered from the Browne's wallets.[**]

---

[*] *Robert Cotton later states that no other cars passed his house before or after Miles Crum arrived. Broadus is the only logical escape route from Rattlesnake Road.*

[**] *At least this is the claim made by Anne Browne.*

Russell drives back through the giant arches marking the entrance to Crystal Beach. He turns right and heads south on old US 19 towards Clearwater, driving carefully to avoid suspicion.

Russell's whereabouts for the next few hours are unclear. He may drive straight to the Crain's home. Or, he may go somewhere else first. At some point, however, on the afternoon of August 7th, Russell pulls the 1946 Ford back up to the Crain residence on Curlew Creek Road.

As he does, Sam Crain, Furrell Crain, and Wilburn Crain are sitting on the front porch. Russell ambles up to the three and lifts his left foot, propping it on the edge of the porch. He leans his left elbow down on his knee and begins talking with the men. The three notice a large, bloody gash above Russell's left thumb.

When asked what happened to his hand, Russell tells the men he slammed it in a car door.

"I want to think it was in the afternoon," remembers Wilburn Crain. "He put one foot up on the porch. And as he stepped up, we noticed, I can't remember if his left or right thumb was bleeding. And he had blood from his hand, I guess, on his clothes. He said he caught it in the car door. Of course, my father probably read through that pretty quick."

It is unclear if Russell changes out of his clothes before arriving back at the Crain's house. Was the blood Wilburn Crain remembers seeing Russell's? Or was it the blood of the Browne's? It seems reasonable to assume that Russell injured his thumb at some point during his attack on the Browne's or Crum's.

Regardless, after arriving back at the Crain's, he leaves a bloody shirt and trousers in his room, clothes later believed to have been worn at the murder scene. He then shaves off his mustache, of which he was so proud only days earlier. He washes up and sits down to a family dinner with the Crains. The convict talks and laughs with the family as though nothing out of the ordinary has happened.

What transpires next is according to the testimony of Sam Crain.

After dinner, Russell approaches Sam Crain. The car he is driving is "borrowed" from a friend, he tells Crain. He must return it tonight. Will Crain meet him in Tampa and give him a ride back?

---

* *From author's personal interview with Wilburn Crain, May 2024. Other sources indicate it was Russell's left hand that was cut.*

Sam Crain agrees.

At approximately 9:30 p.m., after a one-hour drive from his home in Dunedin, Crain meets Russell in the Seminole Heights neighborhood of Tampa.[*]

Seminole Heights is a quiet suburb about four miles north of downtown Tampa. In the 1940s, the close-tied community is on the up and come. Having sprouted at the peak of the popular bungalow home in the 1910s, the suburb boasts the highest number of the fashionable houses in the area. The high ceilings, low-pitched roof, wide eaves, and large airspace underneath make the small wood-frame buildings ideal for the warm, tropical climate of Tampa Bay. Although the intricate streetcar system was dismantled three years earlier, residents of Seminole Heights need not leave their community to enjoy a plethora of shops, schools, churches, restaurants, and grocery stores.

Seminole Heights, by no coincidence, is in very close proximity to the home of Russell's Aunt, Maude McCord.

Sam Crain has no idea Russell has parked the car only a block from where he stole it the night before, at the corner of Curtis and Nebraska Street. As Sam Crain watches from the driver's seat of his car, he sees Russell transfer a supply of groceries from the trunk of his "borrowed" car to Crain's vehicle. These include five-pound sacks of sugar and flour. He is then disturbed to see Russell move two shotguns, one regular sized, and one with the stock and barrel sawed off, to Crain's trunk.[**]

The two return to Crain's house. It's after 11 p.m. Whether with help from Crain, others or just himself, Russell moves the shotguns and groceries from Crain's car into "his" bedroom at the Crain home.

After that, having not slept in at least thirty hours, Rastus Russell settles in for a good night's rest.

---

[*]   *By 9:30 p.m. on Sunday night, all major routes out of Pinellas County are roadblocked with checkpoints looking for Russell. How he avoids or gets through these checkpoints remains a mystery. While the crafty Russell knows the back roads of Pinellas and Hillsborough Counties by memory, there are only so many routes off the Peninsula.*

[**]   *The Tampa Tribune, August 10, 1949.*

16

Special Section: Suspicions and Mysteries in the Case of Rastus Russell

The version of events you have read thus far is a composite of perspectives from witnesses, police, and newspaper reporters.

Where possible, we have deferred to the viewpoint of eyewitnesses or those directly involved, as opposed to newspaper reporters working on a deadline for a story.

However, it is here we get the first taste of inconsistencies in stories, a taste of things that at first seem inconsequential but, when taken in perspective, simply do not add up.

Some of these may be due to victim trauma, not thinking straight, or remembering incorrectly. Others, however, leave one to question the motive of the person recounting the event.

There are no more inconsistencies than in the testimony of Anne Browne. Granted, Mrs. Browne had just been through a horrific event, was severely injured, and likely had a concussion. But she continued to give interviews up to a month after the event, often telling the story differently.

Shrouded in mystery is Rastus Russell's first visit to the Browne's home, approximately three months prior to the Norman Browne murder. Anne Browne first tells police he was there to repair a well. Later, she says no, he helped Mr. Browne repair the well. Then she says he came to look at the house, even recounting a story he told about seeking a house for a friend. Later, we hear another story that he had simply stopped for some water for his car.

Russell, for his part, will later state that he never repaired a well at the property.

Raising more suspicion is Browne claiming she did not know Russell's name. This was supposedly his second visit to the house. He spent three hours chatting and having coffee with the Browne's that Sunday morning. He was supposedly interested in buying their home. And he never said his name? Not even an alias? And they never asked?

Mrs. Browne never states, at least publicly, why Russell believed there was money in the house of two people who were supposedly dead broke. Unfortunately, the Pinellas County Sheriff's Office, as well as every local police department, claim they no longer have any records from that era. However, as we will discover later, Russell clearly planned the Sunday morning visit to the Browne's and expected to return with some sort of windfall. The Browne's were not chosen randomly, as was reported at the time, because of their isolated location.

Next is Rastus Russell's mysterious relationship with the Crain family. Sam Crain states that Russell rented a room from him for one week – and that was his sole relationship with Russell. But Crain does not even own or pay rent at the home. He, himself, is a tenant. He is not in the business of renting rooms. How does he come to know Russell well enough to give him a bedroom in his home next to his sons and daughters?

Wilburn Crain, in his 2024 interview, states that Russell was friends with two of the Crain brothers and was a frequent visitor at the Crain home. Why does Sam Crain never mention this?

Sam Crain's story of what happened the night of the murders is peppered with inconsistencies.

According to Todd Tucker, Crain states that the first time he saw the sawed-off shotgun was sitting in Russell's room. Yet he says in a separate interview that he watched as Russell loaded groceries and two shotguns into the back of his (Crain's) car the night of the murders. Was he not suspicious then? Did he not think it odd that Russell was returning a "borrowed" car by leaving it in a parking space in Seminole Heights?

A separate theory suggests it was Dorothy Crain, and not Sam, who met Russell in Tampa that night and brought him back. Indeed, several of Russell's farm co-workers tell police it was *they* who helped Russell move the groceries from his car that night.

So, either Russell's co-workers are lying, or Sam Crain is lying.

If it was, in fact, Dorothy who picked Russell up that night, Sam Crain may have taken the blame himself in an attempt to distance his young daughter from any connection to the heinous crime, and Russell himself. Both Dorothy and Sam Crain both state later that they were frightened of Russell, and simply did what he said.

Another reporter's account has Russell returning to Tampa that night and coming back to the Crain home at 3 p.m. the next day. However, the account presented here comes from the investigator's interview with Sam Crain. In addition, while Russell did live with his Aunt Maud in Tampa, she states she did not see Russell after 11 a.m. on Sunday morning. As Russell was only known to stay at his aunt's and the Crains, it seems logical that Russell spent Sunday night at the Crain's house.

In addition to this, we are asked to accept that Sam and Flora Crain, having a sixteen-year-old daughter supposedly kidnapped and missing for two months, simply accept the alleged kidnapper into the family upon his sudden return. Not only that, they also gave him a room in their home, ate dinner with him and did favors for him, such as meeting him nearly an hour away in Tampa and then driving him back.

It is possible that the Crain's accepted that their daughter eloped and choose to welcome their new "son-in-law" and daughter home instead of causing a family trauma or upsetting their daughter. But the circumstances seem to leave some lingering questions. The Crains seem to explain everything by stating they were "terrified" of Russell. But Sam Crain and his sons do not seem like the types who are easily intimidated.

We also wrestle with the question as to whether Dorothy was kidnapped, or left willingly, and if so, if she participated and/or knew about any of Russell's crimes.

In a tangled web of inconsistencies, only one conclusion seems obvious: Rastus Russell's relationship to the Crain family is deeper and more complex than is reported in the media at the time. Sheriff Tucker will later have the same suspicions.

Lastly, we must address the strange inconsistencies in the stories of both Anne Browne and Thelma Crum. Both claim that after Russell left, Thelma Crum ran into the house, cut Anne Browne loose, and even tied her injured arm in a tourniquet before running for help. Crum even claims (through J.B. Swan) that she cut Browne loose with the very knife used by Rastus Russell to kill Norman Browne.

Yet Constable Carey states that Browne was still tied up when he entered the bedroom. Carey, by all accounts, is a straightforward lawman and has no reason to lie. Of the three, he was the only one in a sound state of mind at the time.

Nonetheless, why would Anne Browne and Thelma Crum each tell the same story if it were untrue? Even if both were delirious at the time, why would they both remember the story the same way?

As I dug further into the research, none of these questions had a clear answer.

For some, I was able to come up with a reasonably sound theory.

Others would reveal semi-obvious conclusions as the story unfolded.

A few could remain mysteries for the ages.

17

August 8, 1949
Tarpon Springs Hospital
Tarpon Springs, Florida
Morning

It is a hot, sunny Monday morning when Hillsborough County Sheriff's Deputies arrive at the hospital room of Miles J. Crum.

Crum has amazed the medical staff at Tarpon Springs Hospital by surviving the night. However, they still only give him a ten percent chance to live. He is in critical condition with a gaping shotgun wound to his lower abdomen.

Further down the hall, in another room, Thelma Crum clings to life. Mrs. Crum is also in critical condition with a serious head wound. Her face is badly cut, and she is suffering from at least a concussion. Doctors are unsure how much damage has been done and remain concerned.

Baby Judy Crum is also at the hospital being tended to by nurses. While the infant is bruised from her fall to the ground, doctors believe she is otherwise unharmed.

Back in Tampa, working in conjunction with Pinellas Sheriff Todd Tucker, deputies have arrested two suspects in the murderous rampage.

Each matches the general description of the killer. Each was driving a vehicle that resembled the one described by Anne Browne. Each license plate has a similarity to the number scratched on the wooden wall of the Browne's garage.

Further arousing the suspicion of the deputies is that beach sand has been found in one of the suspect's vehicles – the same type of sand that is common around Crystal Beach and the Browne's sandy yard. Clothing is also found in one of the cars.

One of the suspects is of particular interest to the deputies. His wife reported him missing for the past twenty-four hours.

The deputies and Tucker are hopeful they have their man. It is up to Miles Crum to tell them if they do.

Crum is weak and barely able to speak. But he is eager to identify his attacker.

As a feeble Miles Crum tilts his head sideways to see, the deputies parade the handcuffed suspects in front of him. Crum examines each thoughtfully.

After the suspects are taken outside of the room, the grocer tells the deputies he believes neither are the assailant who shot him.

The deputies, disappointed, return the men to Tampa and release them. The clothes in one of the vehicles are kept for further examination.

Carey and Tucker, receiving the news, go back to the drawing board. They don't have to wait long for their next clue. The Browne's milkman, the one delivering milk the day before, calls Tucker. He has a plate number. It's different from the one scratched on the wall by Anne Browne.

Later that morning, the case breaks wide open. Todd Tucker gets another call from Hillsborough County Deputies in Tampa. They believe they have the car used in the murder.

Carey, who has not slept since Saturday night, and Tucker confer in Tucker's office with State Attorney Chester B. McMullen.[*] Then they jump in Tucker's car and head east, speeding across the Courtney Campbell Causeway towards Tampa.

---

[*]   *The Tampa Tribune, August 8, 1949.*

18

August 8, 1949
Seminole Heights Neighborhood, Tampa
Morning

The sidewalk in Seminole Heights is already sizzling from the morning sun as H.L. Russell stares in amazement at the sight before him.

His 1946 black Ford Sedan, the car he reported stolen the night before, has mysteriously reappeared less than a block from where it vanished – the corner of Curtis Street and Nebraska Avenue.

Suspecting he's been the victim of joyriding kids, Russell climbs into the driver's seat and drives his vehicle home.

He then walks inside his house, calls Tampa police, and cancels his pick-up order. His vehicle has been located, he tells them.

Shortly afterward, Russell's young son points out a disturbing detail that his father hasn't noticed. The license plate on the car is a Pinellas County plate. Russell's plate is from Hillsborough County.

Russell also notices that his jack, spare tire, and white wall rims are missing from the vehicle.

H.L. Russell runs back inside and calls Tampa Police again.

Tampa Police dispatch Detective Inspector Stephens. With law enforcement officers across the region on the lookout for a black Ford Sedan in connection with the Crystal Beach murder, Stephens rushes to the H.L. Russell home on New Orleans Avenue.

Upon inspecting the vehicle, Stephens quickly finds bloodstains and traces of flour and sugar on the inside of the car.[*]

---

* *Tampa Tribune, August 9, 1949.*

19

Monday Morning, August 8, 1949
Crain House
Curlew Creek Road, Dunedin, FL

S am Crain is readying himself to start his workweek at the Pasco
Packing Plant – the enormous citrus packing and shipping company headquartered in Dade City, Florida, with an outpost close to
Crain in North Pinellas County. As Crain sits at his kitchen table
having breakfast, his daughter Dorothy and her "husband," John
Calvin Russell, are back at Crain's house for the first time in two
weeks. They are asleep.

As Crain enjoys his meal, he opens the morning edition of The
St. Petersburg Times. There, on page one, he is greeted with the headline story of a horrific murder yesterday in Crystal Beach, only a few
miles north of him. It gets his attention. While Crain has seen his
share of dust-ups, a bloody murder scene is relatively unheard of in his
small town.

While the story is disturbing, Sam Crain has no idea how alarming
it is about to become.

When he reads the description of the killer and the weapon used,
it is likely a chill runs down the Army veteran's spine.

The description of the perpetrator sounds very much like his
one-time roomer and now supposed son-in-law, John Calvin Russell,
or as Crain knows him, Jim Sullivan.

Crain reads about the sawed-off shotgun and becomes almost
certain that Russell is involved. It all starts to come together - The
early Sunday morning disappearance, the trip to Tampa to drop off the
car, the loading of groceries and shotguns out of the car, the shaving

of the mustache of which the swaggering Russell was so proud only days before.[*]

Crain knows a sawed-off shotgun is in his house. He's seen it leaning in the corner of Russell's bedroom. He fears he could not only be harboring the murder weapon but the murderer himself.

Crain grabs the newspaper and scurries to his car parked outside the house, the same car he used to bring Rastus Russell back to his home the night before.

He drives to the home of Oscar Godwin.[**] Godwin is the foreman of the North Pinellas facility at which Crain and his sons work. Relatively short like Crain, Godwin is described as quiet and a "real nice guy."

He is Crain's supervisor and friend.

Crain shows Godwin the article and nervously tells Godwin he believes Russell, his daughter's "husband," is the killer. He explains his trip to Tampa the previous night and tells Godwin he has seen the sawed-off shotgun, along with another shotgun, in Russell's bedroom.

Together, the two pour over newspaper accounts of the horrific murder the day before. With each detail, they become more convinced that Russell is the killer. But before notifying authorities, they decide to make sure.

Crain and Godwin hatch a plan to investigate. Crain, however, is worried. He's always suspected Russell was a dangerous individual. After all, this is the man who virtually kidnapped his sixteen-year-old daughter for two months, returned to his home, then took her again to Tampa to live – with Crain apparently helpless – or too fearful to do anything to stop it.

But if Russell is indeed capable of such a horrific act as the Crystal Beach murder and shooting, his family could be in danger. They are playing with fire now. The two friends must be careful.

Godwin and Crain drive back to Crain's house on Curlew Creek Road. It's near midday when they arrive. The heat of the sun is scorching

---

[*]   *St. Petersburg Times, August 9, 1949.*

[**]   *It is unclear as to whether Crain drives to Godwin's home or reports to work where he encounters him. Nor is it clear if the two call off work or they are not scheduled to work this day.*

on their backs as they walk to the entryway of the home. It will soon hike the temperature to another sweaty 90-degree afternoon.

Rastus Russell is up and about, inside the house. The open windows allow the still, humid air from outside to drift through the home, making it slightly more comfortable for its occupants. But not much.

Crain, carrying a yardstick, explains to Russell that Godwin has come to help him measure the rooms for some repairs he's been planning.

Russell seems unconcerned.

The two put on an acting job, wandering from room to room, feigning concern for the lengths and widths of the walls.

As they go about their work, a county road truck rolls to a stop in front of the house. For whatever reason, Rastus Russell walks outside the house to talk to the driver.

As he does, Crain and Godwin duck into Russell's bedroom. There, they find a sawed-off .12-gauge shotgun and another standard .12-gauge shotgun, along with a bag of groceries. The sawed-off gun is missing a chip of wood out of the remainder of its stock.[*]

Now certain Russell is the killer, the friends know they must call the authorities. But Crain is worried about his family – especially his wife, who is eight months pregnant with the couple's eighth child. A raid on his home might not only lead to a violent confrontation in which his family could be harmed, but a conflict could cause his wife considerable emotional trauma. Crain does not want Russell apprehended at his house.

They must find another way.

The two citrus workers brainstorm together. When they finish, they have devised a plan that will doom Rastus Russell.

---

[*]   *St. Petersburg Times, August 9, 1949.*

20

August 8, 1949
Afternoon
Crain House, Curlew Creek Road

It's the height of another sweltering mid-afternoon when Sam Crain tells Rastus Russell about an "idea" he has for his family today.

Sam Crain would like scallops for dinner. He asks Russell to go scalloping at the Dunedin Flats with Dorothy and Crain's sons. If they leave soon, they can be there in time for the low tide, the best time for collecting the mollusks.

Russell agrees.

Crain tells Russell he will meet the group at the flats around 7:00 p.m. to pick up the scallops.

Shortly afterward, Rastus Russell, Dorothy Jean Crain, and her two older brothers, Allen Garfield Crain and Furrell Richard Crain, begin the hike west on Curlew Creek Road toward the flats.

All are dressed in swim trunks. Russell sports light trunks with a white, tank top undershirt. Dorothy wears dark shorts with a white T-shirt, dark sunglasses, and a white baseball cap. The Crain boys both wear white ball caps.

The group is carrying at least two metal wash tubs, rope, and other gear. It is a considerable haul given the flats are an approximate two-mile walk from the Crain house.

In a shallow, fertile corner of St. Joseph's sound, the Dunedin Flats are situated between the village of Ozona and the outskirts of Dunedin. It is a spot where freshwater Minnow Creek, about twenty-five feet wide, empties into the saltwater sound. The flats meet the shore close to the main road of Old US 19, making them fairly accessible to the public.

The abundant grass beds that grow in the mucky silt bottom of the flats make them a perfect breeding ground for baitfish, sea trout, redfish, and scallops. At low tide, a person can walk nearly a mile from shore, picking up the tasty shellfish by the handful in the shallow water.

Russell and the Crain siblings will hike nearly a mile west on Curlew Creek Road before turning right on Old US 19 and walking north, then veering off the road and west again to reach the flats.

The flats are also a popular place for marinas and fish camps – facilities for fishermen to store and launch boats or clean fish such as mackerel, snapper, or deep-water grouper when they return. Several surround the spot where the Crain's scalloping party is headed today.

Sam Crain watches as three of his four oldest children disappear down the dusty road with a killer.

It is unclear at the time if the Crain children know anything about Russell's violent spree the day before, or their father's discovery. It is also unclear if they are willing participants in the plan to capture Russell or if they are aware of their father's plan. However, a retroactive piece written later by reporter Bob Pritchard states the Crain siblings knew exactly what was going on and were given specific instructions by their father. It seems likely this was the case.

After watching the foursome set off West, down Curlew Creek Road, Crain leaves the house. He has no phone at his home. It is unknown where he goes to find one, but he does. From there, he calls the Pinellas County Sheriff's office.

21

August 8, 1949
Mid Afternoon
Barlow's Filling Station, Palm Harbor

T.B. Barlow is back manning his filling station in Palm Harbor. It's a lazy Monday afternoon, one day after the chilling Crystal Beach murder rocked his community. Barlow is just finishing an oil change when a call comes through on the phone at his station.

Wiping his oily hands, Barlow picks up the phone on his office desk. It is his friend, Sam Crain.

An excited Crain drops shocking news on Barlow. He believes the killer of Norman Browne is staying at his house. He tells Barlow he has notified the sheriff's office, but he'd like Barlow to come investigate.

Barlow, like Dewey Adair, is one of Palm Harbor's unofficial community leaders. Both are business owners, members of the local Masonic Lodge, and Adair, at least, is documented as a "special deputy" to Constable Walter Carey. Special deputies are citizen volunteers drafted into service on an as-needed basis by the constable. Although I could not find any documentation on Barlow, it is likely that Barlow is also a special deputy and as a friend of Crain's, why he was Crain's second call.

Barlow tells Crain to sit tight and leaps into action. He starts working the phone to round up a posse.

Meanwhile, the Pinellas County Sheriff's office is having trouble reaching Sherrif Todd Tucker. Tucker is in Tampa with Constable Walter Carey. The two are working with other officers, canvassing the area in Seminole Heights where the killer's stolen car was found.

In 1949, phone lines in North Pinellas County were still on the party line system. That means if someone else is on the line, you can't get through. One must often keep trying until he gets an open line. In addition, there were no radio systems in sheriff's cars in 1949. Any message for Tucker taken by Tampa Police headquarters will have to be personally delivered to Tucker after he is located in the field. As such, Barlow decides to contact the closest law enforcement officer he can find.

Dunedin Chief of Police Eugene Sheets is at the Clearwater courthouse when a call from Barlow comes through for him. Barlow quickly explains what Sam Crain has told him.

Sheets runs to his car and races north to Barlow's service station in Palm Harbor. It takes him approximately twenty-three minutes.

The Browne killer potentially being located is big news. A general alarm goes out.

Other officers from around the area begin converging at Barlow's. These include Chief George McNamara of Clearwater Police, who coincidentally has just located the Hillsborough County license plate that Russell switched off his stolen car at, ironically, Barlow's Station the day before. Other officers responding are county patrolman J.F. Peacock and Largo officer Whritenour.

Having established a command center at Barlow's, Chief Sheets finally gets through to Walter Carey.[*]

An eager Carey tells Sheets that he (Carey) and Sheriff Tucker are on their way. He instructs Sheets not to begin the raid on the house until the pair arrives from Tampa.

This is an indicator of the chain of command that seems to be in place in 1949 Pinellas County Law Enforcement. While various law enforcement agencies are involved in the hunt, Carey appears to be the one in charge. Whether this is due to his renowned detective skills, Carey's position as constable, or the fact that the crime happened in Carey's juristiction, it is obvious other officers are deferring to Carey in the case, even Tucker.

---

[*]   *How this comes about is unknown. However, it seems likely that as the message finally gets through to Tucker and Carey, Carey calls Barlow's station.*

But Sheets can taste a breakthrough. He doesn't want to risk it slipping through his fingers. He pleads with Carey. It's getting late in the day. He feels the hunt should get underway immediately.

Carey concedes the logic. He tells Sheets to proceed, and he'll get there as fast as he can.

As Carey and Tucker speed back across the bay, Sheets, Whritenour, McNamara, Peacock, and T.B. Barlow man their vehicles and proceed in a convoy towards the home of Sam Crain, three miles away.*

Upon arrival, they are led upstairs to the bedroom of Rastus Russell by Sam Crain and Oscar Godwin. It is now approximately 5:00 p.m.**

---

* *If the timelines provided by Crain and Barlow are both correct, the convoy of police cars would have passed right by the flats where Russell and the Crain children were scalloping.*

** *The details of how the raid on the Crain house came about are one of the blurriest of the story and required some deductive reasoning and puzzle-solving by the author. Newspaper accounts are at odds, if not contradictory to one another. The version presented here seems the most likely and logical after researching all accounts. However, some accounts have officers arriving at the Crain home and instructing Sam Crain to set up the scallop fishing trip, with Russell only returning to the home at 5:30 before leaving on the trip. However, whenever possible, we have used the accounts of actual witnesses or participants, not reporters. This book uses Sam Crain's version of events.*

22

August 8, 1949
Tarpon Springs Hospital
5:00 p.m.

T he Tarpon Springs Hospital is a two-story, twelve-bedroom facility located on Old US 19 between Palm Harbor and Tarpon Springs. When the facility opened in 1927, it was only the second hospital in Pinellas County.

Occupying three of its twelve beds, all members of the Crum family continue to struggle with their wounds.

Of them, Miles's condition remains the gravest. But after two separate blood transfusions, the heroic grocer has at least stabilized.[*] He is being fed intravenously. Crum was able to briefly speak with police earlier in the day, viewing two suspects in the crime that left him wounded. But he rests now, unconscious again.

Thelma Crum is recovering from head trauma and concussion. She is not out of the woods yet and remains in critical condition. She is also traumatized and being treated with sedatives. She has been too weak and emotionally disturbed to speak with detectives.

It is little Judy Crum of whom doctors have become concerned. What was first thought to be only bruises on the seven-month-old now appear to be more serious. Doctors become worried when, earlier in the day, the child suffers a series of seizures. While the extent of the injury is still unknown, doctors suspect some type of brain or spinal injury.

---

[*]   *Only four years after the end of World War II, Crum is the beneficiary of several advancements in gunshot treatment, antibiotics, and blood transfusions during the war.*

Ten miles to the south of the Crum's hospital beds, Anne Browne lays in critical condition at Mease Dunedin Hospital. The deep gash on her left wrist has been repaired to the best of her doctors' abilities. The ugly wound is now stitched, the wrist and arm tinted in shades of black, yellow, and blue. Cuts and bruises cover her head and face, the result of multiple blows to the area from a shotgun butt. Mrs. Browne is believed to be suffering from a concussion as well. But she is alive and seems eager to assist in the capture of her husband's killer.

23

s Barlow, Chief Sheets, and the other officers spread out through Rastus Russell's private bedroom, they find several pieces of key evidence.

As Barlow himself explains to reporters later:

"We found a 12-guage pump sawed-off shotgun, with both the barrel and the stock sawed off. The pin found at the murder scene by Peacock fitted the gun found at Sullivan's house."[*]

As per Sam Crain, Barlow is still under the impression that the perpetrator's name is Jim Sullivan.

Barlow also notes a chip of wood missing from the stock of the sawed-off shotgun.

"We also found a regular 12-gauge shotgun there. This one is identified as having been stolen at the Browne home," Barlow continues.[*]

The officers also find a bag of groceries identified as having come from the Browne home.

To seal the case, the team recovers a pile of bloody clothing that Russell has left on the bedroom floor, having not even bothered to wash it.

---

[*] *The Tampa Tribune, August 9, 1949. It is curious that with several uniformed officers on site, Barlow is giving the interview to the press. This further suggests he is working as a special deputy for Carey.*

What they don't find is Rastus Russell, or as Crain and the officers know him, Jim Sullivan.

He has gone scallop fishing, Crain tells them. He also tells them exactly where to find the killer. And where Russell is, he can't get far. Crain and Godwin specifically selected the Dunedin Flats, knowing it would be nearly impossible for Russell to escape in the water.

Seizing the evidence, the search team leaves Crain's house to reconvene at Barlow's. There, they will form an attack plan.

By now, the word is out. The service station is swarming with deputies and law enforcement officers from around the county. A posse of armed citizens has reorganized and is also arriving to assist in a potential capture or even shoot out with the suspected killer.

Still without any sign of Sheriff Tucker or Constable Carey, McClamma and Sheer begin deploying a skirmish line of officers and citizen militia along Old US 19 from the north end of the Dunedin Flats nearly a mile down the two-lane road to the south end, sealing off any escape route for the suspect.

The flats are separated from Old US 19 by a thin jungle of mangrove swamps, vines, cypresses, palm trees, and underbrush. A few dirt roads run through these tropical forests. These will be the best access routes when officers decide to go in.

It is now nearly 6:30 p.m. A cloudy, overcast sky has given way to a light, drizzling rain. The humidity is unbearable. And as though a dinner bell has been rung, swarms of mosquitos descend on the waiting officers and citizen soldiers, biting soaked, sweaty skin. Frustrated officers lined along the highway swat at the minuscule vampires as itchy, red welts rise on their arms, legs, and necks. The wait is a miserable one.

No one quite knows what everyone is waiting for.

But they won't have to wait much longer.

24

August 8, 1949
4:00 pm
Office of the Clearwater Sun, Clearwater, FL

The following chapter is taken almost entirely from the personal account of reporter Bob Prichard of the Clearwater Sun. Prichard directly participated in the capture of Rastus Russell. Prichard's account of the incident was printed in the Clearwater Sun on August 9, 1949.

I t is mid-afternoon on Monday, August 8, when Bob Prichard, a reporter for the Clearwater Sun, gets a call from the Associated Press. The wire service asks Prichard if he can investigate the report that the suspected slayer in Sunday's murder-torture in Crystal Beach is a marijuana addict. The story has become national news, and the marijuana angle makes it even more intriguing.

Prichard tells the AP he'll check it out.

As the comment is attributed to Pinellas County constable Walter Carey, Prichard heads north to the Tarpon Springs Police Department, a location where Carey can sometimes be found.[*]

When he arrives, Prichard finds it odd that no police officers are at the station. Instead, he finds a group of civilians huddled around the open police radio, intently listening to crackling calls back and forth on the radio as though following a baseball game.

---

[*] *While the Tampa Tribune quotes Carey earlier in the day specifically saying he believes the killer is a marijuana addict, he later tells Prichard that those "rumors" are untrue. This is discussed in a previous chapter.*

Apparently, in the small town of Tarpon Springs in 1949, this is a form of accepted entertainment.

"Has anyone here seen Carey?" Prichard asks.

The men all glance at each other strangely. One answers, "No, we haven't seen him."

They then turn back to the radio.

Prichard pivots and walks back to his car. He decides to go look for Carey himself. Prichard is a veteran reporter, has worked with Carey before, and knows several spots where he might find the constable.

As Prichard retreats out the door and approaches his car, a man from the group inside follows him out. The stranger leans up against Prichard's vehicle as the reporter opens his door.

"Where are you going?" the man asks in a casual voice.

"Out to look for Carey, of course," Prichard replies.

The man casts a sidelong glance towards the police station, then leans in towards Prichard.

"Get down to Barlow's service station at Palm Harbor as soon as you can," the stranger blurts in a sharp whisper. "All hell's broken loose down there! But don't tell anybody I told you."

Prichard thanks the man, leaps into the driver's seat, and stomps the gas. Flying down Old US 19 at speeds approaching 70 miles per hour, Prichard swerves around slower drivers to get to his destination as quickly as possible.

When Prichard arrives nearly ten minutes later, the scene in front of him confirms that all hell has indeed broken loose.

An army of police from around Pinellas County is amassed at Barlow's, intermingled with armed citizens, police vehicles, pickup trucks, and cars parked at every angle and in the street. The armed posse wears revolvers and carries shotguns, rifles, and submachine guns.

This group is open for business, and Prichard immediately realizes something big is going down.

As Prichard scans the crowd for a familiar face, he spots Tarpon Springs Chief of Police Costas Manos standing with a group of men. Manos is talking with Clearwater Police Chief George McClamma.

Manos gives Prichard a nod and waves him over to the group. He knows Prichard and knows the newsman must be itching for an explanation.

When Prichard approaches, Manos gets to the point.

"We think we've got him," he tells Prichard in an excited voice, "but things are moving so fast I can't tell you anything about it now."[*]

Prichard still doesn't know the story, but he knows it could be big. He runs inside the service station to the phone and tries to phone the offices of the Clearwater Sun. He needs a photographer there now. But again the old party line system, antiquated even in 1949, thwarts him. Prichard dials the rotary phone over and over to no avail. He curses the phone system and tries again.

Finally, he gets through. Prichard's editor slams down the receiver and immediately dispatches a photographer.

As Prichard steps outside to rejoin the group, a white Cadillac rolls up beside Barlow's. Out of the driver's side door steps Tarpon Springs Mayor Fred H. Howard, a revolver strapped to his side.

"Let's go!" he says, encouraging his men. "If we're going to get him, let's get him now!"

Prichard, Howard, and Chief Manos pile into a Tarpon Springs patrol car driven by Patrolman Elmer. Manos sits in the front seat, with Howard sliding into the back seat beside Prichard.

Joining a convoy led by Clearwater Chief McClamma, the foursome cross over Old US Highway 19 as the procession heads down a sideroad towards Ozona. As they approach St. Joseph's Sound and turn left towards the Dunedin Flats, Prichard realizes he's the only one in the car who is unarmed.

As he does, he kicks a hard object lying near his feet, wrapped in an oilcloth bag. Prichard reaches down and opens the bag, finding it contains a Thompson Sub-Machine gun.[**]

---

[*] _From account of Bob Pritchard._

[**] _The Thompson Sub-Machine gun was invented by John Taliaferro Thompson for use in trench warfare during World War I. However, when Thompson left development to actually fight in the war, the Thompson was left on the design table. When Thompson returned from the war, he eventually patented his invention and began producing the weapon in 1920. Combining both speed and power, the Thompson fired powerful .45 caliber bullets in rapid succession, making it a devastating weapon in close quarters. However, with the war over, demand for Thompon's invention was tepid. Much to the inventor's dismay, the weapon was adopted for use by gangsters and criminals in_

Prichard had just finished shoving .45 shells into the weapon's greasy magazine when the car pulled up to George's Fish Camp.

George's Fish Camp is a local favorite launch of both commercial and recreational fishermen. It sits at the edge of Ozona, where Minnow Creek empties into the Dunedin Flats and offers a commanding view of the grass beds.*

Three miles out, on the horizon, one can see the palm trees of Honeymoon Island, a favorite beach and picnic spot for local boaters. Honeymoon Island separates St. Joseph's Sound from the Gulf of Mexico, protecting the calm, shallow waters of the sound and ensuring an ideal breeding ground for sea life.

Before Prichard opens his door, Chief Manos gives him a quick overview of the situation. There is a report that the killer is scalloping in the flats near the fish camp with five other people.**

With armed men stationed a mile down Old US 19 to prevent escape, the team led by McClamma, which encompasses dozens of officers and citizen volunteers, will surround the murderer while he's in the water.

Prichard swings open the car door and hops out. Locked and loaded, he has now become a participant in his own story.

---

the 1920s and 30s, including John Dillinger and Bonnie and Clyde. Sensing they were outgunned, the FBI started using Thompson's to combat the organized gangs. Thompson submachine guns finally fulfilled their intended purpose in World War II, when the military began using them. The weapons were a particular favorite of US Marines fighting on Japanese-held islands in the Pacific. Throughout the 1930s and 40s, Thompson's or "Tommy Guns," found their way down to local police departments. They were used by police into the late 1940s. As late as the 1970s, Thompson's could still be found in many local police department inventories, although by then, they were rarely used.

* George's Marina still exists today in Ozona, as does its original building. However, it is now a private marina and goes by the name of Coastal Ozona Marina. Dredging in and around the Dunedin Flats in the 1950s killed off many of the grass beds and abundant fishing they provided. Most commercial fishermen moved further north. Today, the marinas that remain in Ozona cater mostly to recreational boaters.

** There are, in fact, two individuals other than Russell and the Crain siblings who are with the group. Who they are is unknown.

Men all around him swarm out of vehicles and begin dispersing in all directions, taking stations behind bushes and trees. Out in the flats, six figures can be seen in the distance, wading through the shallow water.

Prichard sticks close to Manos, and the two men crouch down in the brush. While the sun won't set for nearly two hours, the sky is bleak and cloudy. A moderate rain is now falling on the pursuers. While the sun cannot be seen as it begins to fall in the western sky over Honeymoon Island, a light pink stripe colors the dark horizon, hinting at its presence above.

The men wait in their positions, the rain drenching them to the skin. The same mosquitos tormenting their comrades back on Old US 19 are now feasting on their blood.

The team hopes the rain will bring the scalloping party back to shore. But the figures in the water seemed unmoved. As their position becomes more uncomfortable, the men begin to become restless. What are they waiting for?

Then, they find out.

A tall, wiry figure wearing a rimmed hat and small, round glasses steps forward, not far from Prichard. The man carries a double-barreled shotgun, the business end propped loosely on his shoulder. He carries an air of authority, and the men seem to fix their attention on him. Prichard knows who it is. Constable Walter Carey has finally arrived from Tampa.

Like a field general taking command of his army, Carey carefully surveys the scene, watching the tiny figures wading offshore. The men seem to know this is Carey's show and wait for his instructions.

The constable flips the shotgun off his shoulder, the pump slapping into the palm of his left hand. He turns to the group of officers that have aligned behind him.

"Come on." Carey growls in his cool, Southern drawl, "Let's go get him."

25

August 8, 1949
Dunedin Flats, Dunedin, FL
7:00 p.m.

I t is just after 7:00 p.m. when Walter H. Carey and his three-man assault team go tromping into the muddy flats of Dunedin. The rain has taken a merciful pause. The tide is low, and the stale, sulfur smell of salt water, fish, and dimethyl sulfide permeates the heavy air.*

The seawater has retreated nearly forty yards offshore, creating a waterless, mushy tidal plain the officers must cross before reaching the sound. They reach the edge of the water and begin wading into the sea. A former fisherman, Carey is no stranger to saltwater. Before leaving the dry shore, he removes his shoes and socks, as do his men.

As they enter the water, raindrops again begin falling, pelting the still saltwater that surrounds them. The going is slow as the armed men sink ankle-deep in the tidal muck. Sand, silt, and seawater envelope feet and coat pantlegs.

An army of nearly thirty-five officers is spread up and down the shore, preventing the killer's escape, should he elude Carey's team. They are backed up by a growing mob of armed citizens, some abandoning their posts back on the highway to move closer to the action. As word spreads, curious onlookers and media are also arriving by the minute.

---

* *Dimethyl sulfide is a natural chemical produced by bacteria as they digest dead phytoplankton. At low tide, you'll also smell chemicals called dictyopterenes, which are sex pheromones produced by seaweed eggs to attract sperm. Both chemicals emit a mildly unpleasant odor.*

After a long slog, approximately 100 yards offshore, Carey and his team are within shouting distance of the six figures in the distance. As Carey approaches, an officer onshore blasts a hefty blow of his police car siren. Somebody fires a shot in the air.

The noise attracts the attention of the scallopers.

Carey waves his arms, signaling the group to come ashore.

There is a pause. Then, the figures seem to separate, with three of the figures drifting to the right. The remaining three begin a slow trod through the knee-deep water towards Carey.

As the distant figures get closer to Carey, he sees they are two young men and a girl.

Anxious officers clutch their weapons tightly as Carey's team surrounds the three. After talking briefly, the men direct the scallopers to shore. They are Furrell Richard Crain, Dorothy Jean Crain, and Allen Garfield Crain.

As the Crain siblings shuffle through the water towards officers onshore, Carey turns his attention back to the three remaining scallopers. Holding his shotgun by the neck in his right hand, Carey raises his left and again waves the group in.

"Come on in!" he bellows.

But the trio seems to ignore Carey's commands. They continue to wade through the thigh-high salt water.

Carey and his men continue advancing.

Suddenly, one of the scallopers breaks from the trio, running wildly through the water and then diving head forward. He begins swimming frantically into the Sound towards Honeymoon Island, nearly three miles away.

One of Carey's men opens up with his .45 caliber sidearm. Five shots ring out through the still, rainy air. The men see tiny splashes plunk up around the swimmer's head. But none of the shots connect.[*]

A roar erupts from the shore.

"That's him! That's him!" come shouts from the crowd.

---

[*] *Some accounts attribute the shots fired to Carey himself. But as Carey was carrying a double-barreled shotgun, it seems unlikely he would hold it in one arm and draw a pistol with the other. However, it is doubtful the officer would have fired without orders from Carey.*

The atmosphere is now electric.

Carey spins around and yells back to the shore, "Somebody get a boat!"

As officers and the crowd hear the command, a commotion ensues as word spreads down the line.

Sheriff Tucker, hearing Carey's urgent request, leaps into action, asking if anyone in the crowd has a boat.

Out of the crowd steps Walter Pryor. Pryor volunteers his vessel, a twenty-six-foot, open motor boat, for the cause. Pryor knows the vessel well. He built it. But the boat is not docked at George's. It's tied up just down the street at Minnow Creek Marine Ways.[*]

Tucker, Pryor, and three other men hop into Tucker's car and speed out of the clearing towards Minnow Creek Marine Ways, less than a mile away.

Officers and spectators watch anxiously from shore as the swimmer gets further away. When the man is no longer visible from shore, many fear he has either escaped or drowned. Carey and his men can only continue wading slowly through the grass beds.[**]

Nearly fifteen minutes pass with no sign of Tucker. Nervous murmurs begin to rumble through the crowd. Rain continues to fall on the heads of the spectators.

Finally, the whine of a boat engine echoes over the flats, its blades cutting a foamy wake through the water.

As relieved shore-bound officers look on, Todd Tucker, Clearwater policeman B.J. Ferguson, Clearwater policeman W.D. Booth, citizen volunteer Mac Hart, and Pryor race toward Carey and the escaping suspect.

Pryor cautiously guides the vessel through the shallow water, knowing low tide can be a treacherous time, even for his small boat. He guns the engine as much as he dares, keeping a keen eye for sandbars. But the flats at low tide can confound even the most experienced captain.

---

[*] *From 2024 interview with Wally Ericson. Ericson knew Pryor and bought the boat from him after the Russell incident. Ericson later sold the boat. He saw it years later, rotting under an oak tree, ruined.*

[**] *The identity of the other two scallopers is unknown. It is possible they are simply random people who happen to be scalloping at the same time as Russell and the Crains.*

Just as Tucker's team seems about to save the day, a sickening grinding sound echoes over the water as the boat grinds to a halt.

The watercraft has run aground on a patch of mud.

26

astus Russell is a strong swimmer. Growing up in Palm Harbor, the young Russell spent his childhood in and around the salt water of St. Joseph's Sound and the Gulf of Mexico. He is quite comfortable in a marine environment.

And the Dunedin Flats are his home turf.

Russell is making incredible progress as he paddles over the shallow grass beds and into the deeper waters of the Sound. Honeymoon Island is still about a two-mile swim from his present location.

Back at the Flats, Todd Tucker and his men have clamored to the stern of the motorboat. As they furiously rock the vessel up and down, the engine puffs and struggles to free itself from the sea muck that has entrapped its propellor.

Finally, the blade kicks loose, and the boat thrusts forward. Pryor gasses the engine to full throttle and the five men go tearing out over the flats again, the front of the vessel lifting upwards as it accelerates into the deeper water.

The rain is picking up. As Tucker scans the horizon for his prized fugitive, millions of tiny pinpricks dot the water's surface, obscuring his view.

Tucker looks back towards shore. There, he sees Chief McClamma standing on a bluff, scanning the horizon through binoculars. While Russell has disappeared from view onshore, McClamma can still see him with the bifocals. He waves Tucker and his crew towards the quarry.

As the boat blows by Carey and his team, Carey points towards Honeymoon Island. Tucker's crew slightly adjusts their angle of attack and race forward.

As Rastus Russell glides through St. Joseph's Sound, the desperation of his situation must be descending on him. He knows the sound of a boat engine at full throttle and hears it growing closer in the distance. Looking ahead, he sees the tops of palm and pine trees on Honeymoon Island. But it seems one million miles away.

Russell takes a deep breath and dives under the water's surface. He swims as deep as he can. And then, as he paddles his arms to keep himself down, he begins to release the air in his lungs. As big air bubbles gurgle past his ears and eyes, Russell waits for darkness to come.

But lungs starved of oxygen become painful. Whether out of pain or of conscious reconsideration, Russell breaks wildly back to the surface. Once there, he gasps desperately for air.

Then he kicks and continues his swim. As the grind of the motor creeps closer, the convict attempts this maneuver two more times, each time losing his nerve at the last moment.

The engine is now upon him, and he hears the throttle ease back as the vessel approaches him.

As the boat drifts up on Russell, Sheriff Tucker roars, "Stop where you are!"

Rastus Russell turns to see four guns trained on his head and body. Exhausted and out of breath, the fugitive stands up on a sand bar, lifting his torso out of the waist-deep water. He throws his arms in the air.

"I tried to drown myself three or four times," he tells the officers in a tired voice, "but didn't have the guts."*

Sheriff Todd Tucker has his man.

As excitement sweeps through the crowd onshore, Pinellas County Deputy Sheriff Bob Fulle watches the scene unfold from a telescope. As he does, he gives a play-by-play to his fellow officers and the hungry crowd around him.

"They're getting nearer.........you can only see his head.......now the boat is near........He's got his hands up!"**

---

*   *Clearwater Sun, August 9, 1949.*

**   *St. Petersburg Times, August 9, 1949.*

Russell resigningly wades towards the boat. As he grasps for the sides, officers reach down and haul him aboard. Russell sits dripping wet in his swim trunks and tank top. For whatever reason, his tank top is ripped or removed, either by accident or by Tucker's men. Then, the officers cuff his hands behind his back.

"What's this all about?" Russell demands, seemingly perplexed.[*]

Without answering, officers lay Russell face down in the boat. The engine zooms to life again, and the boat wheels into a U-turn.

As the victorious Tucker steams back to shore, his captive becomes defiant.

"I'll bet you son of a bitches thought you had a good time trying to catch me!" he goads them.[**]

Russell continues to ask why he is being detained. He fires derogatory comments at the officers as they glide closer to shore. He also asks to see his "wife," Dorothy Jean Crain. His banter goes unanswered.

As the boat approaches the dock back at George's Fish Camp, the crowd on the shores of Ozona has swelled to over 1,000 people. Newsmen and photographers clamor for position as the boat drifts up to the dock.

As uniformed officers Ferguson and Booth lift the shirtless Russell from the bottom of the boat, the killer loses his swaggering tone. Seeing the mob of onlookers armed with both rifles and cameras, he pleads with his captors, "Please protect me. Don't let the crowd get me!"[***]

While the rain has now eased, a gray, cloudy sky has obscured the impending sunset, still nearly an hour away. Beneath the dark clouds above Honeymoon Island, the pink stripe of sky has grown more pronounced, creating the illusion of dusk.

It's approximately 7:30 p.m., nearly thirty-one hours since Norman Browne was killed.

---

[*]   *Tampa Tribue, August 9, 1949.*
[**]   *Clearwater Sun, August 9, 1949.*
[***] *The Tampa Tribune, August 9, 1949.*

27

As Rastus Russell is lifted onto the wooden dock of George's Fish Camp, an explosion of flashbulbs pepper the fugitive and his captors. Photographers stand, crouch, and kneel, all firing off shots as fast as they can shoot and reload. The images of the shirtless, muscular Russell walking handcuffed with officers will appear in newspapers around the state and make the cover of at least two national magazines.[*]

The fugitive's hulking body and thick arms make the photos all the more sensational for the times. In fact, Russell's wrists are so big that normal handcuffs will not fit him.

Rick Carey remembers the comments his grandfather (Walter Carey) made about the fugitive Russell.

"He said that this man (Russell) was the strongest man he'd ever met in his life. He said his wrists were so big that you couldn't really get handcuffs on him. They had to put leg chains on his wrists, (chains) that would go around somebody else's legs."[**]

As reporters and citizens shout taunts and questions at Russell, the fugitive again becomes defiant.

"What's all this fuss about?" Russell asks again to no one in particular. "I haven't done anything."[***]

With Russell's wrists cuffed in front of him, Sheriff Tucker, wearing black trousers, a tucked white button shirt, and a black bowtie, stands to the right of the suspect. Tucker grabs Russell's right arm

---

[*] *Official Detective and Uncensored Detective each feature Russell on their covers in early 1950. Those feature articles were obtained in researching this book.*

[**] *From 2024 interview with Rick Carey.*

[***] *The Tampa Tribune, August 9, 1949.*

above the elbow with his left hand. On the other side, Deputy Bob Fulle loops his right hand around Russell's left arm. Fulle dons the same outfit as Tucker, sans the bowtie. A freshly lit cigarette dangles from the deputy's lips as the two lawmen escort their captive through the sea of angry, curious onlookers.

"Get those damn photographers away from me!" Russell demands.

As Tucker orders the crowd to stand back, other officers flank the trio, helping to dissuade spectators from getting too close. Tarpon Chief Manos, dressed in full uniform complete with tie, takes up position on Fulle's left.

As flashbulbs continue to pop and questions continue to fly, Rastus Russell ducks his head and stares at the ground. As the lawmen make their way to a waiting car, Russell grows frustrated.

"Make them stop shooting those flashbulbs!" he bursts. "They've had enough fun."

Tucker and Fulle hustle the barefoot Russell to Tucker's waiting car. As they jump in the back seat with Russell, two other deputies sit in the front. The car whisks the five men back up the dirt road to Old Highway 19.

The deputy turns right and heads south towards the Clearwater Jail.

28

While Tucker and his team are chasing down Rastus Russell in the water beyond the Dunedin Flats, Furrell, Allan, and Dorothy Jean Crain are wading up onto the muddy shoreline near George's Fish Camp.

As they walk through saltwater puddles and thick hedgerows of dead, brown-green seagrass, they are accosted by a wave of law enforcement officers and reporters.

While police are not yet sure of the Crain's relationship with the suspect, they allow reporters to question the trio as they come ashore.

Seeing the photographers, Dorothy pulls the shade of her white cap down over her face. When reporters ask her to remove it, the teenager is defiant.

Then a photographer bellows a question. Is she trying to hide something? Turning on the girl, others pile on.

Dorothy grabs the top of the cap and rips it off her face, a scowl greeting reporters from underneath. Her wavy light brown hair tumbles out, the ends falling just below her shoulders. She stands sullenly as photographers snap away.

The siblings stand together for the media circus. Eighteen-year-old Allen is on the right. A shirtless Furrell stands tall in the middle, his hands perched confidently on his hips. Dorothy stands on the far left, her arms dangling at her sides. Her cap is now removed, but dark sunglasses still hide her brown eyes. Her white T-shirt is tied in a knot near her navel, the sleeves cut off at the shoulder.

At the further demands of the crowd, Crain removes her sunglasses as well.

As the cameras snap, reporters shout questions at the overwhelmed girl. Is she really the killer's wife? Did she help with the murder? What is the killer's name?

Dorothy remains defiant and vague in her answers, giving several names for Russell. She quickly stops talking altogether.

Likely running with Dorothy's limited comments, various news reports initially list the suspect's name as Jim Sullivan, Johnny Russell and James Russell, all known aliases of Russell.

All three Crain siblings are taken into custody by deputies. They are told that, for the time being, they are being held as "material witnesses."

The Crains are ushered into cars and whisked away to the county jail in Clearwater.

They are long gone by the time Rastus Russell is hauled ashore nearly an hour later.

29

August 8, 1949
Pinellas County Jail
Clearwater, FL
8:30 pm

B uilt in 1918, shortly after the adjacent courthouse, the Pinellas
County Jail stands three stories high. It houses multiple holding
cells. The brick building is known to hold maximum security prisoners
on the third floor. Because of its location in downtown Clearwater, the
facility is often referred to by locals as the "Clearwater Jail."

By 1949, the structure is outdated and in need of repairs. Because
of this, a new, modern jail is now under construction directly across the
street. County leaders hope to have the new, more secure facility open
within a year.

But it's not open yet.

When Sheriff Todd Tucker ushers Rastus Russell into the first
floor of the jail, it's nearly 8:30 p.m. Sun reporter Bob Prichard is
right behind him. Russell's dark hair and bathing trunks are still wet.
He stinks of fishy salt water and seaweed. A thin coat of sand and dirt
covers his feet from his long walk to the car. A two-inch gash is visible
on the back of his left hand, above his thumb.*

Once through the doors, Tucker turns his captive over to Pinellas
County Jailer Harvey Nash. Typically, prisoners are uncuffed once they
are securely inside the jail. But as Nash looks Russell up and down, he
decides to leave this suspect's cuffs firmly in place until the prisoner is

---

*   *From personal interview with Wilburn Crain.*

inside his cell. He takes the barefoot, shirtless Russell by the arm and thrusts him into the elevator that leads to the cells upstairs.

Prichard can no longer contain himself. As the jailer and prisoner enter the elevator car, the reporter jumps forward, notepad in hand.

"What's your name?" he asks.

The suspect stares at Prichard.

"Russell," he replies.

"What's your last name?" Prichard retorts.

"That's my last name," Russell answers, irritated.

"What's your first name?" Prichard fires before the steel doors slam shut.

"James," Russell replies before his face disappears.

Back in Dunedin, Police Chief Eugene Sheets huddles with other officers in his downtown office. The men are holding a key piece of evidence: The sawed-off shotgun retrieved from Russell's room at the Crain house. Sheets also holds the firing pin found by Officer Peacock in the Browne's yard yesterday.

When Sheets inserts the pin into the butchered pump shotgun, it fits perfectly.

It is now nearly certain that the shotgun found in Russell's room was the same gun used to shoot Miles Crum.

Sheets and the other men in the room are now confident in one thing: They have their man.

Once upstairs in the jail, Russell is processed into the facility. He is fingerprinted and photographed. He is given clothes to wear.

Nearby, Dorothy, Furrell, and Allen Crain wait anxiously in a holding cell. They, too, are given new clothes, discarding their wet and salty bathing suits. Sam and Flora Crain have arrived at the jail.

States Attorney Chester B. McMullen has been notified and is en route to the courthouse next door. Here, questioning of the Crain's will begin tonight, behind closed doors.

Russell, of course, will be questioned too. But before that, Tucker and Walter Carey have a visit planned for him. They're going to see Anne Browne.

* * *

With some preliminary information on his prisoner now in hand, Jailer Harvey Nash sets out to learn more about James Russell. With no computers or internet, Nash's research is limited to hard records from the courthouse and his phone. But it is now after 9 p.m. on a Monday night. He'll have to wait until morning before he can reach any outside sources of information.

For tonight, he'll be limited to what is contained in the courthouse files. Fortunately, there is plenty. Within a short time, Nash learns of Russell's many run-ins with the law in Pinellas County. He also learns his prisoner's real name is John Calvin Russell. He discovers Russell's stays at both Chattahoochee and Raiford. He learns Russell's nickname, "Rastus."

When he shares the information with Tucker and Carey, the men know they have just captured a very dangerous man. And Walter Carey realizes for the first time that the alleged killer he's been tracking for the last thirty-one hours is the same man who attacked his brother eight years earlier.

Indeed, Tucker and Carey both remember Rastus Russell. But they haven't seen him for a long time. And he looks drastically different from the car thief and thug they remember from 1941.

* * *

It's late Monday night when Rastus Russell is escorted back down the elevator and into the main lobby of the Pinellas County Jail. During an initial questioning, Russell denies any knowledge of the Brownes or the murder the previous day.

Tucker and Carey aren't buying it. They want a positive identification and don't want to wait until morning. Russell will see Anne Browne tonight.

As Russell and his handlers step outside the building, they are confronted by an ocean of reporters and curious citizens. As the lawmen weave through the throng, a voice from the crowd shouts to Russell.

"Hey Rast," calls the man, "What they got you in for?"

"They got me in for a terrible crime," he shoots back, "but I didn't do it."[*]

The handcuffed Russell then smiles and laughs with reporters. He again asks to see his "wife," Dorothy Jean Crain.

The lawmen shove Russell into the backseat of Tucker's waiting sedan. It's a twelve-minute ride north on Old US 19 to Mease Hospital in Dunedin. The rain has stopped, but the moisture hangs heavy in the nighttime air. Rain makes nature happy, and the high-pitched shrill of crickets combines with the jubilant coo of tree frogs to produce a symphony in the still darkness.

Tucker's car turns left out of the jail and speeds off, its red tail lights fading into the balmy night.

---

[*]   *St. Petersburg Times, August 9, 1949.*

30

It's approximately 11:00 p.m. on Monday night when Tucker, Carey, and deputies arrive at Mease Hospital. The ward where Mrs. Anne Browne lays is quiet. Most patients are asleep.

In addition to her wrist and headwounds, two fingers on her right hand are also broken and have been placed in a cast.

When the lawmen arrive at Browne's room, Browne tells them she does not have her glasses. She cannot see properly without them. She tells Tucker they are back at her home in Crystal Beach.

Disappointed, Tucker and his men head back outside. Tucker dispatches a deputy to Browne's home to retrieve Browne's glasses and other personal items. Tucker decides the time spent waiting at the hospital can be more profitably used forging a chain of circumstantial evidence. They will let Mrs. Browne rest tonight. Russell will keep until morning.

* * *

It's after midnight early Tuesday, August 9th, when two headlights cut through the pitch-black darkness on Rattlesnake Road and pull into the yard of the Browne house.*

---

*   In 1949, Pinellas County Sheriff's Deputies drive their own vehicles. It is not until 1961 when the department gets its first county provided patrol cars. The new cars come installed with police radios – a relatively new technology at the time. Some of the municipal departments involved already have in-car radios. Ironically, it is Tucker

The electricity is still out, and only the outline of the white house can be seen in the wooded blackness. The trees and brush surrounding the secluded home hum with life as all manner of nocturnal woodland creatures and insects hunt, feed, and mate in the tropical night.

A lone deputy climbs out of the driver's seat. Sent by his boss, the deputy's mission is to retrieve Mrs. Browne's pocketbook, which, according to Mrs. Browne, contains her glasses. Browne will need the glasses to identify the Sheriff's suspect tomorrow morning.

An earthy, musty smell wafts through the air, the combined natural scent of dirt, water, and fallen wood decaying in the summer heat with palm fronds, pine needles, and oak leaves.

Navigating by the light of his flashlight, the deputy climbs the wooden steps of the house where Miles Crum was shot thirty-six hours earlier. The sound of his hard-soled shoes climbing the wooden steps seems magnified in the dark, as does the creak of the Browne's front door as he opens it.

Inside, the home remains in the condition it was when Russell left. Debris remains scattered across the floor. The officer enters the old house and turns his light into the Browne's bedroom to the left of the front door. It is located in the Northwest corner of the house.

Bloody sheets still lay strewn across both beds, a deep, thick pool having solidified on top of the bed where Norman Browne was butchered. The body fluid has baked in the tropical climate for a day and a half. A sweet, sickening odor permeates the room.

Pushing the light around the room, the officer spots Mrs. Browne's pocketbook on the nightstand between the two beds. While it contains Mrs. Browne's glasses, it is missing $30 in cash removed by one Rastus Russell the day prior.

But there is a problem.

Atop the pocketbook sits one of the Browne's two cats, "Kippy."

Startled, the animal's eyes reflect red in the beam of the flashlight. The officer recoils when the cat becomes aggressive. It hisses, swats, and growls when he reaches for the purse.[*]

---

who spearheads the push for in-car radios, which he begins installing in deputies private vehicles in the early 1950s.

[*]   *An Interview with Mrs. Anne Browne, Dunedin Times, September 9th, 1949.*

After a short standoff, the defensive feline retreats, allowing the deputy to complete his mission.

Mrs. Browne will have her glasses by morning.

* * *

It is after midnight when Rastus Russell is finally locked in a solitary, padded cell for the night.

In the meantime, interviews with members of the Crain family are well underway. Sam Crain tells State Attorney McMullen his long and sordid tale of John Calvin Russell.[*]

What is known is that Sam Crain told McMullen and the other interviewers that he rented a room to Russell, that his family lived in fear of Russell, and that Russell "took" Dorothy Crain against her will and kept her for two months. Crain portrays his family as victims who are dominated and controlled by the crazed Russell. For his part, Sam Crain did take out a warrant against Russell when he disappeared with his daughter.

But a deeper dive reveals that Russell's relationship with the Crains is not so cut and dried.

At the time of this writing, Sam, Furrell, Dorothy, and Allen Crain had all passed away (Dorothy passed only nine months prior to the beginning of this book at age 91.)

As mentioned earlier, however, brother Wilburn "Bill" Crain was twelve years old at the time of the murder. Mr. Crain, at age eighty-six, agreed to sit for an interview for this book in 2024. The details he provided were fascinating.

As stated earlier, Rastus Russell was a friend of both Furrell and Allen Crain and garnered a soft spot with Sam Crain. Wilburn describes Russell as a regular around the Crain household in the summer of 1949, hanging out with the Crain brothers and working on cars in the front yard. Both Sam Crain and Russell were good with cars which may have created some comradery between the two.

---

[*]   *While several attempts were made to access the transcripts of those interviews for this book, the Pinellas County Circuit Court told us they no longer exist.*

According to Crain, Russell was polite and good-natured around the Crain home. He never remembers anything out of the ordinary about him.

How much of this is shared with Tucker, Carey, and McMullen in 1949 is unknown.

In her interview in 1949, Dorothy tells the lawmen that Russell did not take her to California but only to his aunt's house in Tampa. She says she did not attempt to escape because she was terrified Russell would harm her or her family.

But several of Dorothy and Sam Crain's statements are inconsistent, at best. And none of them explain why Russell is seemingly welcomed, with open arms, back into the Crain home upon his return with Dorothy in July of 1949.

As we will see later, Dorothy's argument that she was never in California may be questionable. It is also notable that Sheriff Todd Tucker himself claims later that he has "definite evidence" that "the girl" was in the stolen car with Russell and rode around with him after the Lester Lambert robbery.

Just because the Crains know Russell does not mean they are criminals or in cahoots with him, of course. That being said, Russell is a skilled and notorious car thief. And in at least one of Russell's suspected robberies, witnesses report the suspect had two accomplices. In one case, the accomplices are reported as a man and a woman.

Wilburn Crain also relayed a curious story in our 2024 interview. Crain says that in the days in or around the Browne murder, a car was found burning in the woods near the Crain house. Crain claims it was a "northern" car, remembering a midwestern license plate. He says the car was a coupe, and a pair of skis were found in the back seat. While no reports of this could be found in researching this book, Crain was adamant it happened. The fact that Russell had just done time for car theft in the Midwest, had just traveled from the Midwest months earlier, and told the Browne's, Miles Crum, and Lester Lambert he had committed crimes in Chicago all lend weight and mystery to Crain's memory of the burning car.

If that, however, had any connection to the Crain brothers or Rastus Russell, we can only speculate. It is possible the Crain brothers had no knowledge or involvement in any of Russell's criminal activities and that the burning car had nothing to do with Rastus Russell.

Sam Crain gives curious accounts of his dealings with Russell as well. Crain tells police he first suspected Russell of the Browne murder when he read the description of the killer in the morning newspaper and "remembered" seeing a sawed-off shotgun in Russell's room (as if this were not strange enough without a murder in the morning paper.) Yet in an interview printed in The Evening Independent days later, he tells the story of driving Russell all the way to Tampa on the night of the murder, somehow eluding roadblocks set up all over the county. This is to supposedly return a "borrowed" car. Crain then gives the more spectacular testimony of watching as Russell loads groceries and two shotguns out of the "borrowed" car and into Crain's car. Is Crain not suspicious then?

Sheriff Tucker later reports that some of Russell's farmhand buddies come forward on the night of Russell's capture and tell a story of helping Russell unload stolen groceries from his car. They, too, claim they were "terrified" of Russell. Is it possible that these men helped unload Russell's stolen car in Tampa into Sam Crain's car? Or is it possible they met Russell back at Crain's house late Sunday night and helped Russell unload groceries into Sam Crain's home, out of Sam Crain's car?

Possible, of course.

But Crain makes no mention, at least in the reported version, of any other persons involved in Russell unloading his vehicle.

It could simply be inconsistent reporting – that Crain told a more coherent story to detectives behind closed doors.

What really happened that night may never be known. But the facts as they are presented do not fit neatly together into a puzzle, especially with Tucker's revelation of Russell's coworkers being involved.

Sam, Furrell, Allen, and even Dorothy Crain may or may not have had any knowledge or even participated in Russell's criminal escapades. Or, one or more of them may have simply "presented things in their best light" in order to downplay their prior relationship with Russell.

Whatever the case, one thing is clear: Sam Crain draws the line at murder. And when told what to do, his children obey their father.

For their part, McMullen, Tucker, and Carey are content to have captured a vicious murderer and eased the minds of a terrified public. The Crain's helped them do it.

For tonight, that is enough for the lawmen to take them at their word.

31

I t is approximately 8 a.m., Tuesday, August 9th, when Sam Crain's four-door sedan bounces along the bumpy dirt road off Old US 19 and pulls up to the Dunedin Flats. Crain is visiting the location for the second time in fourteen hours.

Unlike the raucous scene the night before, the shore is calm and quiet. Shorebirds such as White Ibis and Pink Spoonbill prowl along the shallows where water meets sand, searching for a bite of breakfast. The only sounds Crain hears, other than the morning call of songbirds and Osprey overhead, are the sporadic splashes of leaping Mullet common to the grassy waters.

These he can hear clearly as there is little to no wind. While the temperature is a cool 72 degrees, mild for an August Dunedin morning, the humidity remains an oppressive eighty-seven percent.

Crain is weary after a long, traumatic day and a worrisome night. His son Furrell and daughter Dorothy are being held in the Pinellas County Jail, although Crain has been told "only for questioning." His other son, Alan Garfield, was allowed to return home last night with his parents.

Rastus Russell, or as Crain knew him, Jim Sullivan, the man who was once known as a friend to his family, is now almost certainly a murderer. He is being held in a cell not far from his children.

And it is Sam Crain who played the key role in putting him there.

All of that being the case, the killer is now behind bars, and no one in Crain's family has been harmed.

The plant worker walks purposely along the shoreline until he comes to two large tubs of scallops, pulled haphazardly ashore yesterday evening by deputies. Crain recognizes the tubs as his own. Gathered by three of his children and Russell, the scallops have spoiled in the overnight heat.

Crain tilts the tubs and dumps the smelling mollusks back into the sea.[*]

Lifting the empty wash tubs back into the trunk of his car, Crain slams the trunk closed and heads back home. It's going to be another long day.

* * *

Back at the Pinellas County Jail, Rastus Russell has a long day ahead as well.

Sheriff Todd Tucker and Constable Walter Carey have their prisoner scheduled for several visits today. First on the list is the office of Assistant Tax Assessor Lester Lambert. In addition to the Browne murder, the officers suspect Russell may be to blame for Lambert's robbery.

When Russell is escorted into the taxman's office, Lambert's eyes light up with recognition.

"I'm positive he's the one!" Lambert tells the Sheriff. "I'm just as positive as anyone can be of an identification. As far as I can see, he is the right guy."[**]

Russell hangs his head. He says nothing.

Satisfied, the officers haul their suspect back outside. They likely have Russell on at least one charge. But now it's time for the main event.

The officers, their entourage, and a slew of reporters depart in a caravan to Mease Dunedin Hospital.

There awaits Mrs. Anne Browne. And on this bright and sunny morning, she has her glasses.

* * *

---

[*]   *St. Petersburg Times, August 11, 1949.*
[**]   *Clearwater Sun, August 9th, 1949.*

132

Mrs. Browne is awake and alert as a slew of law enforcement officers enter her hospital room. She has been eagerly awaiting their arrival.

Surrounding her bed are Sheriff Tucker, Constable Carey, Deputy Sheriff Wilmer James, Deputy Sheriff Robert Fulle, Jailer Harvey Nash, and at least one reporter, Leonard Merreli, of the St. Petersburg Evening Independent.

As the crowd of lawmen part, two step forward holding, the handcuffed arms of John Calvin Russell. His swagger of the day before is gone. As he is pushed towards Mrs. Browne, the killer is trembling all over. He stares at the floor.

As Mrs. Browne scans the haggard-looking captive, Russell raises his eyes to meet hers. Through her reacquired glasses, Anne Browne casts an icy stare into the face of the man who killed her husband.

"That's him," she growls. "That's the man!"

The widow can't contain herself. "You still have that mean, sarcastic look on your face!"

Tucker gently probes the wounded woman, "Mrs. Browne, are you positive this is the man?"

"Yes, Sheriff. I am quite positive," she shoots back. "He's the man."*

Russell cowers in the face of the woman's withering accusation. He stares intently at Mrs. Browne, his body still shaking. His lips are moving as though he is trying to say something to his victim. But what he says is inaudible, even to those standing next to him.

Tucker thanks Mrs. Browne.

She'll never see Rastus Russell again.

---

* _The Evening Independent, August 9th, 1949._

32

With the primary witness now identifying Russell as the killer of Norman Browne, Tucker and Carey whisk their suspect back to the jailhouse.

There is much work to be done. The sheriff and constable are eager to begin a deep questioning of Russell. In addition, the sheriff will need to have formal charges drawn up in which to hold the former asylum inmate.

Later today, Tucker plans to take Russell to Bay Pines Veterans Hospital, where Miles Crum has been transferred. Crum remains in serious condition and has been placed inside an oxygen tent. His survival remains questionable.

Anne Browne's identification of Russell as the killer has set off a media storm. In addition to Russell's dramatic capture last night, the event has become national news. The sensational story has been broadcast to newspapers across the US and the world through wire services such as the Associated Press and the United Press.

Smiling from behind his office desk, Tucker takes the opportunity to crow a bit to the media.

"Great credit is due Crain and Godwin," Tucker tells the reporters. "In fact, these men are largely responsible for breaking this case. However, I cannot praise too highly the work of my deputies as well as the deputies under Hillsborough Sheriff Hugh Culbreath. Constable Walter Carey did some excellent work, and so did Clearwater Police Chief McClamma and his men. Matter of fact, the whole affair was an example of perfect coordination and cooperation. A brutal murder has been solved."*

Inside the jail, it's time for Tucker and Carey to get down to business. They want answers. Now they will finally get some uninterrupted quality time with their suspect.

Inside the interrogation room, they find Rastus Russell to be surprisingly accommodating.

Russell breaks down under intense questioning from Tucker and Carey. He admits he was the one who robbed Lester Lambert, took his wallet and watch, and tied him to a tree. He insists, however, that he acted alone.

In an act of contrition, he tells the lawmen where they can find Lambert's wallet and valuable papers - they are hidden at his aunt's home on Louisiana Avenue in Tampa. His watch can be found in his room at Sam Crain's house.

As the men continue to hammer Russell with questions, he opens up, admitting to several crimes throughout Pinellas and Hillsborough counties. These include at least three car thefts, two robberies, and a burglary. In all the cases, Russell is adamant he acted alone.

He is insistent that his "wife," Dorothy Jean Crain, had no knowledge or involvement in any of his crimes.

Russell admits to robbing an "old man" near Silver Springs. He also admits to robbing a "juke joint" near Sulphur Springs, a curious admission that will draw scrutiny later.

However, when questioning comes around to what the detectives really want to know, the torture and murder of Norman Browne and the attack on the Crums, Russell becomes "hazy and faint."

At first, he denies any knowledge of the Browne murders or being at the Browne house.

Then he claims he was at the Browne house that Sunday morning, that somebody else drove him there, but he did not commit the murder or attack on the Crums.

Later, he says he was there but doesn't remember anything.

It is possible that, in some respects, Russell is telling the truth. If he is indeed suffering from some type of mental illness, he could either

---

* *The Evening Independent, August 9th, 1949.*

have blacked out during the event (via a "Jekyll and Hyde" episode) or simply blocked it out after the fact. This would explain Russell's hazy recollection of the morning.

It is also possible that Russell was indeed intoxicated at the time of the attack, the alcohol reducing much of the memory of the violent act to a blurry dream.

Or, it is possible that Russell thought by admitting to the lesser crimes, but denying the more serious charges, his claims of innocence would appear more viable.

That Russell had the wherewithal to steal a car the night before the crime, then stop and switch license plates minutes before, suggests that the robbery of the Browne's, at least, was premeditated. During the crime, Russell drives all the way to his aunt's and then all the way back (an approximate 90-minute round trip) to finish it.

After the crime, Russell has the presence of mind to dump the bloody car, change his appearance, stash the shotguns, avoid police roadblocks all the way to Tampa, and then all the way back. All of these together strongly suggest that Russell was not blacked out through either mental incapacitation or drug or alcohol use.

Regardless, Russell steadfastly refuses to acknowledge any guilt for the Browne murder or attacks on Miles or Thelma Crum.

Then, nearly incriminating himself, he infers that Dorothy Jean had nothing to do with the Browne murder.

He does, however, freely admit to being at the Browne's house three months earlier. He claims he did not repair a pump. And while he will not admit any knowledge of Browne's murder, Russell oddly admits to stealing the car suspected of being used in the murder.

Tucker provides no further details on this part of Russell's answer.

Later in the questioning, the prisoner gets agitated. He demands to see his wife, Dorothy Jean Crain. When Tucker denies the request, Russell becomes irate.

Frustrated, the detectives suspend their interrogation.

✳ ✳ ✳

Later in the afternoon, Hillsborough County Sheriff Deputies arrive at the front door of Maud McCord in Tampa. The aunt of Rastus Russell allows the deputies to enter.*

Following the instructions relayed by deputies in Pinellas County, the Hillsborough officers find Lester Lambert's belongings, minus his cash, exactly where Russell said they were.

While in the house, the deputies begin questioning Mrs. McCord. Hillsborough County Deputy Henry Canto asks McCord if she keeps any weapons in the house.

McCord tells them she keeps a shotgun for protection. It was kept in a cloth sack hanging on the wall.

Mrs. McCord shows the officers the white sack. When deputies open the bag, they, as well as McCord, are stunned to find not a shotgun but a wooden replica of one. A piece of wood has been craftily cut and then affixed with a broom handle to mimic the shape of a barrel. When placed inside the bag, the wooden shape looks like a real shotgun.

Officers seize the wooden gun. But that is not all they find. Upon searching the garage, officers discover evidence gold.

They find the wooden stock and steel barrel that was sawed off of the shotgun. It will later be compared to the .12 gauge found in Rastus Russell's bedroom at the Crain house.

The pieces will match perfectly.

McCord also tells officers of her nephew's strange arrival on Sunday morning, August 7th, only to abruptly depart again, telling McCord he had to go on "another little job" in Pinellas County.

Back in Clearwater, officers have identified the blue hat with the comic strip inside found at the murder scene as Russell's. In addition, the stolen Pinellas County license plate found attached to the back of the 1946 Ford, the same one Russell used on the day of Norman's Browne murder, has become a final piece of damning evidence.

It matches the numbers Anne Browne scrawled on the wooden wall of her garage.

---

* *It is unclear whether the deputies have a search warrant or are simply investigating Russell's claim that Lester Lambert's belongings are in the house. It is known, however, that Walter Carey is a stickler for having search warrants, knowing that without one, evidence cannot be used in court.*

33

August 9, 1949
Pinellas County Jail

It is late Tuesday morning when Constable Walter Carey, Sheriff Todd Tucker, and Jailer Harvey Nash once again come to retrieve Rastus Russell from his cell.

Russell has been moved from his private quarters on the third floor of the jail into a four-man cell with three other prisoners. One report claims Russell was moved because he made too much noise banging his handcuffs against the metal bars of his individual holding cell. However, most inside the jail claim Russell has been well-behaved thus far.

His new home is in the maximum-security wing on the third floor of the jailhouse. This section is deemed the "escape-proof" portion of the jail. His cellblock contains four other cells. A thick steel door controlled from a switchboard outside the cellblock separates the rest of the jail from this section.

The new jail across the street cannot open soon enough. The "old" jail that holds Rastus Russell currently contains three times the number of prisoners for which it was designed. With no air conditioning, temperatures inside can reach sweltering levels in the summer.

For relief, the windows are opened to allow outside air to flow through. This is of little relief in the summer, as the rare breeze outside is often as hot or hotter than the stifling air inside. The windows of the cellblock provide a view of the sidewalk across the street. Male prisoners shout, hoot, and whistle at female pedestrians who happen to venture past. For this reason, many avoid this section of Clearwater's streets.

The jail is dirty. There are many complaints about the food. The overcrowding and poor conditions create strife inside the facility. Flaring tempers and violence are common.

For Rastus Russell, this has not yet been a problem. Periodically, the cell doors on his block are opened, and the prisoners are free to mingle with each other inside the block. Far from creating any trouble, the suave Russell is quick to befriend several of his cellmates.

When the officers arrive, Russell goes willingly. He is being permitted to call an attorney today.

Carey and Nash cuff Russell's hands in the front, then lock the cuffs to a tight leather strap that has been fastened around his waist. The three escort the restrained prisoner out the metal door of his cell.

The men are dressed in typical Florida summer clothes, designed to breathe and deflect heat. Carey sports a short-sleeved, white cotton shirt tucked neatly into dark trousers. On his head rests a sporty summer fedora, white with a black stripe above the brim. Atop his nose rests his signature, round, wire-rimmed glasses. Russell and Nash also wear short sleeved white shirts. Russell wears light-colored trousers. Nash wears his own summer fedora.

Russell will get to call his attorney. But there is a little matter to be addressed first.

As the three step out of the cell, a group of reporters and photographers are waiting. Carey and Tucker know they are there. The media has been permitted upstairs for the event.

When Russell sees the cameras once again awaiting him, he abruptly turns his back, at one point nearly doubling over to hide his face.

Carey bends down and tries to persuade Russell to stand up and face the erupting flashbulbs.

He refuses.

"This thing is bad enough," Russell barks, "without having my pictures splattered all over the newspapers!"[*]

Beside him and facing the cameras, Walter Carey ceremoniously produces a warrant. Holding it up for all to see, Carey loudly reads the document charging John Calvin Russell with the first-degree murder of Norman Y. Browne.

Photographers snap vigorously away.

---

[*] *St. Petersburg Times, August 11, 1949.*

Humiliated, the killer rages at his captors, "When I get out of here, and it won't be long, I'm going to smash every damn camera in the country!"*

Carey must feel a sense of satisfaction. Not only has he got his man for all to see, he is charging the man who injured his late brother with a crime that could send him to the electric chair.

The next day, a photo appears in the St. Petersburg Times of Carey reading the warrant. Behind him, jailer Harvey Nash appears to be smiling. Taking up a third of the shot is the back of Rastus Russell, his face pointed at the floor, hidden from view.

* * *

With the photo op complete, Jailer Harvey Nash ushers Russell down to the jail office. Sheriff Tucker, who presides over the jail and supersedes Nash, has instructed Russell to be allowed to call Tampa attorney Pat Whitaker, Sr.

Since yesterday, Rastus Russell has been insisting he be allowed to contact Whitaker.

Under the law, a man charged with a crime carrying the death penalty (which Russell has) has the right to an attorney. If the accused cannot afford one (which Russell cannot), the Circuit Judge may select an attorney to represent him. However, the state is not compelled to pay for an attorney selected by the defendant.

Russell is entitled to ask for a preliminary hearing before Magistrate J.S. Register of Tarpon Springs. Or, he may simply waive a hearing and plead not guilty.

When Nash asks Russell if he wants a preliminary hearing, Russell tells him he does not want any hearing until he can get Whitaker to represent him. When Nash tells Russell the court will appoint him an attorney, Russell becomes insistent.

"If they appoint .... or .... (Russell names two prominent Clearwater attorneys), they will only get me sent back to Chattahoochee. I would rather go to the electric chair than be sent back there."*

---

*   *St. Petersburg Times, August 11, 1949.*

Yesterday, Russell told Sheriff Tucker that he "knew" Whitaker and wanted a good lawyer.

Whitaker, however, is more than just a good lawyer. Pat Whitaker, Sr. is a real-life Perry Mason. Known as the most "able criminal defense attorney in the South," Whitaker's ability to sway a jury with his colorful, flamboyant style is legendary. So famous is Whitaker's style of arguing, other attorneys flood the courtroom any time he tries a case, simply to observe his presentation.

One of the attorney's signature moves is "accidentally" losing his dentures in the midst of a thundering oration, thereby garnering a sense of shared humanity with the jurors. Stories of Whitaker's courtroom prowess serve to enhance his reputation, including once winning a case by convincing a judge that a mullet is not actually a fish (it is.)

It is said that the famous lawyer has saved more men from the electric chair than any other Florida attorney. His power is likely enhanced by the fact that he also happens to be a Florida state senator.

In truth, only about one percent of Whitaker's firm, made up of himself and his two brothers, Tom and D.B. Whitaker, consists of criminal defense. However, high-profile criminal cases bring notoriety to the firm. Thus, is it not uncommon for Pat Sr. to take them on a pro-bono basis. The time incurred is more than recouped in free publicity.

Rastus Russell's case is certainly high profile. It would seem a perfect candidate for the prominent attorney.

Whether or not Russell "knows" Pat Whitaker, Sr. may never be known. There is no record of Whitaker representing Russell in any other case. Nonetheless, it is a curious statement for the convicted felon to make. Russell's uncle from Thonotosassa is a prominent attorney and Mason.

When Russell calls Whitaker's office on Tuesday, August 9th, the famous trial attorney is out. Russell speaks with Pat's brother, Tom Whitaker.

Tom has read about the case in the newspaper. He is lukewarm and non-committal when talking to Russell. The attorney tells the prisoner to call back on Monday when Pat is in the office.

Russell hangs up the phone. With Nash and assistant jailer Townsend escorting him, Rastus Russell trudges back towards the elevator, his chains rattling as he shuffles across the floor.

Later, Tucker briefs the media.

"Tom did not seem very enthusiastic about taking Russell's case," he tells them.

34

I n 1949, Bay Pines Veterans Hospital is a state of the art, federally funded facility with approximately 150 beds. Originally constructed in 1933 as a home for disabled soldiers, the hospital has expanded rapidly since its influx of patients during and after World War II.

Located on Seminole Point, just Northwest of St. Petersburg, its massive campus consists of fourteen Mediterranean-style hospital buildings. The facility owns over 700 acres of prime real estate over-looking the Gulf of Mexico. From the outside, its beautiful, modern buildings on its waterfront, palm tree acreage could easily be mistaken for an exclusive resort rather than a hospital.

While Miles Crum has not been overseas, he served fifteen and a half months in the army, being discharged as a sergeant shortly after the end of the war. He has been transferred here to receive treatment for his traumatic wound. Surgeons are still not optimistic about Crum's condition. But they are now giving him a fighting chance.

It is late afternoon by the time Sheriff Tucker, Carey, and deputies ride up to the main office of the hospital. Rastus Russell sits cuffed between deputies in the back seat of the cruiser.

As the officers present the silent prisoner to the ailing Crum, the grocer looks up from his hospital bed.

"That's him," he tells Tucker. "I'll never forget those eyes and that face."*

---

* *The St. Petersburg Times, August 10, 1949.*

Crum's life prior to his encounter with Rastus Russell was a quiet one of pressing routine. He and Thelma often worked hours of 6 a.m. to 9 p.m., six days per week. This left little time for a social life or activities such as going to the movies. Crum doesn't know it yet, but his life of obscurity has been thrust into the spotlight. He will not be comfortable with the attention.

* * *

With Rastus Russell now identified by two separate witnesses as the perpetrator at the Browne house on Sunday, Todd Tucker feels his case against the thrity-four-year-old is clinched.

But something else is nagging him.

Back at the jailhouse, Furrell and Dorothy Crain remain behind bars. While Tucker earlier stated that the two were being held as material witnesses, he has suspicions that one or both of them may have deeper involvement with Russell. Today, he has hardened his tone, saying that the pair remain in custody "pending placement of possible charges against them."

This was after interviews with the siblings at the courthouse on Monday night.

Tucker and Carey are particularly interested in a robbery that occurred the same night Lester Lambert was robbed and tied to a tree, nearly three weeks ago. A small tavern in Oldsmar, not far from where Lambert was carjacked, was robbed by two men and a woman. One of the men used a sawed-off shotgun. Lambert later stated to police that his kidnapper appeared to be looking for his companions during their long ride back to Curlew Creek Road.[*]

Russell abandoned Lambert less than a mile from the Crain home. This is also the same night that the Crain family supposedly saw their daughter for the first time in two months after disappearing with Rastus Russell before welcoming the young man back into their home.

The coincidences are not lost on the lawmen.

With Russell tucked safely back in his cell, Tucker turns his attention to the Crains. He resumes questioning of Dorothy Jean.

---

[*]   *St. Petersburg Times, July 28, 1949.*

While the teenager provides little information in the way of useable evidence, she shares some extraordinary insights into Russell's character with the Sheriff.

Dorothy says that Russell once told her that he would "kill himself" if he ever felt hemmed in by the law – a promise he attempted to keep at the Dunedin Flats.

She also tells Tucker that Russell told her his mother was always "too busy to bother with him" when he was a child. He felt "picked on" when people resented his abuse of animals (such as pulling the heads off chickens or cutting the tails off cats.)

The girl's comments about Russell hint at a more intimate relationship between the two than is presented later.

While little else is known about what the Crain share with Tucker in the interviews, Tucker tells the media afterward that he plans to confer with State Attorney Chester M. McMullen regarding the Crains' possible involvement in the Browne case or some of the earlier robbery cases to which Russell has admitted. Whatever Furrell and Dorothy Crain tell Tucker, it is a lot more than is shared with the public. Otherwise, Tucker would never make such a comment to the media.

In regard to Russell's suicide threat, Tucker isn't buying it. He knows Russell had the chance to kill himself back in the Dunedin Flats. If he couldn't do it then, he isn't going to do it now.

Tucker states as much the next day.

"Are you guarding Russell against suicide?" asks a curious reporter.

"No, we're not," Tucker responds coldly. "I don't think he has the nerve to kill himself."[*]

* * *

With two witnesses positively identifying Russell as the culprit in Sunday's violent attack, Carey and Tucker want to get the third and final witness to ID him today.

Thelma Crum remains hospitalized in Tarpon Springs. But Mrs. Crum is not having a good day. In addition to her physical injuries, Crum is suffering emotional trauma from the event. She has also just

---

learned that her infant daughter, Judy, is not improving. Doctors now report the child in "alarming" condition and fear serious internal injuries may have occurred. Thelma Crum is nearly hysterical.

When Tucker phones the hospital to request the visit, he is asked to hold off.

"We were told that Mrs. Crum cannot undergo the strain of attempting to identify Russell at this time," Tucker tells reporters. "However, this development is relatively unimportant insofar as our case against Russell is concerned. He has been positively identified by the widow of the murder victim as well as by Crum."

It's been a productive day. Tucker and Carey can wait on Thelma Crum.

35

August 10, 1949
Clearwater Courthouse, Clearwater, FL

While detectives continue to collect overwhelming evidence against Rastus Russell, State Attorney Chester McMullen has the job of prosecuting Russell and making it stick.

Three days after the murder, McMullen is already putting his case together.

Chester Bartow McMullen is a forty-six-year-old firebrand former prosecutor for Pinellas County. In 1931, at age twenty-eight, he was elected as State Attorney in a landslide victory. He has held the position ever since. He still holds the record of being the youngest state attorney ever to take office within the Sixth Judicial Circuit.

Like Rastus Russell, McMullen's roots run deep in Florida. His grandfather, Daniel McMullen, was one of Largo, Florida's first homesteaders. His father was Pinellas County's first tax collector. His brother, Melvin Arthur McMullen, served as state attorney from 1915 to 1921.

Like his other family members, McMullen has ambition. While he has not discussed it publicly, the young attorney is mulling a run for a seat in the US House of Representatives next year. A hard conviction in a spectacular, nationally covered murder case certainly wouldn't hurt that cause.

Even without a run for Congress, McMullen knows he must come down hard on this one. The gory, disturbing manner of the murder has ignited the public imagination – and horror. Sending Russell back to Chattahoochee will not do. For Rastus Russell, the prosecutor will accept only one outcome: The electric chair.

In 1923, the Florida Legislature passed a law replacing hanging with the electric chair. In that same year, an oak chair was constructed and placed inside a death chamber at Raiford State Prison. Popular myth held that the chair was constructed by inmates using wood from trees around the prison. In fact, Florida's first electric chair was actually constructed by Cooks Cabinet Shop in Jacksonville.[*]

Born out of a marketing battle between George Westinghouse and Thomas Edison, the first electric chair was constructed in the 1880s. It was seen as a technological miracle. At the time, both pro and anti-death penalty advocates saw it as a more humane alternative to public hanging.

That is debatable.

Decades later, research contradicting the "instant, painless death" argument for electrocution began to accumulate. It suggested that because the skull insulates the brain from an electric current, some inmates might experience a slow-motion death of boiling body parts, paralyzing muscle contractions, and intense pain.[*]

When William Kemmler becomes the first prisoner put to death in the electric chair in 1890 New York, it becomes a macabre affair.

As horrified witnesses looked on, Kemmler's body smoked while blood flowed from his eyes. The death chamber smelled of charred flesh.

Westinghouse is contrite and slightly embarrassed afterward.

"They could have done better with an ax," he ruefully acknowledged.

Yet, in the first part of the 20th century, the population in the US is growing rapidly, as are crime and homicide rates. The public is demanding law and order. The electric chair is seen as a frightening deterrent to violent crime.

Fourteen states are already using the new device by 1923. In that year, Florida Sheriffs, tired of presiding over hangings, persuaded the Florida legislature to replace the rope with the chair.

Dr. Ralph Greene, Sr., a Florida state health official, installs the components of the state's first chair. Greene describes building the head electrode like a "helmet . . . with felt, mesh wire and straps." It featured homemade accessories, such as a leg electrode made from an old Army boot and some roofing copper. The final wiring is done by Westinghouse.

---

[*] *St. Petersburg Times, The Story of Old Sparky, September 25, 1999.*

Initially, the Sheriff where the condemned's crime occurred is taxed with "flipping the switch." But as Sheriffs became resistant to carrying the burden, the legislature replaced the Sheriffs with a black-hooded executioner in 1941. The anonymous person is paid $150 per execution.

There has always been something "eerily medieval" about electrocutions in Florida and elsewhere, notes Craig Brandon, author of *The Electric Chair*. As the condemned walks down a forty-foot corridor to the Florida death chamber, the warden, guards and hooded executioner follow silently behind. *

Robert Snyder, a professor of American Studies at the University of South Florida, explains the psychology of the electric chair and its use in 20th-century Florida.

"There's always been a sense in Florida that if you feel you have been victimized, you have an obligation to protect your honor by avenging what has taken place," Snyder says. *"A sort of bestial spirit resides deep within the heart of people in Florida. When it comes to meting out punishment, this naturally translates into continuing use of one of the more brutal, callous ways of legally executing a person."***

By 1949, an average of six prisoners a year meet their fate in "Old Sparky" or "Old Smokey," as Florida's chair is known.***

Three days after the most sensational murder case his county has ever seen, Chester McMullen believes he has enough evidence to make Rastus Russell one of them.****

---

*   *St. Petersburg Times, The Story of Old Sparky, September 25, 1999.*

**   *St. Petersburg Times, September 25, 1999, citing author Brandon.*

***   *Source: Florida Department of Corrections, https://fdc.myflorida.com.*

****   *The electric chair was the sole means of execution in Florida from 1924 until 2000, when the Florida State Legislature, under pressure from the U.S. Supreme Court, signed lethal injection into law. Although no one has been executed in Florida's electric chair since 1999, prisoners awaiting execution on Florida's death row may still be electrocuted at their request. The chair is currently located in Florida State Prison on the outskirts of Starke. Source: Wikipedia.*

An Eager Posse waits on the Shoreline of the Dunedin Flats

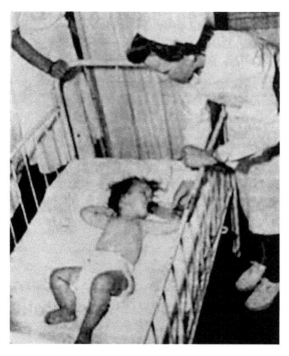

Baby Judy Crum at Tarpon Springs Hospital After the Russell Attack

Crain Family on Front Porch 1948, Furrell on far Left, Dorothy on Far Right

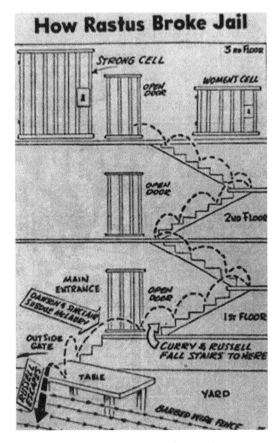

Diagram Showing Russell's Jail Escape

Dorothy Jean Crain left, Alan Garfield Crain right and Furrell Crain - head visible behind Alan, arrive at Police Headquarters

Dorothy Jean Crain

Dorothy Jean Crain

Dunedin Flats, 1940s. The road in the bottom left corner is Old US 19 where a line of Deputies was posted to prevent Russells escape.

*Fence over which Russell Escaped. New Jail
Construction can be seen in Background.*

Florida National Guard Arrives to Hunt Russell

Furrell and Dorothy Crain Pose for Photographers on the Dunedin Flats

*HL Russell Stands Beside the Black Ford Rastus Russell used
in the Browne Murder. The two are not related.*

Judge John Elmer Bird

*Miles and Judy Crum. Despite the writing on the photo this is
likely in 1949 only weeks before the Russell incident.*

Miles Crum's Store, 1949. Note Crums Jeep on the Right

Miles Thelma and Judy Crum in Happier Times

Modern Map of Crystal Beach showing Location of Browne Home in 1949

*Outside Browne Murder House. Arrow shows
bedroom where the Brownes were found.*

Outside Murder Scene of Norman Browne

Outside Raleigh Allen Store

Pinellas County Deputy Sheriff Bob Fulle Examines Evidence
Found in Russell's Room. Note: Murder Weapon at top of
Table. The Shotgun underneath is Mr. Brownes.

Rastus Russell

*Rastus Russell is brought ashore at Dunedin Flats,
August 8, 1949. Sheriff Tucker on Left.*

*Rastus Russell is Escorted from the Dunedin Flats after his
capture. On his left is Todd Tucker. On his right is Deputy Sheriff
Wilmer James and Tarpon Springs Police Chief Manos.*

Ray McClaury

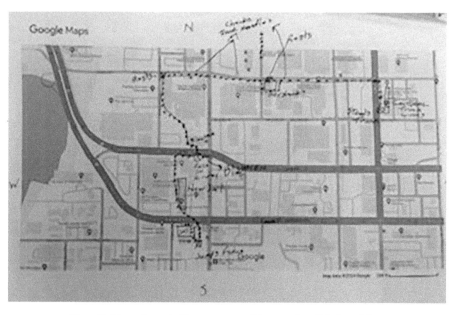

Russells Run through Clearwater as illustrated on Modern Map.

Sam Crain

Sheriff Todd Tucker

Sheriff Tucker and wife, Nellie May Tucker look at a photo of Tuckers
son 1940s. Tuckers son survived the Pearl Harbor attack in 1941.

Tarpon Springs Police Dept 1949 – Chief Manos 2nd from
right – Courtesy Tarpon Springs Historical Society.

The Hunters: Carey (Left) and Tucker (Right)
Share a Lighter Moment at Citrus Park.

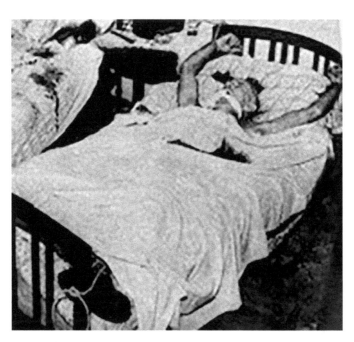

The Macabre Murder Scene of Norman Y. Browne.

Tracking Russell in Citrus Park: Frazier (left,)
Tucker (on Right with Shotgun on Shoulder.)

Waiting on the Crain Porch for Russell. Charles Crain is Second from Left.

Walter Carey Photo

Walter Carey Reads the Charges While Russell Turns his Back to the Cameras

Rastus Russell

36

H olding what he feels is an iron-clad case against Rastus Russell, Chester McMullen wants to move fast in prosecuting the accused murderer.

His first step will be convincing Circuit Judge John U. Bird to recall the grand jury.

A grand jury is a group of sixteen to twenty-three citizens selected like any other jury. In 1949 Florida, they serve an eighteen-month term and meet several times throughout the year, typically for two-to-three-day pre-scheduled sessions. A grand jury's job is not to determine guilt or innocence. It is only to determine "probable cause" for a trial.

The grand jury can typically hear several cases over the course of a meeting. However, the body typically only hears major felony cases.

The grand jury meets in complete secrecy. Only the prosecuting attorney is present, along with any witnesses he chooses to present to the jurors. The prosecutor's only job is to show there is enough evidence to proceed to trial.

If the jury agrees, an indictment is issued. To get an indictment, the grand jury does not need a unanimous decision. It only requires a simple majority agreement.

A grand jury hearing can be seen as a trial run of its case by the prosecution. Although no defense attorney is permitted in the hearing, an indictment can allow the prosecution to advance directly to trial.

Chester McMullen would very much like that.

But there is one problem. The grand jury in Pinellas County just met weeks ago. It is not scheduled to meet again until December. That is too long for McMullen.

171

He plans to meet with Judge Bird this afternoon and ask him to recall the grand jury for an emergency hearing of Russell's case. Getting cooperation from Bird will be key in bringing Rastus Russell to a speedy trial.

* * *

Across the street at the county jail, Russell continues to be interrogated by Tucker, Carey, and deputies. In addition to admitting to a variety of crimes in both Hillsborough and Pinellas Counties, the prisoner confesses to one that baffles his interrogators.

He tells them he "stuck up a juke joint" near Sulphur Springs, a neighborhood on the northern outskirts of Tampa. He claims he did the crime early in July. He also tells them he "robbed an old man" three or four weeks ago near Ruskin, a rural town several miles south of Tampa.

Hillsborough Deputy Sheriffs are called to question Russell about the robberies. However, when they investigate later, they find no record of any tavern robberies in the location or times that Russell specified. They also find no record of any "old men" being robbed in Ruskin during the same time period.

Investigators find the admissions strange, chiefly because most of his other confessions did indeed coincide with unsolved crimes.

One crime that has gone unsolved is the robbery/beating of eighty-two-year-old W.J. Graham last month in Tampa. The severely beaten Graham was found in the Sulphur Springs area of Tampa. He held on for a few weeks, then succumbed to his injuries just yesterday, August 11th. Whoever did the robbery could now be charged with murder.

J.L. Glissen, an employee of the City of Clearwater gas and water department, thinks he has an answer. Glissen read with interest newspaper reports of the attack in Crystal Beach. He has also read of Rastus Russell's admission to robbing Lester Lambert only weeks earlier.

Glissen is a close friend of the Graham family. He notices marked similarities in the attacks on Graham and Lambert. When he notices the location of Russell's (aunt's) home in Tampa, he becomes alarmed.

W.J. Graham is a retired pensioner of the Tampa Electric Company when he goes out for a late evening stroll early in July

1949. Graham is in the habit of taking a walk before going to bed at his home at 6900 Central Avenue in the New Seminole Heights district of Tampa.

Witnesses report that a car stopped, picked up Graham, then drove north toward Sulphur Springs. Graham was found the next morning, lying in a coma, along the road near Sulphur Springs. Doctors said Graham had been brutally attacked with a "blunt instrument."

Graham never regains consciousness enough to identify his attacker.

When Glissen reads the accounts of the Browne's, Crum's, and Lambert in the papers, he contacts Sheriff Tucker.

Glissen tells Tucker of his suspicions. The kidnapping and robbery bear a strong resemblance to the Lester Lambert robbery. (While there is no report of Glissen mentioning it specifically, he must certainly have also drawn a connection to Russell clubbing Thelma Crum over the head.) He tells the Sheriff that Graham had less than seven dollars in his pocket at the time of the robbery.[*]

Tucker is intrigued. New Seminole Heights is less than three miles from Russell's known home at the time, 914 East Louisiana Avenue – Aunt Maud's.

Thus, when Russell tells the story of the "juke joint" and the "old man" in Ruskin, the interrogators become suspicious. Did Russell simply use elements of a real crime in "admitting" to two fictitious crimes?

Then, they get an even wilder story from Dorothy Jean Crain. As their questioning of Ms. Crain has continued since Sunday night, the teenager has become more forthcoming in her testimony about Russell. She freely admits to living with the handsome Russell for nearly three months.

Tucker relays a story that Crain told to him.

She tells Tucker that Russell came home one night last month boasting of robbing a "rural juke joint."

Tucker explains, "She said Russell claimed he had been jumped by six male patrons of the resort and had emerged victorious after a terrific hand-to-hand struggle."[**]

---

[*]   *How he would know this is unclear.*

[**]   *The Evening Independent, August 12, 1949.*

The officers are skeptical. In fact, they now suspect that Norman Browne may not, in fact, be Russell's only murder. Together with Tampa deputies, the lawmen voice the theory that Russell "confessed" to the Sulphur Springs tavern hold-up in an effort to throw off suspicion of his connection to the Graham death.

Deputy Sheriff Wilmer James, one of the first on scene at the Browne murder, is clear in his conviction.

"The very nature of the crime," James declares, "bares Russell's trademark."[*]

In hindsight, the officer's theory makes sense. The similarities between the Lambert robbery and the Graham robbery are striking. The method in which Thelma Crum was attacked is identical to the method that Graham was struck. Warren Newbern, robbed eight years earlier in Palm Harbor by Russell, was hit on the head with a bottle.

Russell's modus operandi appears to be committing his crimes close to home. He steals the car (by his own admission) used in the Browne murders less than a mile and a half from his aunt's home in Tampa. He ties Lester Lambert to a tree almost within shouting distance of his room at Sam Crain's house. The Browne's home is about three miles from Sam Crain's house. As a teenager, he burglarized, stole cars, and shoplifted within blocks of his mother's boarding house in downtown Palm Harbor.

Russell is known to have been living at his aunt's house with Dorothy Jean Crain at the time of the Graham attack. Its location to Graham's house is about as far as the Browne's house from Sam Crain's. In short, very close.

More interestingly, if Russell's strategy is admitting to lesser crimes to cover for major crimes, as he appears to be doing in the case of Norman and Anne Browne, why would he not use the same technique for Graham?

Unfortunately, unlike the Browne murder, there is a dismal lack of evidence or witnesses in the Graham murder.

And with the focus on prosecuting Russell in the Browne case, the Graham murder seems to have been put on the back burner.

---

[*] *The Evening Independent, August 12, 1949.*

In all of the record searches done for this book, no further mention of W.J. Graham, his murder, or Russell's connection to it could be found.

It was presumably never solved.

37

Sixteen-year-old Dorothy Jean Crain has been in the Pinellas County Jail for four long days.

She has been told she's being held as a "material witness." In reality, Sheriff Tucker has not made up his mind about her. Was she involved with any of Russell's crimes? Or was she really an innocent victim, kidnapped and living in fear for her life, as she originally told police?

The truth seems to be somewhere in between. Tucker is not only looking for more insights into Russell, but trying to decide if the girl should be charged with any crime.

Her testimony today seems to reveal two truths. First, while Dorothy doesn't admit to participating in any of Russell's shenanigans, she certainly had knowledge of at least some of them. Secondly, hers and Russell's relationship seems to have indeed been a romantic one, and not a kidnap situation.

That being said, it is still difficult to assign much blame to the teenager. The girl was likely easy prey for the handsome, charismatic thirty-four-year-old. Tucker must be bouncing this around in his head as she opens up about her life with the suspected killer.

Regardless, despite daily visits from her parents and her brother Furrell being held in a nearby cell, Dorothy must certainly be wearing down. The Pinellas County Jail in 1949 is hardly a place for a teenage girl used to the relative comfort and safety of living at the Crain homestead on Curlew Creek Road. It is brutally hot. It stinks. Although the men's cellblock is separate from the women's, she shares quarters with all manner of criminals.

At this point, she is likely ready to give Tucker whatever he wants.

And today, she gives him a juicy nugget of a story.

As Tucker explains the next day to the Evening Independent, "The girl told us a lot of things."

Tucker then relays a startling and insightful story in his own words.

"Last Saturday morning, according to the girl's statement, a young woman taking orders for portraits for a Tampa photographic studio called at Russell's home in that city."

Tucker is referring to Maud McCord's house in Tampa.

"Miss Crain was interested in having some portraits made but called her 'husband.' Russell came to the door and talked to the saleslady."

This is a revealing statement by Dorothy Jean Crain. Not only does she refer to Russell as her "husband," she is interested in having a portrait done of them together. This more resembles newlyweds living a normal life together than a girl who was kidnapped and held against her will.

Tucker continues by quoting Russell speaking to the sales person.

"I haven't any money today," Russell tells her, "But you come back Monday, and I'll have plenty of dough.'"

This exchange took place on Saturday, August 6th, one day before the Browne murder.

Dorothy tells Tucker that Russell "returned" early Sunday evening with at least $60.

Tucker continues, "Russell gave Miss Crain's father $2 to buy gasoline to drive him to Tampa. He gave his landlady $15 and $10 more to the girl. She said he still had a lot of money left.'" *

If true, this is a fascinating revelation by Dorothy Jean Crain.

By "landlady," Tucker is presumably referring to Maud McCord. This would mean Russell returned to McCord's house after the murder. He did this not only to pay his "rent" but also possibly to pick up Dorothy. According to Sam Crain, Russell stayed at the Crain house on Sunday night after Russell and Sam Crain returned from Tampa with two shotguns in the trunk of Crain's car.

Sam Crain also claimed that Russell showed up at the house late Saturday night and left early Sunday morning.

---

* *The Evening Independent, August 12, 1949.*

Dorothy's story casts some possible doubt on Sam Crain's version of events the night before and after the murder of Norman Browne.

It is possible that Russell left Dorothy at their "home" at Maud McCord's house and went to Sam Crain's house alone on Saturday night. Crain claimed Russell did not sleep that night and only stayed a few hours in the very early morning.

It is also possible that Russell left Dorothy at McCord's house all day Sunday, only to return Sunday night, pay his aunt Maud, pick up Dorothy, and then head to Seminole Heights, where he dumped the car and met Sam Crain. This would mean that Dorothy was present with Russell and Sam Crain when Russell was loading the two shotguns into Crain's car on Sunday night.

He could have stopped to pay Maud on his way to meet Sam Crain in Seminole Heights on Sunday. Or, some reports say Russell left the Crain house on Monday prior to the scalloping trip. Perhaps this is when he drove back to Tampa to pay his "landlady," Aunt Maud.

The most probable scenario, however, is that Russell did indeed bring Dorothy with him to the Crain house on Saturday night, where she remained until at least Monday before the scalloping trip. If this is the case, Tucker may have used the word "returned" to mean Russell returned to the Crain house on Sunday, not Maud McCords. There, he gave Dorothy $10, then paid Sam Crain $2 for gas to take him to Tampa.

As mentioned prior, Wilburn Crain states in his interview for this book that Russell did indeed return to the Crain house on the day of the murder with a bloody gash on the back of his hand. Why would he return to the Crain's if his "wife" Dorothy was at McCord's? He likely would not.

Secondly, in her interview about the day of the murder, Maud McCord talks about Russell but never mentions Dorothy at the house on Sunday, at least as reported in the press. She also states that after Russell appeared and then left quickly on Sunday morning, she did not see him again that day.

But how would Dorothy know Russell gave his "landlady" (McCord) $15? Either Russell told her, Russell took her to Tampa with him Sunday night and stopped to pay McCord on his way to meet Sam Crain, or, Russell and Dorothy went together to McCord's on Monday.

Tucker likely knew the answers. But he wasn't sharing them with the press.

More intriguing is Ms. Crain's claim that Russell had "a lot" of money on him when he returned on Sunday. Early reports say that the only money taken from the Browne's home was $30 from Anne Browne's pocketbook. The Evening Independent reports the amount to be "exactly" $60.

How much does Dorothy mean by "a lot?"

$33? $100? $5,000?

Tucker doesn't specify. But it introduces an intriguing possibility. What if Russell did *indeed* get what he came for at the Browne house? What if there *was* a large sum of money there?

And what if Rastus Russell either found it or Norman or Anne Browne relented and told him where it was?

After all, we only heard Anne Browne's version of events. If there was a large pile of illegitimate cash in the house, would she share that information with police?

Did Anne Browne, seeing her husband lying dead, relent and tell Russell where to find the cash, and in return, Russell spared her life?

Is that why she only received a cut wrist instead of her husband's fate? Russell easily could have killed her. She was bound by both feet and one hand. Did he start to stab at her, demanding the money, and after feeling the searing pain of the blade cutting through tendon and arteries on her wrist, finally cry out, "Under the floorboard in the kitchen!" or some such statement?

While newspapers erroneously report that the Crum's arrival "interrupted" Russell's attack on Mrs. Browne, the victim states in her own account that Russell was sitting on the porch with the shotgun resting on his lap when the Crum's arrived.

Did Russell's statement, "You keep your damn mouth shut, or I'll come back here and kill you too," occur after he got his money?

These two factors alone indicate Russell made a conscious decision not to kill Anne Browne.

Reports from the crime scene indicate a lock box was found on the floor of the Browne house. It appeared as though someone had tried to pry it open. But it was left at the scene, unopened.

Why wouldn't Russell take the box with him? He could have been frazzled by the encounter with the Crum's and forgot it. He could have assumed there was nothing worthwhile inside. Or, he could have already found what he was seeking and, thus, simply discarded it.

And if a larger sum of legitimate money or other valuables were taken, why would Anne Browne not report this to investigators?

These unanswered questions lend some credence to a story Wilburn Crain told me. He dropped a bombshell that Russell was at the Browne's home because the Browne's "owed a debt." It was a rumor I heard oft repeated in my interviews with old-time residents of both Crystal Beach and Thonotosassa.

But Crain filled in the story with startling detail:

"...up north, and I don't know, when I say up north, I don't know which city we're talking about. It could have been New York, it could have been Philadelphia, wherever. But it was some big town up north. This Browne and his wife owned a jewelry store and they had a lot of expensive jewelry. They hired, this is what we heard, they hired Russell to break into their store, steal the jewelry, and hang onto the jewelry, and they would get the insurance money...they would give him a big chunk of money from the insurance money...That never happened. He broke into the store, stole the jewelry, returned the jewelry to them and waited on the money from the insurance company. Well, if there was any payment from the insurance company, it went to the Browne's. It never went to Russell...I can say the story here is, Russell run em' down. He located them where they were at and demanded his money. That's why he was evidently going through the house and asking 'wheres the money? Where's the money?'"

When I asked Crain how he learned of this story, he couldn't remember, other than he likely heard his father talking about it.

"I can't even say at this point that Russell didn't tell all this to my father," says Crain. *"that he was involved in a robbery and these people owe him some money. I'm sure he didn't tell my father he killed a guy, but he might've told him the story of...I don't know...Listen, there was something that was of monetary value somewhere."*

If there is any truth to Crain's story at all, it could lend weight to Dorothy's claim that Russell returned on Sunday with "a lot" of money.

---

*   *From 2024 interview with Wilburn Crain.*

Or, it could mean nothing. Dorothy's definition of "a lot" of money could be $15 or $20.

What Dorothy Crain's story does accomplish is to further implicate Rastus Russell in the murder of Norman Y. Browne.

But, it does highlight the fact that Russell was expecting to have "plenty of dough" come Monday. It is unlikely he would have gone to all the trouble of stealing a car, switching plates, and staying up all night if he was only expecting to get $30 or $60.

Russell seemed certain there was a large sum of money at the Browne house.

The question is, why?

If Crain's story is to be believed, it would seem to answer many of those questions.

For instance, if Russell's plan was to rob the Brownes, why would he spend three and half hours on Sunday morning sitting at the dining room table having coffee, taking Mr. Browne to "get a paper," and showing the Browne's his car?

Why did he have to find a shotgun in Browne's bathroom before taking them hostage?

Why does Norman Browne scream, "I'll keep the son of a bitch quiet!" shortly before his death. What does that mean?

If his plan is to simply rob the Browne's, why not take in his own weapon and do it right away? Why sit and talk for three and a half hours? If his plan was to kill the Brownes, why would he only have one shell in his shotgun, which, at the time he took the Browne's captive, was still in his car?

What if Russell's plan was not to rob or kill the Brownes, but merely to collect what was owed him – or some other party?

Was Russell's three-and-a-half-hour morning coffee with the Brownes actually a negotiation that did not progress to Russell's satisfaction? Was Russell's showing the Browne's the sawed-off shotgun in his car a veiled threat as to what might happen if the debt was not settled?

Or, did Russell believe there was money or jewelry in the house, perhaps from the robbery, and was trying to trick the Browne's into revealing its location? Perhaps after three and a half hours, Russell gives up and decides to take a more "direct" approach.

It presents some intriguing possibilities. What is certain is that Russell is convinced there is money in the house. And he spends three and a half hours conversing with the Brownes as though they are old friends. He drives Browne to "get a paper." Do you spend three and a half hours with a person and ride with him to "get a paper" if he is a complete stranger?

If you believe the official version of the story at the time, that this was a random robbery, none of these things add up. If you consider Wilburn Crain's story, they add up perfectly.

Russell will not admit to the murder of Norman Browne, at least not yet. But he will make some curious statements in the coming days that will add even more fuel to the "debt owed" story when examined seventy-five years later.

38

T he Dunedin Cemetery is a peaceful, Eden-like garden, located
atop a gently sloping hill just south of the small town.

Amidst the cheerful songs of bright red cardinals, bluejays,
and blackbirds perched within the moss-draped oak trees, a hatted,
slow-moving figure struggles across the summer green grass, draped in
a black dress.

The newly widowed Anne Brown is supported on one side by
her only child, Elizabeth "Betty" Browne. Betty rushed to Florida
from New York City upon hearing of her family's tragedy. Today, she
will witness her father's funeral.

The event is a private affair. The only others present are the
Reverand Richard E. Colter, pastor of the First Presbyterian Church
of Brooksville, and Attorney Andrew S. Horton. Norman Browne
appointed Horton as his guardian shortly before his death. Browne's
one brother and six sisters are not in attendance.

There has been no open casket, public viewing, or services at the
Moss Funeral Home. Norman Browne's carved and broken body has
been sealed inside his casket to spare the family any further trauma.

While Anne Browne has not yet been discharged from Mease
Dunedin Hospital, doctors have allowed her to attend her husband's
funeral.

While a thick oak canopy mercifully shielded the party from
the sun as they parked, they now stand absorbing the full force of the
morning heat in the open middle of the graveyard.

In addition to her dress, Anne Browne wears a black, wide-
brimmed sun hat tilted slightly over the right corner of her face, either

to block the sun or hide her injuries. The hat features a string of decorative beads that snake around the top. On her nose sit her round, dark-rimmed eyeglasses. Around her neck, a double-strung necklace of faux pearls.

The two Brownes and the attorney listen silently as Colter gives a short eulogy followed by a prayer. The four bow their heads as Norman Browne is committed to the earth.

His grave will be marked by a modest, block marker.

It remains there to this day.

* * *

Thelma Crum has also been permitted to leave her room today at Tarpon Springs Hospital. Crum has shown improvement in both her physical and psychological state in the last twenty-four hours.

Today, she will be traveling South to St. Petersburg.* There, for the first time since the attack, she will visit her husband. While Miles Crum still has a long road ahead of him, doctors are encouraged he has made it through the last four days, which included a sensitive surgery to repair his intestines.

After visiting the critically wounded Miles at Bay Pines Veterans Hospital, Thelma has a stop to make on the way home. She will be calling at the Pinellas County Jail and the office of Sheriff Todd Tucker to identify her attacker.

Unlike Anne Browne or Miles Crum, Thelma Crum has a sensitive constitution. She does not wish to face her attacker eye to eye as did her husband and Mrs. Browne. Sensitive to her wishes, Tucker has arranged for a special identification process.

The grocer's wife will sit in Tucker's private office overlooking the jail yard while a handcuffed Russell is paraded around the enclosed grounds.

When Russell is brought into the yard, Crum identifies him at once.

---

*   *It is unknown who is driving Thelma Crum. She is certainly not traveling alone. It is possible that a deputy escorts Mrs. Crum.*

Tucker and Constable Carey thank her. Thelma Crum quickly retreats from the unpleasant affair, returning to her now familiar room at the Tarpon Springs hospital. In a nearby room, her daughter remains in critical condition.

39

August 11, 1949
Pinellas County Courthouse
Clearwater, Florida

C hester B. McMullen is on a war path.

McMullen, under pressure from the media, publicly states his intentions in prosecuting Rastus Russell today. He leaves no uncertainty in his comments.

Russell has already told jailers he would rather go to the electric chair than back to Chattahoochee.

McMullen intends to grant him his wish.

But you cannot send an insane man to the death chamber. Thus, McMullen's first task in his prosecution is to establish that Russell is indeed sane.

"As far as I'm concerned, he's sane," McMullen proclaims to reporters. "I think he's got plenty of sense, although he undoubtedly is abnormal."

The State Attorney continues, "I think I have all the evidence needed to prove both that he is sane and that he is guilty of murder."

While McMullen presents a stiff chin to reporters privately, he must harbor some concern.

This is not the first time the state's attorney has encountered Rastus Russell. McMullen was on the job back in the early forties when Russell was a common entry in local arrest reports – including the assault in Palm Harbor that pulled an attempted murder charge. Back then, McMullen watched Russell's attorneys successfully argue insanity in at least two cases. Russell has had at least three stays in mental institutions, not even counting his childhood trip to the "home for the feeble-minded." He was declared insane by a committee in Pinellas County fourteen years earlier.

The former prosecutor has no doubt that Russell's defense attorney, whomever it may be, will again lean heavily on an insanity defense to spare his client an appointment with "Old Sparky." Any decent defender will be able to make a solid argument for it, one that could easily sway a jury.

But McMullen has some bullets of his own. Russell clearly showed premeditated intent and had clarity in his actions after the crimes in attempting to cover his deeds.

"Every act committed by Russel, both in the Crystal Beach cases and the kidnap-robbery of Lester Lambert, in my opinion, showed cunning planning and the rational impulse to escape from the law," McMullen declares.

Nonetheless, yesterday morning, the aspiring Congressman sent an urgent request to officials at Chattahoochee where, fourteen years ago, a board of doctors in Pinellas County sent him after adjudging him insane.

"I have asked the hospital people to advise whether or not Russell knew right from wrong at the time of his discharge," McMullen tells reporters.

The answer comes quickly.

Dr. J.H. Therrell, superintendent of Chattahoochee, tells McMullen that during Russell's stays in 1934 and 1939, doctors on the hospital staff evaluated him. Both times, he was judged sane.

"Both times Russell was here, the staff unanimously declared him without psychosis," Therrell tells the Tampa Tribune the next day.*

That's all McMullen needs to hear. If the experts at Chattahoochee have declared Russell sane twice, it is a fact on which he can lean heavily at trial.

McMullen must also be pleased to hear that Tucker and Carey have completed plans to bring Russell before Magistrate J.S. Register in Tarpon Springs next Monday for a preliminary hearing. With a grand jury indictment required for all cases carrying the death penalty in the

---

* *The Tampa Tribune, August 12, 1949.*

state of Florida, the preliminary hearing is largely a formality. But it will start the ball rolling.

The present grand jury is scheduled to leave office in December, with no further meetings scheduled. Unless they are called back into special session, the Browne murder will be investigated by the new grand jury, which will take office on December 5th.

McMullen can't wait that long.

Once the preliminary hearing is complete, McMullen will ask Judge Bird to recall the grand jury to hear the case against Russell.

But McMullen has been down this road before with Russell and Bird. Eight years earlier, in addition to an auto theft conviction, he had the convict charged with burglary and attempted murder. Had it stuck, Russell would either be doing time at Raiford or still locked safely behind the walls of Chattahoochee. Either way, Norman Y. Browne would likely still be alive.

But Russell was in neither of those places on August 7, 1949. That is because eight years earlier, Judge John U. Bird set him free.

* * *

While McMullen is under pressure to bring justice to Rastus Russell, Judge Bird is now feeling some heat of his own.

John U. Bird comes from a large family with a long heritage in the South. The Bird family has lived in Florida for several generations as has his mother's family, the Ulmer's, who originally came from Louisiana. Bird's grandfather was a Confederate soldier in the Civil War.

Bird grew up just outside the tiny town of Monticello, Florida. He moved to Clearwater in 1912 and served as both city attorney and prosecuting attorney before being elected as county judge in 1928.[*]

By 1949, Bird is an esteemed judge in Pinellas County. But the media is digging into Russell's past legal troubles in Pinellas County. And they are not liking what they are finding.

How is a guy like Russell, who has been in and out of prisons and mental institutions, who has been arrested numerous times, at

---

[*] *The History of Florida: Past & Present*, The Lewis Publishing Co., *Vol. III, page 189, 1923.*

least once for violent assault, running loose amongst the citizens of Pinellas County?

It's a question that will be debated for at least the next decade. There is plenty of blame to share in the entire system, including those at Chattahoochee.

But today, the focus has fallen on Judge Bird. In particular, reporters are curious to know why Russell was permitted to virtually walk out of the state after violently assaulting and attempting to rob Walter Newbern in Palm Harbor in 1941 and assaulting a law enforcement officer in the process – namely, Walter Carey's brother, Rufus.

In answering McMullen's charge of attempted murder, Rastus Russell plead not guilty by reason of insanity. To support his case, Russell's attorney, Joseph Nichols, brought forth records showing

1. That Russell was sent to the colony for feeble-minded children in 1925
2. That he was adjudged insane in December 1934 and committed to Chattahoochee (during that trial, in which he was charged with burglarizing E.H. Kirkland's filling station, Russell's mother, Claude Estelle Baker, testified before Judge Bird that "John Russell is insane,")
3. That Russell escaped Chattahoochee six months later and remained at liberty, having never been reestablished as sane.[*][+]

It worked.

On April 30, 1941, Judge Bird issued an order committing Russell back to Chattahoochee, "there to be held until ordered released by the court."

But then things get strange.

For some reason, Russell is not sent to Chattahoochee. Instead, he is held in the county jail.

Five weeks later, Russell is called to appear before Judge Bird again. Afterward, the following order was entered by Bird:

---

[*]   *Tampa Tribune, August 12, 1949.*

[+]   *No explanation is ever given as to why Russell was not pursued and returned to Chattahoochee.*

"It is considered and ordered that the defendant, John Russell, be released provided that he leave the state at this time; that he pay the cost of court amounting to $107.10 and report again to this court on December 1, 1941."

This is an odd order, considering the man Bird is setting free has just successfully argued that he is insane, is charged with attempted murder, and also battered a law enforcement officer while being arrested for the crime.

The minutes list both Sheriff Todd Tucker and State Attorney Chester McMullen as present for the order, with Bird presiding.

Russell, upholding his end of the deal, leaves the state. He spends some time in Ohio and then migrates to Chicago, where his uncle, Paul O. Baker, resides.[**] Baker is the younger brother of Russell's mother, Claude Estelle Baker McCoy, and works for the city of Chicago as a health inspector.

Even stranger, however, is what happens in December of 1941. On December 1, Russell does not report back to the court as ordered. Does Bird issue a warrant for his arrest?

There is no record of that.

Instead, he issues this order:

"It is considered and ordered that this cause be placed among the inactive cases of this court."[***]

For the charge of attempted murder, Russell could have faced a twenty-year prison sentence. Instead, he is essentially set free.

No reason or explanation is given.

On Saturday, August 13, 1949, Chester McMullen releases a "resume" of court records pertaining to John Calvin Russell.

The media takes particular interest in the 1941 ruling by Judge Bird.

---

[*] *Tampa Tribune, August 12, 1949.*

[**] *It is unknown if Russell makes contact with Baker while there and if so, the nature of their relationship.*

[***] *Tampa Tribune, August 12, 1949.*

When questioned about the matter, Bird says he "could not recall" the details but was certain that he had never ordered Russell to leave the state.[*]

He claims that he might have told Russell that he was *permitted* to leave the state. Later, he says that Russell asked permission to leave the state to visit his sick mother in Illinois. Bird claims he said he was permitted to leave the state and that the clerk had misunderstood him and incorrectly recorded in the minutes that he was *ordered* to leave the state.[**]

Russell, however, tells a different story. At his preliminary hearing for the Browne murder, he tells District Magistrate J.P. Register that Bird sent him to Ohio after holding him in the Pinellas County Jail.

"I received a one-way, no refund ticket to Akron, Ohio, and went there," Russell testifies. "I was afraid after that to come back to this state. I spent most of my time in Illinois."[***]

When asked why an insane man charged with attempted murder was released, ordered only to pay $107.10 in court costs, Bird is at a loss for an answer.

Again, he states he cannot recall. Bird simply declares there "must have been some reason" why the man could not have been convicted of the crime against him.[****]

McMullen, for his part, claims he cannot recall the details of the case either. Whether this is truly the situation or McMullen is simply trying to avoid getting on Bird's bad side, is unknown. What is clear is that Russell's history in Pinellas County will certainly put pressure on Bird to recall the grand jury. If McMullen is sensing momentum shifting his way, there is no need to rock the boat further.

The final barb in Bird's foot? Russell never even paid the $107.10. It is still listed on the Sheriff's ledger as uncollected.

---

[*] *The St. Petersburg Times, August 14, 1949.*

[**] *It is not known if Claude Estelle Baker McCoy was "sick" or why she was supposedly in Illinois in 1941. Claude Estelle Baker McCoy dies the following year in Tarpon Springs, FL.*

[***] *The Tampa Tribune, August 18, 1949.*

[****] *St. Petersburg Times, August 14, 1949.*

Two days later, Bird, having gone back and studying the file, makes a statement to the Clearwater Sun, attempting to clarify the record.

Bird claims that an error in the minutes of the court is responsible for the confusion.

According to the Judge, the court "permitted" Russell to leave the state, but the court reporter erroneously entered the word "ordered."

Bird tells the Sun that he now remembers the case, and although he initially ordered Russell to Chattahoochee, they did not have a place for Russell at the time. He says Russell then "remained around Clearwater" from his commitment date in April until July.[*]

The statement is vague, not specifying if Russell was held in the County Jail during that time.

Bird says that in July, Russell appeared before the court to ask permission to leave the state, telling the Judge he wanted to visit his sick mother in Illinois. Bird says he granted the request, permitting Russell to leave the state, provided he reports back to the court by December 1.

He cannot understand how the wrong word got entered into the minutes.

While Bird's explanation sounds feasible, it still doesn't explain why he would allow a prisoner accused of a violent crime and deemed mentally unstable to simply go free. And if Russell was only allegedly leaving the state to visit his "sick mother," why was he given almost half a year to do so? Why not a week?

It also doesn't explain why his case was simply discarded on December 1 when Russell did not appear before the court as ordered.

Lastly, it is a direct contradiction of Russell's version of events.

Regardless of whether Rastus Russell was "ordered" or "permitted" to leave the State of Florida in July of 1941, his simply being allowed to walk away from an attempted murder charge carrying a potential twenty-year prison sentence, sane or not, remains one of the most perplexing mysteries in the story of John Calvin Russell.

---

[*]   *Clearwater Sun, August 17, 1949.*

40

Friday, August 12, 1949
Pinellas County Jail

While McMullen assembles his case in the County Courthouse, Rastus Russell is planning his future.

He tells Sheriff Tucker he would indeed like a preliminary hearing, but not until he has a lawyer.* He is holding out hope that Pat Whitaker will represent him. He hopes to talk with Whitaker on Monday morning.

While Russell has already become somewhat of an infamous celebrity in the outside world, on the inside, he is treated like any other prisoner.

In fact, he shares a cell with three other murderers: Lawrence Minutoli, James Eldridge Porter, and Glen William Heck. Like Russell, the three are charged with first-degree murder. The foursome seems to coexist peacefully.

Russell has turned up his charm, impressing even the jail staff. Jailer Harvey Nash tells the St. Petersburg Times the killer has been a "model prisoner" since his arrival.

"Meek as a kitten," Nash adds for emphasis.**

The conciliatory Russell even apologizes to Nash for his outburst over photographer Al Hacket snapping his photo days earlier.

"I'm sorry," he tells the jailer, "I was rude."

Sheriff Todd Tucker, however, is not playing into Russell's nice guy routine. Tucker is aware of Russell's history as an escape artist and master lock pick. He orders jailers to keep the prisoner under careful watch.

---

*   *Tampa Tribune, August 13, 1949.*
** *The Evening Independent, August 15, 1949.*

Meanwhile, Tucker and Carey are moving quickly to get Russell scheduled for a preliminary hearing. They set the hearing for Monday, August 15th. Russell will appear before District Magistrate J.P. Register at the Tarpon Springs City Hall and Courthouse.*

The two expect that if Whitaker will not represent Russell, Judge Bird will appoint Russell an attorney.

* * *

Across the street from the jail, Judge John U. Bird sits in his chambers on the third floor of the Pinellas County Courthouse. Staring out his window overlooking the streets of Clearwater, he contemplates the possibility of recalling the grand jury.

The Pinellas County Courthouse is a palatial structure built in true Greco-Roman opulence. While it was erected thirty-one years earlier, in 1949 it remains a jewel of downtown Clearwater. Four massive stone pillars two stories tall mark the front doors of the yellow brick building. The entrance sits one level off the ground, led up to by an official-looking set of stone steps.

Inside, two gymnasium-sized courtrooms are housed under ceilings two stories high. They are lined on both sides by gigantic rows of windows, allowing natural light to brighten the entire venue. The rooms are so well-lit from the outside that the court could easily conduct its business without electricity if need be. However, without air conditioning in 1949, the court, like most public buildings at the time, becomes oppressively hot in the Florida summers. For this reason, the windows are made to open on all sides, although, like the jail, this often offers little relief.

Of the two, courtroom one is the grandest. In an ode to old-world craftsmanship, the room is replete with heavy dark wood furniture and décor. The walls are lined with hand-cut wainscotting on the bottom, wood pillars running up the walls to the hand-carved, decorative crown molding that borders the ceiling. The lush richness of the interior,

---

*   *The Evening Independent, August 12, 1949.*

coupled with the cheeriness of the natural light, gives the room a time-less, classic feel – straight out of "To Kill a Mockingbird."*

It is here that a twenty-six-year-old Rastus Russell appeared before Judge Bird on March 5, 1941, as well as other times throughout his youth.

Bird's chambers exist in a section of the courthouse behind the bench in courtroom 2. It is here the judge now weighs whether to recall his grand jury. While the situation certainly seems to warrant it, recall-ing a grand jury is not something to be taken lightly, even by a judge of Bird's stature.

Bird decides. He'll recall the grand jury, he says. But there is no rush to do so. The grand jury cannot be reconvened until the witnesses are healthy enough to testify. As they are still hospitalized, he will wait before recalling it.

As it turns out, Bird will be recalling his grand jury sooner than he thinks.

On the same day Bird comments on the issue, both Anne Browne and Thelma Crum are released from their respective hospitals. The two women have recovered faster than expected and while not com-pletely healed, are declared well enough to return home.

Brown moves into a private home across from the Dunedin hos-pital where her daughter is staying while in town. Thelma Crum will return to her apartment above the Crum Grocery Store in Crystal Beach.

On this day, Anne Browne gives another interview to the media. She tells the St. Petersburg Times that after recovering at her daughter's temporary apartment in Dunedin, she will move in with Thelma Crum in Crystal Beach and help care for Baby Judy while Thelma attempts to manage the store.

"I believe I owe them that much," Browne proclaims.

She also tells reporters that her home and all its contents will be sold. She talks of its peaceful location, its splendid view of The Gulf of

---

* *The Old Clearwater Courthouse is still in existence today, looking much the same as it did in 1949. Private tours are available if arranged ahead of time. While most legal business is now conducted at Pinellas County's modern facilities, the old courtrooms remain in service and still handle some cases.*

Mexico and Honeymoon Island, and tells what a great home or hunting camp it would make for someone.

But she tells them she never wants to see it again.

41

Monday Morning, August 15, 1949
Pinellas County Jail

T he bright morning sun is already beginning its daily baking of the outer brick walls of the Pinellas County Jail when Rastus Russell is ushered out of his cell.

Russell has been awaiting this moment for nearly a week. He hopes to speak directly to Attorney Pat Whitaker this morning.

If he can secure Whitaker, the most prominent criminal attorney in the state, he might be able to make all of this go away – at least in his mind. Whether Russell truly does have a personal connection with Whitaker or whether he only knows him by reputation, the accused murderer seems to have his heart set on securing the attorney's services.

Sheriff Tucker and Jailer Nash usher the restrained Russell back to the office from which he called last week.

Russell eagerly dials the number.

He gets Whitaker on the line as Tucker and Nash stand nearby. The Sheriff and jailer cannot hear Whitaker on the other end of the line.

But after several minutes of conversation, they see Russell's shoulders drop as he hangs up the phone.

"He turned me down," sighs Russell as he turns towards Tucker.[*]

This presents a dilemma for Tucker. He and Carey got Russell a preliminary hearing for today. But Russell agreed to it only if he had representation. He was apparently assuming Whitaker would take him as a client.

---

[*]   *Clearwater Sun, August 15, 1949.*

It is now John Calvin Russell's decision whether to proceed with the preliminary hearing. It soon becomes obvious it will not be today.

"I asked Russell about the hearing," Tucker told the Evening Independent. "He told me he had not decided what to do, and I told him to let me know as soon as he reached a decision."[*]

While it is expected that Judge Bird will name an attorney for Russell prior to any hearing, deputies announce the next day that "normal procedure" dictates that the judge will not appoint an attorney until the accused is indicted by a grand jury. This news is apparently passed down from Bird himself.

This means if Russell elects to appear for a preliminary hearing, he will do so without an attorney.

---

[*]   *The Evening Independent, August 15, 1949.*

42

S tate Attorney Chester M. McMullen must be grinning inside his second-floor office at the Pinellas County Courthouse. Before McMullen can send Rastus Russell to the electric chair, he expects he will need to prove he is sane.

Two top psychiatrists have just declared Rastus Russell perfectly sane.

On Saturday, Dr. W.C. McConnell of St. Petersburg administered a sanity test to the prisoner. This morning, shortly before ten o'clock, Dr. W.R. Tench of Clearwater also examined Russell and administered his own sanity tests.

Both doctors not only declare Russell sane, they are amazed by his demeanor.

Sheriff Tucker reports the results to the media.

"The psychiatrist found Russell to be in full possession of his mental faculties," Tucker remarks. "In fact, Dr. Tench reported to me that the prisoner was remarkably cool and collected."[*]

The calm Russell is able to vividly describe his experiences at Chattahoochee for his examiners, even giving the names of the doctors who had treated him.

"Dr. Tench told me Russell seemed perfectly sane," Tucker adds.

Rastus Russell has seemingly morphed back into his charismatic, pseudo-intelligent "Dr. Jekyll" personality, using his good looks and engaging manner of speaking to charm his fellow prisoners, jailers, and

---

[*]   *The Evening Independent, August 17, 1949.*

even the psychiatrist examining him. Since being in captivity, he has been able to restrain the violent, impatient, and dim-witted "Hyde" from emerging.

* * *

The day is growing long when Rastus Russell summons a jailer to his cell door. He'd like to talk to the Sheriff.

Several minutes later, the towering Tucker comes striding down the cellblock, an air of authority in each step.

The accused murderer tells the Sheriff he has come to a decision.

He'd like to proceed with the preliminary hearing.

Tucker gets on the phone with the Tarpon Springs Courthouse.

John Calvin Russell will get his hearing. It will be tomorrow.

43

Wednesday Morning, August 17, 1949
Pinellas County Jail

I t's another hot, sticky morning when St. Petersburg Times reporter Ralph Reed enters the Pinellas County Jail. Today, he will conduct the first and only (known) media interview with accused killer John Calvin "Rastus" Russell.

It is not known where Reed interviews Russell inside the jail or who else is present. But Russell provides some enlightening and fascinating answers to questions, some of which provide clarity and some that create mystery.

Russell spends much of the interview wallowing in self-pity.

"I've had a lot of bad breaks in my life," Russell tells Reed, *"And have spent much of my life in institutions."*

He continues, *"I would prefer to die in the electric chair and go to sleep and be out of it all. If I am such a rascal as they say I am, I should go to sleep in the electric chair. It would be more benefit to put me to sleep than to let me suffer."*

When asked about his family, Russell expresses regret. *"What hurts me most,"* he laments, *"is the disgrace I have brought to my aunt in Tampa. She has not been over to see me. No one comes to see me."*

The topic turns to the convict's mother, and Russell becomes emotional. *"I was afraid to come back to Florida and did not even get back to see her before she died."*

Upon uttering the statement, his eyes fill with tears, and he nearly breaks down in front of the reporter.

---

*   *St. Petersburg Times, August 18, 1949.*

"The reason I came back to Florida this year was to visit her grave at Lake Thonotosassa," he adds.

While it is easy to dismiss Russell's lamenting as a sociopathic ploy, Rastus is known to have been close to his mother. His feelings are likely sincere.

If so, it reinforces the theory of the Jekyll/Hyde split personality. The legend of Rastus Russell is one of a psychopathic monster on the loose, looking to kill all in his path, simply for the pleasure of killing.

But Russell is not that. He is not of the same make up as a serial killer such as Ted Bundy or Wayne Gacy. Every crime Russell is known to have committed involves some sort of theft or robbery. In the entire legend of Rastus Russell, he is only known to have killed one person, Norman Y. Browne. Heinous as that crime was, it was not a thrill kill. He killed Browne either out of rage, frustration, or to eliminate a witness. But there is nothing to suggest he killed out of pleasure.

Obviously, Russell has no problem stealing or using violence to get what he wants. But what he wants in most all cases seems to be money or something he can use, such as a car or food.

Despite his acts of violence, the well-documented cases all seem to show some tiny form of doubt or mercy, breaking through the monstrous act being committed. In the case of Lester Lambert, the convict drives Lambert around, wondering aloud what to do next. A pure killer would have killed Lambert.

When tying up the Browns in the garage, Russell leaves to fetch Mrs. Browne a medical kit to assist Mr. Browne. He takes pity.

Despite brutally beating and cutting Mrs. Browne, he spares her life.

This of course, does not excuse Russell's horrific actions. He is a terribly troubled and violent man. But his actions hint at an outwardly pleasant, attractive, charismatic personality, capable of "flipping" quickly into a cold, calculating, violent person out of need or opportunity.

His acts of doubt or mercy could be the conscientious Jekyll trying to break through the shell of the Hyde monster temporarily controlling his body.

As mentioned earlier, it is this author's opinion that Russell did not target the Browne's randomly. His next answers seem to hint heavily in this direction.

When Reed asks Russell if he was at the Browne house on the day of the murder, the convicted car thief pauses thoughtfully and then gives an intriguing answer.

"I can say that I was not there on the day of the murder. But I knew both Mr. and Mrs. Browne."

This is not a shocking statement in and of itself. Anne Browne initially tells investigators that the couple knew Russell because he had come to their home months earlier to fix a pump, or to ask about the house for sale. This, of course, before the story changed that he had come to the house to ask for water for his car.

Russell confirms that he visited the Browne's months ago, but that he had not fixed any well pump.

When asked to elaborate, Russell states that there are "lots of things he could say" but would not talk until advised by an attorney.

While this could be just a wise decision on the convict's part to not incriminate himself, his choice of words is strange; "lots of things I could say."

True, they are coming from the mouth of an accused murderer and convicted felon. But the words suggest there is a deeper story that Russell wants to tell.

When asked about Dorothy Jean Crain, Russell is adamant the girl is his wife. "We were married in Baxley, Georgia, June sixth, this year," he states precisely.

When McMullen asks deputies to check with authorities in Baxley for marriage records, they find no record of Russell and Crain being married there.

Russell matter-of-factly answers questions on a variety of topics.

On his trade: "I'm sort of a mechanic, but nothing to write home about."

On his sanity: "I do not believe I am insane, and I am not a drinker. I have not experienced temporary insanity."

Russell has likely read the newspapers and is aware of the theories the Crystal Beach killer was drunk at the time of the murder, although Walter Carey has since stated publicly that the killer was *not* drunk at the time of the killing. Russell is also aware of his prior pleadings of insanity. These comments, combined with Russell's calm, collected, demeanor on his sanity tests are strong indicators that Russell does not intend to plead insanity this time, even though that may very well be his best defense.

Whether he is serious about preferring the electric chair over Chattahoochee, he is doing and saying things that, whether he knows it or not, are leading him in that exact direction.

Chester McMullen must be pleased with the interview.

Judge John U. Bird, however, could likely have done without it. Bird is still taking heat for his 1941 release of Russell, and the questions surrounding it. His multi-day attempts at explanation have only muddied the waters further.

Now Russell throws fresh fuel on the fire.

With Bird's 1941 actions still in the news cycle, Reed asks Russell his take on it.

"I was never convicted of that crime," Russell tells Reed. "I was waiting in County jail when Judge Bird called me in and ordered me out of state. I received a one-way, no refund ticket to Akron, and went there. I was afraid after that to come back to the state."

This directly contradicts Bird's version of events, that Russell "stayed around Clearwater" because Chattahoochee didn't have room for him and then approached Bird to request permission to leave to visit his mother.

One would think that in 1949, Bird's statement easily could have been fact-checked. A simple check of jail records could tell if Russell was in the County jail from May to July of 1941. But perhaps not. Those records are long since gone today.

It is hard to fathom what Russell would have to gain by making up this story. And yet Bird has all the motive in the world to present an "alternative" version of what may have happened and what he did or didn't "remember."

It makes sense. If Russell's version of events is true, why else would a judge provide a man once deemed insane and charged with a violent crime a free ticket (at taxpayer expense?) to anywhere he wanted to go? And if Bird's version of events is true, why did Russell go to Akron, Ohio? Bird claims he released the prisoner to visit his sick mother in Illinois. Why not send him directly to Illinois?

With both McMullen and Tucker at the hearing, it could have been a cooperative effort.

There is one other, somewhat unlikely, but still possible scenario. When I interviewed several old-time residents of Crystal Beach, a few reported to me the same rumor: That Rastus Russell was the illegitimate child of a "high-ranking judge."

Before the time of young Russell's birth, his mother worked as a teacher at Sutherland College in Palm Harbor. Tarpon Springs is only about four miles up Old US 19 from Palm Harbor. Tarpon Springs contains one of the largest Greek Communities in Florida.

When I asked Wilburn Crain, the only person interviewed for this book who ever met Rastus Russell, what ethnicity he would guess Russell resembled, he told me "Italian or Greek."

When one looks back at Russell's extensive record and then compares his history of escape (and not being pursued) or release, it is more than enough to raise an eyebrow.

Could it be Russell's father was a higher-up in the Court somewhere in Pinellas or Hillsborough County, making a phone call here or there to make things easier on his wayward, illegitimate son as a favor to his mother?

Of course it is.

Could he be of Greek descent and have been from and maybe even served in Tarpon Springs?

Of course he could have.

Russell's grandfather, Thomas Baker, was a prominent dentist, citizen, landowner, and Mason in Thonotosassa, as is his son, an attorney and Russell's uncle. The Masons were the premier civic organization in Palm Harbor in 1949, the Masonic Lodge sitting near the center of town. We know that at least Sheriff Tucker, Dewey Adair and T.R. Barlow were loyal members. This is not to imply that the Masons organization is in any way culpable for the actions of Rastus Russell. But members of any organization talk and at times, do favors for each other.

Membership status of McMullen, Judge Bird, or others involved in Russell's past run-ins, could not be confirmed. But, membership in civic organizations in 1949 is popular and common.

The Klu Klux Klan is also active in Palm Harbor and all of Central Florida in 1949. Many living in Pinellas County at the time had not so distant relatives who fought for the Confederacy. At the time, the organization did not carry the public stigma it has today. It was tolerated as a heritage/political organization, albeit with racial overtones. Its members marched in public parades, and the group donated to civic causes. It is quite possible that some of the characters mentioned in this book were members, although there is no way of knowing for sure.

What is known as the "Old Boys Network" was very much alive and well in late 1940s Pinellas County. When the right people know the right people, mountains can be moved.

Last but not least is Russell's claim that he was "connected" to a drug gang out of Chicago. While on the surface, it may seem to be a fantasy-based boast concocted to frighten his victims into submission, it cannot be dismissed outright. It is known that between 1942 and 1949, Russell spent most of his time in the Midwest, much of it in Chicago, some of it in prison. As mentioned earlier, Russell's uncle, John O. Baker, worked for the city of Chicago.

Russell was arrested in Arkansas in 1942 for transporting stolen cars across state lines from Illinois. It is unlikely he was working solely for himself – trafficking in stolen cars usually involves a seller and a buyer. When Russell escapes prison and runs back to Pinellas County, he is captured by the FBI and returned to Illinois, where he faces "1-20 years" in prison. And despite his escape and running to Florida, he is back on the street in a couple of years. It is unlikely a local judge from Central Florida could have helped in this case. But "connections" in Chicago or Illinois certainly could have.

Did organized crime or contacts inside city government wield some influence in the Chicago and Illinois court system in 1949? Almost certainly. Whether any such contacts aided in Russell's many seemingly light sentences, early releases and unpursued escapes seems like a remote possibility, but a possibility nonetheless.

There is no evidence available to prove or disprove any such theories.

While we like to nostalgically recall the 1940s and 1950s as a time of truth, justice, and innocence, human nature is human nature. The truth is that, just like today, much business, civic matters, legal business, and political favors were done with a wink, a handshake, a bottle of scotch, an envelope full of cash, or a corresponding favor.

What we do know is that Rastus Russell's interview on August 17th only hints at a second layer of truth that seems to exist under the story being presented in the press.

It is a loss for history that we never got to hear Russell's full version of events. Like Lee Harvey Oswald (to whom Russell bears a slight resemblance,) we wonder what shocking secrets he may or may not have revealed: The murder itself, his history with the Brownes, his relationship with the Crains, his deal with Judge Bird and his family's connections (if any.)

After reviewing all the possibilities above, the evidence available and everything about the Judge Bird ruling from 1941, I am convinced that Russell's version of events is probably true.

Despite Bird's strange explanation, the record shows Bird ordered Russell out of the state. And Bird simply moved the case to "inactive" when Russell didn't show up that December.

This does not mean Judge John U. Bird was corrupt or guilty of some sort of conspiracy. Bird was a highly respected Judge in his time and afterward. In fact, it might simply be Bird was trying to protect his community.

With Russell declared insane, Bird sentenced him to Chattahoochee. He must be well aware that Russell has been "kicked back" from Chattahoochee twice, having been declared sane by doctors there. Bird may simply not want to have a known violent man sent to the institution only to be cut loose again in a year or two, having been declared "cured."

He may simply want Russell out of his system and out of his state. So he calls Russell in, tells him to get gone, buys him a one-way ticket to anywhere he wants to go (Russell says Akron,) and tells him if he comes back, he's going to Chattahoochee (a place Russell fears intensely.) Perhaps that part is selectively left out of the record.

For Tucker and McMullen's part, they would be ridded of a headache as well – if this is indeed how things transpired.

Whatever the case, nobody in Florida heard much from Rastus Russell for seven years.

But now the chickens have come home to roost.

44

Rastus Russell has had a rough night.

The night of August 16th is one of the hottest nights of the summer, the outside temperature only dipping to a low of 77 degrees Fahrenheit. As morning arrives, the dew point soars over 75 degrees, pushing humidity to "miserable" levels, the highest ranking on the scale.

The prisoner's cell was stuffy, to say the least, even with the nighttime air wafting through the open windows. Russell was disappointed to be rejected by Attorney Pat Whitaker. Now, with the prospect of being assigned a court-appointed lawyer, he knows he is likely headed to either death row or Chattahoochee.

Even for a killer, heat and anticipation are not conducive to sleep.

As Sheriff Todd Tucker and Constable Walter Carey escort Rastus Russell through the blazing morning to Tucker's waiting car, Russell's hands are again cuffed securely in front and strapped to his waist.

The prisoner is dressed neatly - a white cotton shirt tucked into a clean pair of prison-issue khakis. A brand-new pair of walnut brown shoes encase his feet. There is no record of how Russell acquired them.

His dress notwithstanding, Rastus's face betrays his weariness. Several days' worth of dark stubble gives it a rough appearance. The mustache he hastily shaved off at Sam Crain's house has reappeared, now displaying itself prominently on his upper lip.

His thick black hair parted loosely off center, reveals visible streaks of gray, enhanced by the bright sun.

The prisoner is somber as he shuffles to the car between Tucker and Carey. Tucker opens the rear door of the sedan, and Russell slides into the back seat. Tucker pulls himself in beside his prisoner. A deputy plants on Russell's other side, as another slips behind the wheel. Walter Carey takes shotgun.

Together, the five ride out of the Pinellas County Jail loading area and head towards Tarpon Springs.

Rastus Russell will get his hearing today.

* * *

Tucker may have left the jail but he has left some important instructions behind. While the Sheriff is gone, another notable prisoner will walk out of the jail a free man.

Furrell Richard Crain has been released on Tucker's orders. Nine days after taking the twenty-one-year-old Crain into custody along with his brother Allen Garfield Crain and sister Dorothy Jean Crain, Tucker can find no further reason to hold him.

Furrell's brother, eighteen-year-old Allen, was released almost immediately after the three surrendered to police at the time Rastus Russell was captured.

Tucker believes he has gained all of the information he can from the young Crain. Tucker makes no statement as to why he releases a man he seemed intent on charging only days earlier.

While Sam and Flora Crain must be pleased with their son's release, they continue to pressure Tucker to release Dorothy. The couple tells the Sheriff she is needed at home. Doing without the girl has been a hardship for the family. Besides, they argue, she has done nothing to deserve jail.

Tucker is sympathetic to the couple's pleas. He tells the Clearwater Sun he plans to confer with Judge Bird "today if possible," and if the Judge agrees, he will release Dorothy Jean immediately. [*]

Apparently, Bird does not agree. For Dorothy is not released.

---

[*] *Clearwater Sun, August 17, 1949.*

Tucker explains later that the Crain family is considered a flight risk. Should he release Dorothy, the Crains might pick up and move, robbing the prosecution of some of its key witnesses.

Tucker's concerns could hold some water. Testifying in open court against Rastus Russell might be intimidating or unpleasant, especially for the teenage girl who may very well still have feelings for the suave Russell. Members of the family have told police they are "terrified" of Russell. And Tucker claims the Crain's have "no roots" in Dunedin and could pick up and move quickly.

It is true that as workers in an orange processing plant, the Crain men could likely move to another part of the state and obtain employment almost immediately. It is also true that their house is company provided. They could move tomorrow with no obligation to a mortgage or lease. Nonetheless, quitting jobs and moving a family of 9 across the state, with a pregnant wife, is no small undertaking.

But with a case this big, Tucker (and/or perhaps McMullen or Judge Bird) doesn't want to take any chances.

Thus, while it is possible Tucker may still suspect Dorothy of some involvement in Russell's crimes, it seems reasonable that he would hold the girl as a material witness, at least perhaps, until a grand jury can be recalled.[*]

As Todd Tucker's unmarked personal sedan cruises North on Old US 19, Rastus Russell stares blankly ahead. The vehicle will pass several of the key sites in Russell's antics earlier in the month.

Twenty minutes after leaving the jail, the car passes the intersection of Curlew Creek Road. Tucker asks Russell where Sam Crain's house is located. Russell, not in the mood for conversation, waves his hand dismissively in the general direction of his former residence.[**]

---

[*]   *While holding a material witness in jail is not as common today as it was in the 1940s, it remains a legal and employed technique in many states and jurisdictions across the country.*

[**] *St. Petersburg Times, August 19, 1949. Tucker must simply be making conversation. He must certainly know where Sam Crain's house is located. It is less than a half mile from the intersection the car crosses.*

One minute later, the car passes the Minnow Creek Marine Ways on the left-hand side, near where the prisoner was captured nine days earlier. Russell simply looks the other way.

Seven minutes later, the five men see the pillars on their left that mark the entrance to Crystal Beach. These are the pillars Russell drove between on his way to Norman Browne's house on August 7th. Russell makes no comment.

Twelve minutes later, the entourage arrives at the Tarpon Springs City Hall. The two-story, Red Brick, Greek Revival-style building is somewhat of an all-purpose facility for the Tarpon Springs Community. The first floor of the main building serves as city hall and houses several government and legal offices. On the North side of the building is the Fire Department. On the South side of the building is the Tarpon Springs Police Department, where Constable Walter Carey is known to frequent. Upstairs is the courtroom and the chambers of Justice of the Peace, J.S. Register.

As the officers usher Russell into the chambers of the "JP," the accused murderer stares at the floor, his shoulders hunched forward.

Russell is given a seat close to Justice of the Peace Register, who sits at the head of the table. Taking a seat next to Russell is Clearwater Sun Reporter Bob Prichard, the same reporter who joined his own story by carrying a Thompson sub-machine gun to George's Marina the day Russell was captured.

Before the proceedings begin, Prichard nods at his photographer, Bernalyn Keith of Tarpon Springs. Keith obediently snaps a photo of Russell, the flash from the bulb exploding through the room like a lightning bolt.[*]

Russell, who since his capture has shown a marked distain for being photographed, reacts. Nostrils flaring, the convict rears up and shouts, "Get that lady out of here!"[**]

The two deputies restrain Russell and press him back into his seat.

As the commotion is settling, Russell turns his head to Prichard and speaks quietly.

---

[*] *Unfortunately, there does not appear to be any copy of this photograph available in public records.*

[**] *Clearwater Sun, August 18, 1949.*

"Who are you and what paper do you work for?"

Prichard tells him.

"You and the other reporters have been telling lies about me. I'll get you bastards if it is the last thing I do."*

The room quiets again and Justice Register explains to the accused his constitutional rights.

Register asks Russell if he has secured an attorney yet.

"I have not got an attorney yet," Russell informs the Justice. He elaborates that he has made several attempts to get one.

Russell then listens intently as Register methodically recites Russell's criminal history. The last record is in 1942 when Register reads Judge Bird's 1942 order to move Russell's case to "inactive" status.

"Where have you been since then?" Register asks.

Russell tells him he's served time in Illinois State Prison for car theft. It is not known if Russell elaborates any more than that.

By all accounts, Russell conducts himself well during the proceedings, notwithstanding his outburst at the photographer. He is courteous and polite, speaks excellent English, and participates fully and cooperatively.

When Register reads the charge against him as "murder with premeditated design," Russell calmly interrupts.

"What do you mean by that, Judge Register?" he asks.

Register explains that according to the charge, the accused had planned the murder.

"Oh," Russell responds, leaning back in his chair, looking towards the floor.

When the Justice reaches the end of the proceeding, he asks John Calvin Russell how he pleads to this charge.

Russell replies in a firm voice, "Not Guilty."

---

* *Prichard relays this exchange in a piece he wrote several years later for For Men Only magazine, July 1955. While Prichard dramatizes the piece and plays loosely with some of the facts, there is reason to believe that an exchange such as this did take place. Russell is well known (and will become even more well known) for threatening those who pose a threat to him.*

Russell will be sent back to the Pinellas County Jail where he will await the grand jury being called back to session. There will be no bail. He will now be bound over to circuit court.

45

O n the same day that Rastus Russell pleads "not guilty" to premeditated murder, Sheriff Todd Tucker decides to suspend questioning of the stubborn suspect. While detectives on both sides of Tampa Bay are pleased to be able to close a number of car theft and robbery cases to which Russell has confessed, lawmen and the public will not be satisfied unless the killer of Norman Browne can be brought to justice on a murder charge.

After consulting with State Attorney McMullen, Tucker is confident there is enough to convict Russell of murder without a confession.

"I see no point in talking with Russell any further," he tells the St. Petersburg Times. "We have a complete case against him, not only in the Browne murder but also the attacks on the Crum family and the kidnap-robbery of Lester Lambert, chief clerk in the county tax collector's office."[*]

While Tucker, McMullen, and Carey await Judge Bird's decision on recalling the grand jury, Miles Crum continues to fight his own battle in St. Petersburg. Surgeons at Bay Pines Veterans Hospital announce Crum has shown "remarkable progress" in his recovery. In fact, they now give the grocer a "better than outside" chance of pulling through, a miraculous prognosis given Crum's ghastly wound.

The mild-mannered and cheery Crum must be heartened not only by his own progress but by the fact that his wife and baby, whom he once thought dead, have also survived the terrible ordeal.

---

[*]   *St. Petersburg Times, August 18, 1949.*

Crum also has another reason to be grateful today. The goodwill he has spread to his neighbors in Crystal Beach has come back to him. Crum learns that in his absence, residents of Crystal Beach have rallied to his aid, taking shifts to keep his grocery store open while he and Thelma recover from their wounds.*

In addition, The Clearwater Sun and St. Petersburg Evening Independent have just announced the "Miles Crum Relief Fund," a 1949 version of today's "Go Fund Me" page. Area residents can donate to the fund. The money collected will be distributed to Mrs. Crum to help with hospital bills, purchase new stock for the store, hire a clerk and make payments on "new equipment" Miles installed this year for the store.**

The Crum's come from hearty, old school stock, the kind who take pride in self-sufficiency. Accepting charity is all but anathema to the couple. But the two realize that without help, losing the store is a distinct possibility.

While Miles has shown progress this week, he remains in serious condition and is not yet out of the woods. If he does survive, he will likely be hospitalized for weeks or even months, with no guarantee he'll be able to work again. While it was originally feared that Thelma suffered a skull fracture, this was thankfully not the case. Nonetheless, Mrs. Crum will be unable to run the store until she fully recovers.

Doctors at Tarpon Springs Hospital remain baffled about baby Judy Crum's injuries. One day, she is better; the next, she is worse. They now suspect the baby has suffered a concussion. There is no timeline as to when she will be released. This alone will be enough to monopolize Thelma's time, regardless of her injuries.

---

* *By this time, Thelma Crum is back at home but is still recovering from a head wound and unable to work.*

** *The Evening Independent, August 18, 1949. Crum purchased the store with a GI loan, courtesy of his service in the Army. However, he made some enhancements since its purchase, including the installation of gasoline pumps. While many old residents of Crystal Beach remember the gas pumps as a fixture of Crum's store, a 1949 photo of the store shows no gas pumps installed yet. It is possible that this "new equipment" referenced is the gas pumps, installed after the photo was taken. A 1950's photo of the store clearly shows the gas pumps.*

The Crums concede and graciously accept the assistance of the community. Bay Pines doctors say the financial lift may be just the tonic their patient needs. The next day, Crum takes his first bites of food not consumed through a tube.

The fund has a stated goal of raising $500. It will go on to raise nearly three times that much, a hefty sum in 1949.*

* * *

The next morning, Thursday, August 18, State Attorney Chester McMullen opens his office door to allow local reporters inside. Sitting behind his desk, McMullen announces that after meeting with him earlier, Judge Bird will sign an order calling the grand jury back into special session on August 31.

The jury will be tasked with investigating the murder of Norman Young Brown, in addition to other cases brought before the body.

Bird has stated that all witnesses to the Browne death do not have to testify. With Mrs. Browne and Mrs. Crum both well enough to testify, Bird indicates Miles Crum need not appear.

Should the grand jury believe there is enough evidence to proceed to trial, they will issue an indictment against John Calvin Russell.

Russell, for his part, can already see the writing on the wall. Having lost his bid to secure Pat Whitaker, the prisoner has agonized over finding legal representation. On this day, he seems to have reached a conclusion.

He asks Sheriff Todd Tucker for permission to forgo representation and plead his own case in his upcoming trial.

There is no record of Tucker's response. However, given that Russell will not require an attorney until after he is indicted and the fact that Russell's strange request will likely be decided by Judge Bird, not Tucker, the Sheriff likely advises Russell to wait until after the grand jury decides his case. Tucker must realize that under no circumstances would this be in his prisoner's best interest.

---

*   *Later, a motion is made that the funds should be shared with Mrs. Browne. Thelma Crum eagerly agrees.*

Then again, that is likely not Todd Tucker's main concern at this point.

* * *

On August 22nd, doctors at Tarpon Springs Hospital release eight-month-old Judy Crum to the waiting arms of her mother. Concluding the baby has suffered a concussion, they believe bedrest and her mother's care will eventually cure the child's ills.

They are wrong.

* * *

It is difficult to describe the steam cooker climate of the Florida summer to someone who has never experienced it.

Florida residents often chuckle when northern cities shift into crisis mode and issue "heat warnings" to all residents whenever the daily thermometer eeks over the 90-degree mark. What cities like New York and Boston call an emergency, Tampa, Orlando, and Miami call a mild summer day.

When a Floridian tells a Northerner it is "hot," Northerns often respond that "it gets hot here too in the summer," to which the Floridian will smirk and say, "No…you don't understand."

Daytime temperatures regularly hover between 92 and 95 degrees. Near constant humidity regularly pushes the heat index well over 100 degrees. Dry heat is one thing. Wet heat is quite another. Stepping into the afternoon sun from an air-conditioned building can literally take your breath away.

The pavement, roads, and sidewalks become so superheated that veterinarians' offices fill with dog owners naïve enough to walk their pets on surfaces hot enough to fry bacon. Every year, a number of pets and even children perish simply because a distracted or ignorant adult left their loved one in a car with the windows up. In the Florida sun, vehicles heat to broiling temperatures as fast as an electric oven.

Most modern Floridians shelter indoors during summer months, comfortably cooled by air conditioning. Only those who must go outside, for work or otherwise, tend to do so. There are many days that the stiflingly still air and deep humidity make even going to the beach or pool a miserable experience. Daily thunderstorms are common.

Even to those with outdoor jobs, going without air conditioning at home is considered cruel and unusual in Florida. Here, summer heat is not a crisis. Hellish summer heat is the norm. The air conditioner conking out is a crisis.

The residents of 1949 did not enjoy the luxury of air conditioning. They used creative building construction, open windows, and ceiling fans to deal with the summer temperatures. But for the most part, they simply toughed it out. Over time, they may have become partially accustomed to it. But few would describe summers as anything close to comfortable.

Summer sun reacting with the deep waters of the Gulf of Mexico and the Atlantic Ocean, however, was the same in 1949 as it is today.

As the fiery sun beats down, the water temperature heats up. This creates evaporation, sending more water vapor skyward. This feeds the growth of clouds. When a weather system moves through, such as a low-pressure system off the coast of Africa, it can pick up strength from the increasing moisture in the air. If it gets strong enough, it can form into a tropical system and, potentially, a hurricane.

On August 22nd, 1949, this is exactly what is happening in the Atlantic Ocean about 525 miles due East of Miami. In the Bahamas, a hurricane alert is issued for the approaching storm with estimated winds of 90 to 100+ miles per hour winds. While there are no hurricane categories in 1949, this would rank as a category two hurricane, a "Cat 2," on today's scale.

Unlike today, tropical storms were not given individual names in 1949. However, as the storm approached, President Harry S. Truman visited Miami, and the media jokingly dubbed the cyclone "Harry's Hurricane."

Storm tracking is not as precise either. But two things seem relatively certain. One, with over 500 miles of warm ocean waters between the storm and the coast, the system will almost certainly strengthen before landfall.

Secondly, there is a very good chance that the storm will strike Florida at some point.

For Floridians, this is no laughing matter.

While the city of Clearwater is on the west coast of Florida, residents keep a wary eye on the weather. There is a chance the storm could "loop around" the bottom of Florida and travel up the coast, making landfall on the west coast of the state. While this sounds unlikely, it happens often. Even if this is not the case, the storm passing over or even nearby Pinellas County, even after moving over land from an east coast landfall, can cause serious problems for towns and residents.

But events such as hurricanes distract the attention of public officials, police officers, and even prison workers. For a select few, this can create opportunities.

Rastus Russell knows this all too well.

46

T he official name for "Harry's Hurricane" given by the Weather Bureau is "Hurricane No. 2."

The storm has mostly spared the Bahamas, giving it only a glancing blow as it passed north of Nassau. With the highest winds reaching 75 miles per hour on the island, there is storm damage and power outages. But the effects are not severe.

Florida, however, could be a different story. The storm is expected to make landfall near Fort Lauderdale in less than twenty-four hours. When it does, its winds will have reached 120 miles per hour, making it a Category 3, "major" hurricane on today's ranking scale.

While the exact track of the storm is unknown, storm damage is expected to extend more than 100 miles from the center. The eye of the storm is expected to pass through the state of Florida, exiting just northwest of Clearwater before heading out to the Gulf of Mexico.

While storm preparations are underway in Pinellas County, the mood is not as alarmed as on the East Coast. Residents here know that storms weaken quickly over land. By the time the storm reaches the west coast, its winds will have subsided substantially. And with a western moving storm, there will likely be little to no storm surge here.

Nonetheless, drenching rains and winds at 40-50 miles per hour can still cause plenty of headaches in 1949 Florida.

There is little fanfare at the Pinellas County Jail. The building is a strong, brick structure capable of withstanding much more than a little high wind. Here, it is mostly business as usual.

In fact, the day prior, Sheriff Todd Tucker has taken some time to have a lighthearted chat with the media in regard to his most famous, or infamous prisoner, John Calvin "Rastus" Russell.

He is the "model prisoner," Tucker reiterates.

Tucker has only one complaint, he notes facetiously. His prisoner eats more than any two law violators confined to the prison.

"Jailers report Russell has an enormous appetite," Tucker muses, "Other than that, the prisoner has a good conduct report – since he has been behind bars."*

Russell's cell, which he shares with the jail's three other alleged murderers, is known as "murderers row" to staff and inmates. Russell, however, is said to be getting along well with other prisoners.

Head jailer Harvey Nash also marvels at Russell's enormous appetite.

"He eats enough for two ordinary men," Nash tells a reporter, "In fact, I wouldn't be surprised to see him gain fifteen or twenty pounds before his trial. It's a pity we can't work him."

Other jailers repeat the sentiment. They say they have never guarded a prisoner with Russell's capacity to put away food.

This could go back to the prisoner's early days as an obese teenager. It could be the stress or anxiety of being imprisoned is causing him to revert to childhood comfort techniques. After all, a grand jury is likely to indict him for murder in six days. A number of things can happen after that. None of them are likely to be pleasant for the lifelong criminal.

That might not be the only thing troubling the violent Russell, however.

"There hasn't been a single visitor calling to see him," Tucker reports. "He hasn't even had a phone call. An ordinary man might worry about that. But not Russell. The fact that nobody seems to care what happens to him concerns him not at all."

Tucker's take on this topic seem to contradict Russell's earlier comments where he expressed disappointment that no one from his family came to visit him.

Tucker continues to pontificate. He tells reporters that even Russell's aunt, so proud of the young John only weeks earlier for finally

---

* *The Evening Independent, August 25, 1949.*

"settling down" with a new wife, has not called or written a single correspondence since Russell's incarceration.

"He has an uncle, I am told, practicing law in Chicago," the
Sheriff continues, "But the uncle has made no effort to get in touch
with Russell, nor has the prisoner written any letters."*

Near the end of the interview, Jailer Nash strikes a serious note.
Just because Russell is a "model prisoner," the staff is careful not to let
their guard down.

"We've seen those fellows attempt jailbreaks," said the veteran
Nash. "For this reason, Russell is watched around the clock."

Jailers are well aware of Russell's history as an escape artist.

The *Evening Independent* tries to put readers' minds at ease:

*Breaking out of "murderers row" in the county bastille would be a
tough job – even for a man of Russell's tremendous physical strength. The
cellblock has specially treated steel bars. Even if a prisoner could saw through
the bars, he would be compelled to overpower the jailer at the front door.***

The news outlet, Tucker or Nash, has no idea how ironic the article
will seem in just a short time.

* * *

Inside the jail, Rastus Russell has made a new friend.

Just yesterday, jailers brought in three teenagers charged with
breaking and entering the St. Petersburg Jaycees Club. They are Ray
McClaury, 15, Robert Peterson, 17, and Richard Schall, 16. Because
of overcrowding at the jail, young, non-violent offenders like the three
teens share the same cellblock with violent murderers such as Russell.

While Russell shares a four-man cell with other alleged murderers, for much of the day, the prisoners are free to mingle in the
common area of the cellblock. It is here that the thirty-four-year-old
Russell befriends Ray McClaury.

---

*   *Tucker has his facts mixed up. Russell has an uncle in Chicago and an uncle practicing
      law. But they are not the same person. Both, however, are brothers of Russell's mother,
      Claude Estelle Baker.*

**   *The Evening Independent, August 25, 1949.*

The teenager quickly falls under the older Russell's influence. The expert car thief enthralls the young man with tales of his daring do, and brags that he can outsmart the law.

While young McClaury may think he's found the big brother he never had, Russell has a purpose in mind for the wayward teen.

McClaury is facing his third felony conviction. However, his crimes have all been breaking and entering or burglary. At fifteen, he's likely facing a light sentence if convicted.

Russell, on the other hand, is facing death in the electric chair. At best, he'll almost certainly be sent for an extended stay back at Chattahoochee. The grand jury is scheduled to hear his case in six days. They will likely indict him on a murder charge.

Russell has bragged that he can escape from any jail. He now plans to make good on that claim. The prisoner has no intention of sticking around for grand juries, courtrooms, and certainly not a date with Old Sparky. He has nothing to lose by attempting escape.

Rastus Russell's nice guy, model prisoner routine has been just that – a ruse. While guards have been ordered to watch him closely, he has managed to lure them into thinking he's a benign prisoner, somebody who follows the rules and can even have a good-natured chat. He has even helped jailer Nash with light work around the jail, such as moving boxes from floor to floor.

Russell begins telling McClaury of his master plan of escape. He bills it as a grand adventure, much as he did with Dorothy Jean Crain. He tells the boy he can outsmart any cops and that they'll hide out at a campground until they can escape across the state line.

Enamored and eager to please his new role model, McClaury signs on as Russell's accomplice. A sinister plan begins to take shape. And Rastus Russell knows the timing will soon be perfect.

* * *

On Friday night, August 26th, 1949, "Hurricane No. 2" roars ashore near Pompano Beach, Florida, just north of Miami. Hurling 125 miles per hour sustained winds with gusts up to 155 miles per hour, the storm packs a punch. In nearby West Palm Beach, 2,000 of the city's 7,000 homes are damaged.[*]

The storm rumbles through Southeast Florida, tearing up homes, electric lines, and citrus groves, then takes a Northwest track toward Tampa.

At approximately 3 a.m. on Saturday, August 27th, "Harry's Hurricane" passes through Tampa, the eye then darting just northeast of Clearwater.

By the time the storm reaches Clearwater, it has weakened. Pinellas County escapes with only a glancing blow. But a glancing blow from a hurricane still means 50-mile-per-hour winds, torrential rains, falling trees, flooding, loss of electric power, and in 1949, with lines above ground, loss of phone service.

By Saturday night, workers had cleared most city streets and restored some electrical power. But phone service is still down in many parts of the county. Several sections of the county are without power. There is much cleanup to do.

As residents of Pinellas County learned in 2024 with the passing of Hurricanes Helene and Milton, the aftermath of a storm can be almost as bad as the storm itself. Their 1949 forebears are dealing with this same ordeal in late August of that year.

At the county jail in Clearwater, however, all is well. So well, in fact, that head Jailer Harvey Nash has left for vacation.

This means Jailer Townsend will be in charge. But Sundays are the sabbath. Townsend takes the sabbath off. This means that new jailer, Bryan Curry, will be on duty tomorrow. This should not be a problem. The jail typically has two jailers or a jailor and a deputy on duty at any time.

This is almost always true, unless, of course, it is a busy night and the deputy must respond to a call.

...a busy night, such as the night after a hurricane, with storm damage, power outages, and phone service spotty around the county.

---

[*]   *The Tampa Times, August 27, 1949.*

47

Sunday Evening, August 28, 1949
Clearwater Jail
9:05 pm

S unday nights are typically quiet times at the jail. The jail's weekend rush of new "customers," as deputies refer to inmates, ended in the wee hours of Sunday morning.

Rastus Russell and the other twenty-four inmates who share his cellblock did not get their entertainment today. Normally, the prisoners can look out through their barred, third-story windows and watch workers build the massive new jail on the other side of Chestnut Street. But the builders are off on Sundays.

That doesn't mean Russell did not have an interesting day. In fact, the prisoner had his one and only visitor since his incarceration.

A mysterious man described as "dark and curly-haired" visited the accused murderer this morning. The man leaves in a 1946 blue Ford with a Hillsborough County license plate.

Inside the cellblock, prisoners talk, play cards, and read. Lockdown will be in twenty-five minutes, when all inmates will return to their cells to be locked in for the night.

Downstairs, assistant jailer, Bryan S. Curry, bides his time in the jail office. Curry has been with the Sheriff's Department less than six months. He has only been a jailor, however, for the last few weeks. His boss, Harvey Nash, is away on vacation. The experienced assistant jailer, Jack Townsend, typically handles nightly lockdowns. But again, Townsend does not work Sundays.

The deputy who would normally be with Curry has been working calls tonight, likely related to the storm. He will be back, but Curry does not know when.

231

That leaves the green Curry in charge of the jail by himself.

Not to worry, Curry thinks. It's Sunday night, everyone is tired. The storm is over. Besides, there don't seem to be any real troublemakers in the current group of guests.

In about twenty minutes, he'll start upstairs to begin lockdown, which he will accomplish by pulling a lever on the outside of the cell-block. This will automatically close the cell doors on the inside of the block without Curry having to enter the block.

He will then turn and repeat the process for the women's cell-block, where one Dorothy Jean Crain will bed down for the twentieth consecutive night inside the jailhouse.

* * *

Inside the third story cellblock, Rastus Russell is well aware of who is working tonight, and who isn't. In fact, the crafty criminal has spent the last three weeks observing each guard closely, his habits, his routines, and weaknesses. Russell has made friendly conversations with each, getting to know each one.

One or more of them may have let themselves believe, as Ray McClaury would state later, that Russell was a "good guy."

Todd Tucker knows otherwise. His instructions to his jailers are clear: Take no chances with Russell.

Nash and Townsend follow Tucker's orders to a tee. Every door is locked before another is opened. They never enter the "bullpen" before the prisoners are locked securely in their cells.

But Curry is new. And Rastus Russell has observed that Curry hasn't internalized all of the redundant security procedures as of yet.

Russell knows Nash is on vacation. He knows Townsend is out on Sundays. Somehow, the jail has been left in the hands of a neophyte.

At 9:04 p.m., one of Russell's cellmates, James E. Porter, asks one of the jail trustees for an aspirin.[*] Porter is awaiting grand jury action

---

[*] *Trustees are non-violent, well-behaved prisoners who, in exchange for work performed at the jail, such as mopping floors or washing dishes, are given credit towards fines or time off of their sentences. Trustees are generally given more freedom and less supervision throughout the jail.*

on a murder charge for shooting a customer during an attempted grocery store robbery. Porter suffered a bullet wound to the hand during
the holdup. He now wears a cast on it.

Occasionally, the hand aches and Porter asks for a pain reliever.

Whether Porter is in cahoots with Russell and McClaury or
whether he simply wants an aspirin is unknown. His actions later suggest he is not working with Russell.

Walking down to the jail office, the trustee informs Curry of the
inmate's request.

Curry claims he does not know what prisoner asked for the aspirin. But he opens the jail medicine cabinet and grabs a box of aspirin.
He then exits the office and unlocks the door to the first-floor cellblock. Entering the elevator, the jailer taps the button for the third
floor, where the men's bullpen is located.*

Procedure dictates that Curry lock the barred door to the first-
floor level before going upstairs. But Curry forgets the keys in the office.
Having made aspirin runs many nights before and believing he will only
be gone a minute, Curry leaves the door open.

The steel door to the third-floor bullpen features a small opening six inches wide by four inches deep. The tiny hatch can be opened
with a key so that food and other materials can be passed into the
cellblock without opening the larger door. But again, Curry has for-
gotten his key.

Inside the door, Rastus Russell stands ready. He is dressed in his
prison-issue khaki pants, a short-sleeved, maroon, checkered shirt, and
blue tennis shoes.

In his right hand, he holds a homemade "blackjack" – a steel rod
about ten inches long with a makeshift grip - a layer of gauze bandages
wrapped with adhesive tape. Behind him, the teenaged McClaury waits,
holding a sock stuffed with two bars of soap.

It is here that another question later arises that remains unex-
plained. How does Russell know that Curry will open the whole door?
Tucker claims Curry simply forgot his keys and, rather than go back

---

*   *Some reports claim Russell's bullpen was on the second floor of the jail. While this is*
    difficult to ascertain, witness accounts and a diagram in the St. Petersburg Times show
    three flights of stairs to Russell's cell from the first floor.

downstairs to retrieve them, thought it would be easier to open the entire lever-operated door to pass in the aspirin.

How can Russell know that Curry will forget his keys? We cannot know. The most likely explanation is that Russell has observed the novice jailer make the mistake in the past and assumes he will do it again. It is hard to believe this is the first time Curry has ignored or simply been unaware of procedures.

In an interview afterward, Ray McClaury seems to confirm this theory.

"Russell said we'd attempt the break Sunday night because he had observed jailer Curry's routine and thought the attempt would be successful."[*]

To open the entire door to the cellblock with twenty-five prisoners, four of whom are accused murderers and one of the state's most notorious escape artists behind it, being the only jailer in the jail, with the door downstairs left unlocked, against strict protocol and constant reminders from Tucker, seems like horrific negligence, even and perhaps especially, for a new jailor.

And yet, that is exactly what Bryan S. Curry does.

Curry presses the lever to unlock the steel door. As the latch clicks, Russell glances at McClaury.

"This is it," he preps the adrenaline-pumped teen.[**]

Curry starts to pull open the door. He gets it three inches open when Russell rams his body against the door, smacking it back into Curry's face. The jailer goes stumbling, crashing against the opposite wall of the corridor.[***]

Russell pounces, pounding the stunned man about the head and shoulders with the iron bar.

---

[*]   *Clearwater Sun, August 29, 1949.*

[**]   *St. Petersburg Times, August 28, 1949.*

[***] *McLaury's version of the story has Russell grabbing the door with his hands, shoving it back into Curry's face, and then jumping him.*

"He came at me like a tiger," Curry reports later. "He struck me again and again with a makeshift blackjack..."*+

But the game Curry is quick to react.

Stumbling to his feet, he charges the bulky Russell, tackling him to the floor. Curry lands on top of Russell and begins wrestling him for the blackjack.

Just as Curry appears to be getting control of Russell, McClaury joins the fray, jumping on Curry's back. For whatever reason, he drops his soap-filled sock and instead attacks Curry with his hands, trying to pull him off Russell.**

The other prisoners, stunned by the suddenness of the attack, look on, unsure what to do.

Finally, James Porter, the accused murderer who originally requested the aspirin, decides to assist the jailer. He jumps on McClaury, trying to separate him from the fight with his one good hand.

Curry, blood streaming over his face and neck, is putting up a terrific fight. But Russell still has the blackjack. As they roll about the floor, Russell strikes Curry over and over the face and head with the rusty metal rod.

"Russell must have jabbed me a thousand times," Curry tells reporters later. "...I grappled with him, but his tremendous strength was too much for me."

Realizing he's in trouble, Curry cries out for help.

The battle is now in full view of the women's cellblock. The six women behind the bars, including Dorothy Jean Crain, begin screaming in fear and alarm.

Russell, on top of Curry, turns to the women and roars, "Keep your goddamn mouths shut you goddamn whores!"***

They do.

---

*   *The Evening Independent, August 29, 1949.*

+   *Other reports indicate Russell only struck Curry once in the initial fray, striking him more later as they were rolling down the stairs.*

**   *Curry later claims that he had control of Russell at this point and had McClaury not jumped him, he would have subdued Russell and foiled the escape.*

***   *The Evening Independent, August 29th, 1949. The exact words Russell uses are blanked out, but the manner in which they appear implies the language used here.*

Curry is still fighting. Taking up the fight again, the two are joined by McClaury and Porter, also battling outside the cell. Seeing the stairwell unguarded, McClaury makes a break for it. Porter grabs him, and the two struggle down the stairwell, pushing, pulling, and punching.*

Meanwhile, Russell and Curry are locked in a death struggle. The two go tumbling down the stairs, punching, kicking, choking and pounding. Curry holds Russell close, forcing Russell to take short swings with the rod. But Russell still gets his licks in.

The two roll and brawl down three flights of stairs, through the open door, and onto the first-floor landing.

Finally, having pummeled the determined Curry for several minutes, Russell breaks free from the semi-conscious jailor. He drops the blackjack and leaps over the railing, landing in the lobby. He dashes out the front door of the jail into the prison yard.

Inexplicably, a wooden table sits conveniently placed against the fence to the outside world. Russell leaps onto the table, then pounces onto the ten-foot-high chain link fence.

Climbing to the top, the nimble Russell encounters three rows of barbed wire. The wire, however, is on the outside of the fence, not the inside. This makes it more difficult for an outsider to get into the jail than for an insider to get out. Russell places one foot on the barbed wire, steadies himself, then leaps over. As he does, his left-hand catches on one of the barbs, ripping a nasty gash between his thumb and forefinger.

The inmate lands hard on the sidewalk below, rolls to his feet, and runs. As Curry runs out the door of the jail with a shotgun, Rastus Russell disappears into the night.

It is approximately 9:15 p.m.

---

* *McClaury later claims Russell told him to head down the stairs first to scope out the situation below.*

48

Ray McClaury is not fairing so well.

While Russell is tussling with Curry, McClaury makes it all the way to the first-floor stairwell landing. He has about five more steps to descend and he will be out the front door, having fought off the one-handed Porter. Just when he thinks he's in the clear, he is confronted by two African American trustees, Ben Dawson and Archie St. Clair. The two men have been roused from their cells on the first floor, having heard the commotion upstairs.

Trustees are typically well-behaved, non-violent prisoners who have a certain amount of freedom within the jail, performing jobs such as kitchen work and cleaning.

Seeing McClaury fighting Porter, Dawson carries a hatchet he's snatched from a mount in the kitchen. Approaching the two brawling men, Dawson slams McClaury over the head with the flat end of the tool.

Dazed, McClaury collapses on the floor. The two trustees subdue the teenager with Dawson straddling him, pinning him to the floor. As he does, Rastus Russell and jailer Curry roll down the steps behind them, tumbling onto the very same landing. Russell rises to his feet, drops his weapon, and leaps over the stairwell railing. He lands on the floor about fifteen feet below and is gone.[*]

Battered and winded, Curry stumbles down the first-floor steps and grabs a shotgun from the office. Running out the front door, he watches Russell scurry away. Curry does not give chase.

---

[*]   *St. Petersburg Times, August 31, 1949.*

Instead, he has at least two other prisoners out of their cells (he does not know Porter has attempted to help him) and twenty-two more upstairs in an unlocked cellblock. He must mind the rest of his jail.

Curry asks Dawson and St. Clair to escort McClaury and Porter back upstairs. Bleeding and bruised, Curry staggers into the office and calls Clearwater Police.

There has been an escape.

* * *

Sheriff Todd Tucker is enjoying a quiet weekend at his Largo ranch when an urgent phone call interrupts his evening.

The call must certainly light Tucker on fire. Rastus Russell, the Palm Harbor troublemaker accused of the most gruesome murder in Pinellas County History, the man whom Tucker had so victoriously captured only three weeks earlier, has escaped.

First, his much-needed weekend retreat has just ended in a most unpleasant way. Secondly, the jailers, whom all work for Tucker, have obviously screwed up badly. It is Tucker who will have to answer for them.

Lastly, and most importantly, Tucker now has a dangerous fugitive on the loose in his county, one that will most certainly strike terror into the hearts of its citizens and witnesses.

The Sheriff straps his pistol to his side, bids his wife goodnight, and drives off toward Clearwater.

* * *

Like Tucker, Clearwater resident W.G. Booth is enjoying a quiet Sunday evening at 419 Oak Avenue, about a block from the jail. Like most residents of Pinellas County at the time, his windows are open to allow the cooler evening air to circulate through his home. At 9:14 p.m., his peace is rocked when he hears screams from both men and women coming from the jail.

"Help, Murder! Help! Help!" is what he can make out.

Alarmed, Booth dials the number of Clearwater Police.

"I knew something was wrong, so I called Clearwater Police immediately, and I heard crowds around the jail," he reports.[*]

It is about 9:30 p.m. when an urgent alert interrupts the listening pleasure of Pinellas County's citizens. As residents are winding down the weekend with Sunday night radio shows such as *The Count of Monte Cristo, Corliss Archer,* or *The NBC Symphony*, reality brutally intrudes.

"Rastus Russell has escaped!" exclaims the spokesperson for the Pinellas County Sheriff's office, interrupting the radio broadcasts. "... When Russell escaped, he was wearing a maroon checked sports shirt, light tan trousers, brown shoes. Russell's hair is wavy black; he has a high forehead, a barrel-shaped chest, big shoulders, and big hands."[**]

The news ignites a shock wave amongst residents. Few in the Clearwater – Tarpon Springs corridor will sleep well tonight.

The speaker urges anyone with information to call Clearwater Police at 32351.

They will, in droves.

* * *

Sunday night, August 28th, 1949, is a calm and balmy night in Clearwater, Florida. Hurricane number 2 has passed safely out to sea, ushering in, as hurricanes often do, a period of clear skies. This is such a night, the temperature hovering near 81 degrees. There is little to no wind. Humidity, of course, still hovers uncomfortably high.

If Rastus Russell would have looked up into the nearly cloudless sky, he would have seen a beautiful waxing crescent moon overhead.

But the jail escapee has more on his mind than lunar cycles this evening.

Breathing hard from his battle with Curry and dash to freedom, Russell likely has only one thought.

Run.

He does.

---

[*] *The Evening Independent, August 29, 1949.*

[**] *The Tampa Tribune, August 29, 1949. The report is wrong. Russell is wearing blue sneakers.*

Against all odds, Rastus Russell has pulled off another dramatic prison escape, this one steeped in violence.

In the process, however, he has wounded himself, an occurrence that will make him easier to track. Soaring from the exhilaration of his escape, it is unlikely the killer even feels the deep wound on his left hand or immediately notices the blood trail it is leaving behind.

But Russell is in his element on the run. He is not only an excellent car thief; he has honed his skills at evading law enforcement.

Deputy Wilmer James tells the media that Russell jumped the fence near the southeast corner of the jail.

It is known that Russell ran out of the north door of the jail. Why would he run all the way around the jailhouse to jump the southeast fence, only to head north again? There was a wooden table placed near the fence, which Russell jumped.

Did Russell know the table was there?

He must have. It seems to be the only logical explanation of why he would run to the opposite corner of the yard.

Female prisoners claim they watched Russell run "through" the front gate. But guards insist that would be impossible. Russell's blood trail seems to confirm an exit point at the southeast corner of the jail.

Regardless, Russell knows the police response will be quick and massive. He needs to get out of town, or find a place to hide, fast.

He bolts across Markly Street, then runs through or along the construction site of the new jail. Passing the construction zone, Russell takes cover behind (west side) the county courthouse. His hand is bleeding badly, leaving a trail of blood drops the size of dimes everywhere he runs. He breaks around the north end of the courthouse. Reaching the Northeast corner of the courthouse, Russell does not see the four-foot-deep airway in the ground. He stumbles in.

Sticking out his injured left hand to break his fall, the convict leaves a nearly perfect bloody handprint on the granite foundation stone.[*]

Anticipating bloodhounds on his trail, Russell shows some crafty foresight at this point. He descends a bluff at the foot of Haven Street, splashes into the tidewater ditch, and trudges along for roughly sixty feet before reemerging on Haven.

---

[*] *St. Petersburg Times, August 30, 1949.*

Russell then trots north across Haven Street with muddy shoes and soaking wet pantlegs, leaving sloshy footprints behind. He darts behind the Sinclair filling station, eventually arriving at the rear parking lot of the Fort Harrison Hotel.[*]

By this time, nearly twenty minutes has passed since Rastus Russell jumped the jail fence. Clearwater Police, stationed only blocks away, are already on his tail. Following their quarry's blood trail, officers near the Fort Harrison Hotel hear what sounds like someone climbing a fence near the rear of the hotel's treed courtyard. Rushing around back, they find no one. But they pick up the blood trail, leading through the grass and a wrought iron gate into the courtyard.

While officers are closing, Russell still has a lead on his pursuers. He emerges at the northwest corner of the Fort Harrison Hotel near Pierce Street. Hearing a car, possibly police, Russell steps behind the hedge bordering the building, flattening himself against the wall to avoid detection.[**]

Hours later, Clearwater Police find bloody handprints against the wall and drops of blood splattered on the pavement at this spot. Officers later speculate the splattering came from Russell shaking the blood off his hand or hands.

Out of breath, realizing he is bleeding and likely smarting from his fall into the airway, the escapee takes this moment to collect himself. The amount of blood found later suggests Russell spent at least a few minutes here. He gathers his bearings and plots his next move.

The convict might not know where he is going yet, but he knows he must keep moving. Bolting across Fort Harrison Avenue, he routes east towards Garden Avenue. Along the way, he stops and tries every door handle on the block, leaving a bloody handprint on each one. He finds every single handle locked.

---

[*] *In 1975, the Fort Harrison Hotel was purchased by the controversial church of Scientology. The hotel now serves as the World Headquarters of the Church and has been visited by several of Hollywood's Scientology devotees, including John Travolta and Tom Cruise. While the church has contributed much to the revitalization of downtown Clearwater in the 21st century, it has had to weather poor publicity and non-favorable documentaries about its cult-like culture and treatment of members.*

[**] *Clearwater Sun, August 29, 2024.*

This action suggests Rastus Russell does not have a second half of his escape plan firmly in place. He had one for getting out of the jail. Once out, he is winging it.

The door handles suggest he is seeking a place to hide out of sight, perhaps to address his wounds and make a plan. But locked doors mean he keeps running.

He arrives at the rear of the Hershock Furniture Store on the east side of Garden Avenue. Another collection of blood and prints suggests Russell rests here, too, perhaps catching his breath. He tries several more door handles around the building.

And then suddenly, Rastus Russell's trail of blood disappears.

49

It has been just over an hour since Rastus Russell climbed the fence of the Clearwater Jail.

Downtown Clearwater is electrified.

Sheriff Tucker has arrived on scene. So have over 100 officers from St. Petersburg, Tampa, Clearwater, Dunedin, Largo, and Tarpon Springs, backed up by State Police, and Sheriff's deputies from Pinellas and Hillsborough counties.[*]

When they arrive, they are placed under the command of Sheriff Tucker.

Tucker requests help from the National Guard. 150 members of the Clearwater infantry unit are mobilized, arriving on scene as the varied lawmen pour into Clearwater.

In addition to the guardsmen and law enforcement officers, armed citizens begin showing up, amassing around the jail and police station, and also patrolling city streets on their own accord.

In 1949, the population of Clearwater is approximately 15,000 people. Not only do people know each other, their neighbors, towns-people, members of their civic organizations and churches, there is a tight sense of unity. The people who live here grew up here, went to school together, married into each other's families, and serve the community together.

In 1949 Clearwater, a killer on the loose is a more immediate and personal event than it might be today.

Today, the population of Clearwater is over ten times what it was in 1949. An escaped killer from the county jail today may warrant no

---

[*] *The Evening Independent, August 29, 1949.*

more than a raised eyebrow towards the evening news before switching over to Netflix or Hulu for an evening's entertainment.

To 1949 Clearwater residents, news of Rastus Russell's jailbreak is like being told a rattlesnake is loose in the house – it creates a horrible, frightening emergency.

"People were absolutely terrified," remembers Pat Polaski, a teenager living in St. Petersburg in 1949.

The scene in downtown Clearwater is surreal.

While wailing sirens echo up and down city streets, armed men, professionals and citizens alike, roam its sidewalks. Gaggles of women, some still wearing bedclothes, clog street corners or sit in cars outside police headquarters, waiting for news that it is safe to return home.

Armed National Guardsmen set up a perimeter around the city, standing fifty feet apart on all sides. Roadblocks are established along roadways leading out of the city. Overhead, star shells explode against the night sky, shading the ground in an unreal, apocalyptic light.

Meanwhile, Sheriff Tucker is busy working the phones, trying to track down some bloodhounds. Finally, he reaches Plant City Police, who sends Harvey Frazier with his two tracking dogs, Flip and Flop. Frazier and his dogs were the same team used in the original search for Russell in Crystal Beach.

The dogs are on the way. But they must come from Plant City, nearly 90 minutes away.

Tucker feels confident he has Russell boxed in.

But if there is such as a thing as a criminal Houdini, it is Rastus Russell.

* * *

Circling the Hershock Furniture store, Rastus Russell can hear police sirens blaring all around him. In the rear of the store, he again frantically rattles door handles to the store and surrounding buildings.

Still no luck.

With the slash in his hand gushing blood, Russell strips off his maroon, checkered shirt and peels off his white, tank top undershirt. He then wraps the undershirt around his hand, temporarily halting the flow that is making him easy to track.[*]

Sticking close to buildings and vegetation, Russell continues to run east on Pierce Street. Rounding the corner of Pierce, the escapee cuts south on Myrtle. And it is here that Rastus Russell's tired eyes encounter a most magnificent and welcome sight. In front of him lies Clearwater's Central Truck Lines. At nearly 10:00 p.m. on a Sunday night, there are no apparent persons on the property.[**] But there is a welcoming selection of waiting trucks.

The killer scurries across the street. Careful to stay in the shadows, he goes from truck to truck, checking the door handles for unlocked doors. He tries three, leaving bloody hand prints on each. All three are locked. When he gets to the fourth, a black 1943 Ford pickup, it opens.

There are no keys inside, of course.

But that is no problem for an expert car thief.

In addition to searching for his escaped prisoner, Todd Tucker has another worry. Rastus Russell has sworn vengeance against Sam Crain and his family for setting him up on the scalloping expedition. According to Tucker, Sam Crain was the man Rastus Russell had "sworn he would kill if he ever regained his liberty."[***]

Russell is known to be vindictive and directly threatened Anne Browne should she tell the newspaper about his actions at her home.

After Russell was safely behind bars, Mrs. Browne did indeed give her account to the newspaper.

Miles and Thelma Crum remain the only other witnesses to Russell's crimes.

---

[*] *This is a deduction made by purely by myself. Russell's blood trail disappears for a while near the Hershock store. Later, his blood-soaked undershirt is found inside a truck cab. It begs to reason that Russell removed the shirt to stem the bleeding of his wound and possibly mask his trail.*

[**] *There is, in fact, one employee on sight as comes to light later.*

[***] *While there are no direct quotes from Rastus Russell in regards to retaliating against Sam Crain, Tucker states his prisoner has made threats against the Crains.*

In Tucker's mind, the Crains, the Crums, and Mrs. Browne are now all at risk.

The Sheriff sends deputies to all of the witness's homes.* Both Anne Browne and Thelma Crum are moved to undisclosed locations.

Deputies are posted to guard both Browne and Crum.

Upon hearing the news, Sam Crain is taking no chances. Within an hour of being notified of Russell's escape, he packs up his family and moves everyone to a friend's home in Palm Harbor.

"The police come to our house that night and told us Russell had escaped," Wilburn Crain remembers. *"They told us how he did it, that he had beat the jailer…They come to us and tell us that he's a danger to my father and our family. So my father gets with one of the people that he works with … and he carried all of us over and we stayed overnight several nights."***

But one Crain stays behind. Charles Crain, older brother of Furrell and Alan, has served in both the Army and Navy. Home from the service, Charles is eager to get a crack at the man who took away his sister and is now threatening his family. Armed with a rifle, Charles joins four deputies on the Crain front porch. Tucker has posted the men as a "reception committee" for Rastus Russell. All carry high-powered rifles. Tucker issues a "shoot to kill" order.

Now it's the Sheriff who is done playing nice.

---

*   *At this time, Anne Browne is no longer staying at her home in Crystal Beach. She is staying with her daughter at a temporary apartment in Dunedin.*

**   *From interview with Wilburn Crain, May 2024.*

50

Inside the cab of the truck, Rastus Russell pops off the cover to the crank shaft. Hastily pulling the lace out of his shoe, the expert thief uses the metal tip of the lace to twist the ignition wires.

The escapee is covered in a layer of sweat. He is winded from his jaunt through the city. Despite his makeshift band-aid, his hand has not stopped bleeding.

The pickup truck roars to life.

Russell jiggles the floor stick into first gear, releases the clutch, and creeps his stolen pickup off the lot of the Central Trucking Company. And then, despite over 100 officers of the law, 150 members of the Florida National Guard, and countless armed men and boys frantically combing the streets for any sign of Rastus Russell, he somehow avoids the roadblocks set up around both the city and county and slips into the night. It is approximately eleven o'clock p.m.

The escape artist has just pulled off his most daring and unlikely getaway.

* * *

It is well after midnight when Plant City officer Harvey Frazier arrives in Clearwater with his crack bloodhounds, Flip and Flop. Frazier has raised the dogs from pups and trained them himself since they were very young. The three work as a coordinated team, and the officer is quite confident in their abilities.

Tucker wastes no time putting them to work. Officers have been following Russell's blood trail but have lost it near the Hershock Furniture Store on Park Street.

247

Frazier starts from the beginning, prepping the dogs with a piece of Russell's clothing found in his cell.

The dogs mostly follow Russell's blood trail leading behind the courthouse and across Haven Street. Curiously, the hounds stray from the blood trail, turning west and heading two blocks to the waterfront of Clearwater Harbor before turning and heading east again towards Pierce.[*]

Whether this is an aberration in the dog's pursuit or a diversion by the crafty Russell, perhaps stemming his bleeding temporarily to throw pursuers off his trail, is unknown. Officers later float a theory that Russell may have initially planned to escape by boat into the harbor.[**]

It seems not only possible, but likely this was Russell's initial plan. The jail is only two blocks from the harbor. Once on the water, it would be extremely difficult for officers to track the experienced waterman, especially at night. From the sea, he could make landfall almost anywhere.

While Rastus Russell has been portrayed as a dullard or insane, his actions reflect the thinking of a criminal genius. He often brags about his prowess in outsmarting law enforcement. In his case, the bravado is not unfounded.

The water would have been Russell's quickest and safest route out of town. Thus, it seems unlikely the astute criminal would overlook it as an escape route. The dog's diversion to the waterfront would seem to confirm this was Russell's first choice.

But it was not to be. For whatever reason, perhaps unable to find a boat or unable to start one, Russell doubles back into town.

Russell, however, is not the only one who can see the waterfront as the logical choice for escape. Sheriff Tucker has scrambled officers to guard the waterfront in case of Russell's approach. He has also posted lawmen in and around the train station, suspecting Russell may attempt to take a passenger train out of town.

When a report comes in of fresh footprints at the waterfront near the northern edge of Clearwater, a team is scrambled to investigate. But they are not Russell's.

---

[*]   *The Evening Independent, August 29, 1949.*
[**]   *Tampa Tribune, August 29, 1949.*

Tips like these pour in for the next several hours as terrified citizens react to every strange movement, sound, or unfamiliar person. Teams of officers scurry around the city, following up on each lead.

One of these tips comes from an employee of the Central Trucking Company garage. The man claims he saw the escapee ducking around the buildings.

The Sheriff sends a large contingent of officers and orders the National Guardsmen to surround a several block area from Turner Street to Park Street and Myrtle Avenue to Greenwood Avenue. While the guardsmen guard the perimeter, officers wielding flashlights, pistols, shotguns, and rifles comb through the area that is punctuated by large tracts of high, swampy grass, water, and mosquitos. The Central Trucking Company lot sits on the western edge of this perimeter.

As officers splash through the muddy swamp, they are treated to a diverse chorus of singing tree frogs, armies of crickets, and the occasional hoot of a whippoorwill, all celebrating the rejuvenated wetland that Storm #2 has provided.

But officers find no sign of Rastus Russell.

* * *

Todd Tucker must be having Deja vu when he calls a 2 a.m. meeting with other law enforcement heads, including Chief McClamma of Dunedin and Chief A.J. Reichart of St. Petersburg Police. The leaders are discussing the possibility that the convict has escaped by train. Railroad authorities across the state and as far north as Georgia have been notified and advised to keep a wary eye out for the accused killer.

Tucker believes the violent Russell may seek refuge in a private home, perhaps seizing a firearm along the way. The chiefs also reiterate fears that Russell could seek vengeance against those who have harmed him, including Sam Crain and his family, or those who could harm him, such as Anne Browne and Miles or Thelma Crum.

For whatever reason, the decision is made to dismiss the guardsmen for the night. But tired police officers from around the region continue to check every door, shake every bush, and chase every lead in a frantic attempt to locate the escaped prisoner. The search fans out from the downtown area to surrounding residential neighborhoods. While many men and boys are helping in the search, most residents stay behind locked doors. Those with firearms have them close by.

Even outside the very jail in which Todd Tucker is meeting his colleagues, searchers shine flashlights up into the towering oak trees across the street at the courthouse, just in case their quarry has chosen to hide out in one of their dark canopies. Had Rastus Russell been arrested and convicted only forty years earlier, he would almost certainly have found himself hanging from one of their branches. In 1949, at least two of the mammoth oaks are still known as the "hanging trees."[*]

But there will be no such justice tonight at the hanging trees. In fact, there may be no justice at all. Todd Tucker is beginning to realize a truth he did not want to acknowledge.

Rastus Russell is gone.

✳ ✳ ✳

It is about 4:00 a.m. when Officer Frazier, Flip, and Flop pick up Russell's scent again near the blood trail at the Hershock Furniture Store near the corner of South Garden Avenue and Pierce Street.

As they follow Russell's trail down Pierce Street and cross the Southern Atlantic Line Railroad tracks, the canines become more animated, indicating the scent is fresher.

Flip and Flop pull Frazier and a group of officers that have fallen in behind them into the parking lot of the Central Trucking Company. With rifles raised and flashlights eagerly scanning the landscape, the officers cautiously march onto the lot. When a flashlight beams across a streak of blood near the handle of a pickup truck, everyone freezes.

Moving in to investigate, the policemen find bloody door handles on two more adjacent trucks. The next parking space beside the three trucks is empty. In its place is the large bloodstain on the pavement. It is here that Flip and Flop lose the scent of Rastus Russell.

✳ ✳ ✳

---

[*] *In present day, large oak trees still grow in front of the Old Courthouse in Clearwater. However, none of the old "hanging trees" have survived to present day.*

At about the same time, Frazier's bloodhounds are finding the spot where Rastus Russell escaped in a stolen pickup, St. Petersburg Times newspaper carrier Jim Shelton is on his way to deliver the morning edition of the paper announcing the escape of the infamous convict. Shelton covers the Safety Harbor/Oldsmar area for the Times. He is traveling his regular morning route north on Haines Road.

When Shelton is about a half mile south of the Dunedin Shortcut intersection, he notices an abandoned pickup truck parked along the road.*

Whether Shelton suspects the pick-up has anything to do with Rastus Russell is unclear. When he discovers the truck, Shelton cannot know that the escapee has fled in a pick-up truck. He may find it suspicious, or he may simply feel a civic duty to report an abandoned vehicle.

Either way, a half hour passes before Shelton finally comes across a pay phone on his paper route. He pulls over and dials Clearwater Police. Officer Dave Caruthers takes the call. By this time, Caruthers is aware that Russell may have made his getaway in a stolen pick-up.

Caruthers immediately dispatches officers to investigate. Then he calls Sherrif Tucker.

* * *

A bleary-eyed Todd Tucker is still digesting the news of Frazier's discovery at Central Trucking Lines when he gets the call from Clearwater Police.

An abandoned pickup truck has been found on Haines Road near Oldsmar. Tucker knows in his gut it's his man.

The Sherrif sends seven carloads of officers racing to the scene. He also redeploys Frazier and his hounds to go with them. The dedicated dogs have had only about thirty minutes rest.

Traveling the approximate nine miles to the abandoned vehicle's reported location will take over twenty minutes. As Tucker waits impatiently for a report, he realizes he's caught his first break in the chase.

---

* *Haines Road is the modern-day McMullen-Booth Road. The Dunedin Shortcut is today known as S.R. 580 and further west, as Main Street, Dunedin.*

51

C learwater is not the only town where the world has turned upside down tonight.

In Palm Harbor, where Russell is both known and feared, a call to arms has roused the townsfolk. The area has turned into an armed camp. Indeed, even law enforcement officers speculate Russell may run to Palm Harbor, either because it offers familiar places to hide or to seek vengeance on those he believes responsible for his arrest. With men and their sons outside homes or patrolling streets with hunting rifles and handguns, women and children huddled behind locked doors and windows, few in Russell's hometown will sleep well tonight.

News from the Sherriff's Office will soon confirm their worst fears.

It's close to 5:00 a.m. when Tucker's convoy of officers come tearing up Haines Road towards Oldsmar. A steady rain has started to fall, further hindering the lawmen's visibility in the darkness.

But when the taillights of an abandoned pickup truck reflect in the responder's headlights, the cars converge and surround the vehicle.

At first, there is confusion and exhilaration. There is shouting with several beams from flashlights darting around the truck and its cab through the rain and fog. With rifles and shotguns trained on the cab, an officer approaches and jerks open the door.

The cab is empty.

There is no doubt that Russell was its driver. Inside, the officers find a bloody tank top undershirt discarded in the front seat. The dashboard is smeared and splattered with blood, so thick that it is still dripping onto the truck's floorboard. The left side door handle, side panel, and light switch are smeared with blood.

Upon the discovery, the focus of the chase shifts from downtown Clearwater to the Curlew and Oldsmar area. Officers, including Tucker and County Patrolman J.F. Peacock, race to the scene.

Peacock is the area's forensic expert and is the same officer who investigated the original murder and assault in Crystal Beach.

While Peacock cannot pull a clear fingerprint from the truck, he is confident that Russell was the driver and says the location of the blood spots indicates a wound on the left hand.

Russell apparently ran out of gas, exited the truck, and ran into the woodsy swamp somewhere between Dunedin and Oldsmar.[*]

The area is only about three miles from the home of Sam Crain and less than five miles from Palm Harbor, further fueling speculation that Russell is headed to one of those two places. However, the location suggests Russell was headed to Tampa.

While Tucker doesn't have his man yet, his confidence is growing.

"I knew the minute we found the truck," Tucker says, "that Russell's capture was bound to come sooner or later because when his stolen truck ran out of gas, it meant Russell would have to hitchhike to make his getaway."[**]

Perhaps, but Rastus Russell has not attempted to hitchhike as of yet. He has fled into the countryside. Despite his best efforts, his flight has not gone unnoticed.

Between 4:15 and 4:35 a.m., a man believed to be Russell was spotted three times by residents near the area where the truck was found.

The first saw Russell running across the corner of a citrus grove less than two miles from Sam Crain's house.

The second sighting was by a farm family, alerted by their barking dogs in time to catch a glimpse of a man "fox trotting" down a dirt road leading to a swamp.

---

[*] *The Clearwater Sun reports the truck was found "full of gas and in good condition." However, Tucker himself contradicts this in his statement to The Evening Independent. Thus, we must assume the Sun Reporter got his facts wrong.*

[**] *The Evening Independent, August 29, 1949.*

The third time was by an early-rising farmhand who saw a man he believed was Russell jogging into a Cypress Swamp six and a half miles northeast of Dunedin.

As these were all in the same general area, the sightings are likely real. Unfortunately for the pursuers, this is a miserable area to search, especially after a drenching rain.

In 1949, the area around Northern Haines Road was wet, mucky swampland characterized by moss-draped cypress trees, high reeds, brackish water, tall grass, fallen trees, and all manner of biting insects, animals, and reptiles, including snakes and alligators. Even today, the area around McMullen Booth and Tampa Roads, although dredged for a canal, is still surrounded by swamp. Pursuing officers, up all night and wet from the earlier rain, must be thrilled to go stomping into the muddy morass of biting, stinging life.

But they do.

* * *

As the first streaks of morning light begin to lift the heavy air of the morning, Harvey Frazier's dogs are back on the case. Like their handler, Flip and Flop have not rested and are reaching the end of their tracking effectiveness.

They will be relieved shortly by two new teams of dogs. For now, it's up to Frazier to coax the most from his pride and joys. The rain has erased much of Russell's trail but the dogs pick up a scent not far from the truck. Frazier goes bobbing into the woods, followed by a posse of officers.

Russell has a considerable head start. But the dogs hold up and follow the trail in a northerly direction.

The hounds pick up Russell's trail on a clay road heading north. Rain begins to fall again, lightly but steadily. The dogs excitedly trot ahead, darting left and right as their sensitive noses search for any stray scent of Rastus Russell.

After nearly three miles through muddy woods, orange groves, and leafy thickets, the dogs arrive at the home of Alfred Clark. Clark's home and outbuildings lie at the southwest corner of North Haines Road and Curlew Creek Road.

Clark, alarmed to see an army of police surrounding his home and barn, asks the situation. Officers explain and ask if he has seen anyone. Clark says he has seen no one, and his own dogs, always alert to intruders, have not barked.

Yet Flip and Flop pull to and fro enthusiastically around Clark's home and barn.

Tucker's men search the house and barn but find nothing.

When the contingent of officers and deputies reach the back of Alfred Clark's property, the trail abruptly changes direction.

Frazier's dogs double back, heading in a southwesterly direction. The team follows the tired animals into another swamp near what is known as Possum Creek.

And here, in the lush and watery flats, the dogs lose the scent.

As one officer puts it, Russell's trail "lifts up" here.

When a reporter asks Frazier if the injured convict could have changed shoes to throw the dogs off his scent, Frazier sets the record straight.

He informs the reporter that such a tactic would not work. The dogs work on body scent, he explains, most of which reached the ground from the bottoms of a man's trousers, not the soles of his feet.[*]

In fact, the swampy water and heavy rain have simply erased what is left of the scent trail.

Rastus Russell has once again dodged his pursuers.

* * *

No one is sure exactly where Rastus Russell was in the hours after his escape. But local resident Bill Polaski believes he has an answer.

The 91-year-old Polaski was a teenager living near Curlew Creek Road, only about a mile from the Sam Crain house, at the time of Russell's escape. He remembers going to work on a farm the next morning and his boss laying a pistol on the seat of the pickup truck in which he was riding. Polaski, never knowing his boss carried a weapon, asked why he had brought it.

---

[*] *Clearwater Sun, August 29, 1949.*

"Well," he said, not wanting to alarm the boy, "I know a few things. And we might need it."

His boss was Alfred Boyd, and the Boyd Farm where Polaski worked was right in the bullseye where police were searching for Russell. Boyd, in fact, would later assist in the search, helping lead officers through the property on horseback.

Polaski remembers the time when Russell was on the loose.

"...he would do things and would leave so many little patches of evidence that they came to say, 'Well, Rastus has been working here at night.'"

But it is Polaski's recounting of another man's story that may account for Russell's whereabouts the night and early morning of his escape.

"There was an old man, Mr. McCall. I loved him," says Polaski. *"He lived down the next house before you get to the cemetery* (on Curlew Road, formerly Curlew Creek Road.) *I enjoyed him. Just a good old man. He was such a real old Florida backwoodsman.*

He had this old Hudson. He looked out the window that night and saw Rastus over that old Hudson.

He said up and down, he told people, he said, 'I heard somebody open the door of my car...and I looked outside.'

He said it was a bright, moonlit night.

And he said, 'I looked down, and there was a man in my car!'

He told his wife, he said, 'Go get the shotgun!'

Said she never did.

*The guy took off. To the day he died, he would tell you he thought it was Rastus."**

Polaski's story sounds feasible. In the wee early hours of August 30th, Russell was on the run and known to be in the Curlew Creek area. He was almost certainly looking for a car. Either finding McCall's Hudson unlocked or jimmying the lock, Russell jumped inside.

Whether he ran into difficulties starting the car or saw McCall or McCall's lights go on, the fugitive apparently abandoned the theft attempt.

---

* *From personal interview with Bill Polaski, June 21, 2024.*

52

August 29, 1949
Ozona, FL
Early Morning

Rastus Russell is back on familiar ground, his adopted hometown, Palm Harbor. His move seems counterintuitive, given this is the very place both citizens and deputies are on hyperalert for the fugitive.

Police speculate later that it was Russell's plan to hide out in Palm Harbor until he found the opportunity to get vengeance on Sam Crain for his perceived betrayal of Russell. While this is possible, it seems more likely Russell believes Palm Harbor may offer him a familiar, safe place to hide in order to plot his next move.

Russell is not an unknown drifter. In fact, before he left the state, Russell was a familiar face on downtown streets. Known as the "bad boy" of Palm Harbor, the small-time criminal was said to stand outside his apartment building, staring down passersby in an intimidating manner – causing many to cross to the other side of the street to pass.[*] At the same time, the handsome Russell also has friends in town – he's grown up here and gone to school here. His mother was known as a kind and intelligent resident.

A decade ago, the now-tanned and toned Russell was somewhat of a cult hero to local teenagers. Sometime between high school and his exit from the state in 1942, Russell grows out of his obese body and transforms into something of a bad-boy heartthrob. He seems to have been both attractive and feared, much like the tough hoodlum in high school that every kid secretly hoped would be his friend and

---

[*]   *From interview with Wesley Henry, May 2024.*

every girl secretly hoped would ask her out, yet feared what would happen if she went.

It is a theme that repeats itself throughout Russell's life – "I did what he said because I was afraid of him" – (yet secretly wanted to do it.) The violent criminal seems to have a way of putting those around him under a seductive spell, a potent mix of applied fear and charisma – See Norman Browne, Dorothy Jean Crain, Ray McClaury, Sam Crain, and almost certainly many more – Aunt Maude? Judge Bird? Pinellas Jailers? The secret visitor on the day of his escape? His farm worker buddies? Over and over, we hear this same refrain.

And so it is at the cusp of dawn on Monday morning, August 29th, when a wounded, dirty, hungry, and exhausted Rastus Russell staggers through the high weeds and bushes that hide Willa Mae Skinner's Ozona front yard from the road. Willa Mae is a long-time resident of Ozona (a tiny seaside village at the edge of Palm Harbor, adjacent to Crystal Beach) and has known Rastus's mother, along with her troubled boy, for years.[*]

Answering the knock on her door, Skinner is confronted with the haggard Russell. As she describes later to police, he wears the maroon shirt and khaki pants described in repeated radio bulletins. He also wears a patch on his head, possibly first aid from a wound received from fighting Jailer Curry. Skinner also notes a sizable bleeding cut on Russell's left hand.[**]

Russell asks the older woman for help. Although she does not say specifically what he asks for – it is likely food or a place to stay. The conversation that transpires is not known. Skinner sends Russell away, saying she was afraid of him. Yet tellingly, she then gives her neighbor, Elia Slate, a half loaf of bread for Russell.

Again, the theme plays out. Skinner is afraid of Russell and yet, for whatever reason, provides him with food. Unclear is who Elia Slate is and how Skinner knows she will see Russell. Perhaps Russell tells her he will visit Slate next.

---

[*] *Claude Estelle Baker McCoy spends the last years of her life in Ozona along with her husband, Cecil McCoy.*

[**] *St. Petersburg Times, September 2, 1949.*

Police later believe Russell received help from several residents of Palm Harbor or Ozona, people he has known for years.

Through numerous interviews with Palm Harbor, Crystal Beach, and Thonotosassa residents from the time, one word keeps surfacing: *Monster.*

Why would a man portrayed as a monster, a person who committed a horrific, unspeakable crime, be helped by locals?

One potential clue: For every person who responded with this label for Russell, I asked a follow-up question: "Did you ever meet him?"

To a person, the answer was "no."

Thus, the "monster" label likely came from hearsay or newspaper reports. This does not mean that Rastus Russell was not a monster. He certainly committed heinous acts. But gossip and imagination can create one dimensional images that may not be completely accurate. At the very least, it leaves plenty of room for interpretation.

Willa Mae is quick to add that Russell threatened to hurt her if she turned him in to the law. But what other explanation would she give for not immediately contacting police?

One theory that has emerged from my study of Russell is this: Russell grew up in Palm Harbor, a troubled boy. Perhaps he is mentally challenged; perhaps he has a touch of autism, enough to affect his decision-making, to trigger fits of rage or cruelty, but not enough to eclipse his personal charm. Perhaps those who know him come to understand that Rastus is "different" and accept that Claude Estelle's boy "can't help how he is."

Thus, they both like or pity him and fear him at the same time. One can almost see Willa Mae nervously glancing up and down the street, shoeing the fugitive away, then guiltily preparing a loaf of bread for the "poor, suffering boy."

Yet while some portray Russell as "not too bright," others, including Wilburn Crain, the only person interviewed for this book who ever met Russell, saw him in a different light.

When asked if he thought Russell was slow, Crain told me, "I don't think so. I thought he was pretty sharp....crazy like a fox would be my definition of it."

Another theory is that Russell does indeed have friends or family in high places, friends the knowing locals do not wish to cross, and thus provide the young man with help, or at the very least, look the other way.

Regardless, it is a considerable feat that the convict slips into the militarized town undetected.

Then again, it is under the cover of darkness. And Russell is intimately familiar with every side road, orange grove, and backwoods trail in the area.

* * *

For twenty-three years, Palm Harbor Junior High School was more than just a school. In many ways, it served as a center of community life and activity. Built in 1926, the school is widely considered one of the best in the county. The two-story brick building sits on nine well-maintained acres of flat, high ground.

The interior structure, however, is largely made of wood.

On the stormy night of May 31, 1949, at approximately 11:32 p.m., a bolt of lightning strikes the roof, igniting a fire that quickly morphs into an inferno.

Because of the hour, the blaze gets quite a jump before somebody notices the flames and calls the fire department. Volunteer firefighters from Tarpon Springs, Clearwater, and Dunedin arrive shortly after. But they have a problem.

They have no water.

For whatever reason, pumper trucks from Dunedin and Tarpon Springs lag behind. As a growing crowd of onlookers join helpless firefighters in watching the blaze consume the building, principal Dana D. White arrives from his nearby home. His striped pajama top neatly tucked into a hastily pulled on pair of trousers, White runs into the office of the burning building. Helped by several firefighters, the principal manages to save nearly all the school records before the space is consumed by flames.

With pumper trucks finally arriving, hoses are run to a pond in a nearby grove. But it's too late. Despite an hours-long fight through thunder, lightning, wind, and sometimes driving rain, the building is destroyed.

* * *

In the early morning of August 29th, 1949, the charred ruins of the Palm Harbor Junior High School remain dark and quiet on the northwest corner of town. While the building was gutted three months earlier, much of its brick walls, as well as parts of the interior, remain upright. The basement, a rare feature in Florida structures, is largely intact.

With a cement floor, concrete block walls, and the first floor of the school serving as a ceiling, the basement is still protected from the elements. It would seem to be the last place anyone would look. In fact, it might be the perfect hideout for a fugitive.

Through the darkness, likely just after visiting the likes of Willa Mae Skinner and others in Ozona and presumably securing a breakfast, Rastus Russell ambles onto the grounds of what used to be the esteemed school.

After dumping his pickup on Haines Road, Russell has spent the early morning hours jumping from backyards to barns, wading through swamps and streams, trying to open a car door or two, and finally ending up on the familiar streets of Palm Harbor.

Like a vampire, Russell knows if he does not find a dark place to hide before the sun rises in earnest, he is toast.

The distance from the swamp in which the hounds lost his trail to Palm Harbor is roughly four miles – a distance the athletic Russell has covered quickly. Like his pursuers, however, the bleeding Russell has not slept since early Sunday morning, nearly twenty-four hours. He not only needs a place to hide, but a place to rest and regroup.

The experienced escapee knows the game plan – move at night – rest, and stay out of sight during the day.

Whether Russell has the school as his destination or simply comes across it is unknown.

He is, however, well acquainted with the building. As a teenager, he prowled its halls as a student. It was there, it is said, that the obese boy was a bully, known to seize the lunches of classmates, eat what he wanted, and then grind sand into what remained before returning it to its owner.

Now, the burnt-out shell is a godsend.

By this time, most of the rubble from the scorched building has been removed. Yet, Russell must still navigate through a field of blackened wood and bricks to reach the basement stairwell. Possibly using a cigarette lighter or match to light his way, the exhausted fugitive descends the stairs.

The pitch-black basement is surprisingly unscarred by the fire. Russell navigates its corridors into the boiler room. Laying several layers of newspaper on the concrete floor as a mattress, he employs another layer as covers. Then, safely out of sight, protected from the elements, water, and bugs, Rastus Russell falls soundly asleep.

53

Despite Frazier's bloodhounds losing Rastus Russell's scent in the swampy marshlands about three miles northwest of Sam Crain's house, Sherrif Todd Tucker is not deterred.

In fact, with the rain gone and the midday sun lighting Tucker's search area, the Sherrif predicts Russell's capture is only a matter of hours.

The break of day has brought a wave of resources into the search. Two fresh teams of dogs have arrived to replace the depleted Flip and Flop. More officers and deputies from Pinellas, Hillsborough, and surrounding areas are pouring in to join the manhunt. Clearwater's Company K of the Florida National Guard has rejoined the search after a night's rest. The new day has also brought a throng of local volunteers, eager to help track the accused killer.

With the extra help, Tucker believes he's thrown a "ring of steel" around the three-by-four mile-wide swamp area in which he is certain Russell is hiding.

When a local Coast Guard officer calls Tucker to offer a helicopter to assist in the search, Tucker enthusiastically accepts. Now, in addition to several hundred armed men, trucks, and patrol cars moving in and around the swamp, the rotor hum of a Coast Guard helicopter can be heard buzzing overhead, adding a military feel to the whole affair.

Tucker has also managed to secure two light "Grasshopper" airplanes which buzz back and forth over the swamp, scanning the surface for movement.

With so much search power concentrated in such a small area, most lawmen participating share Tucker's optimism in finding their fugitive.

But the swampy Curlew Creek area is not only in the general vicinity of the Crain home, it is an area with which Rastus Russell is intimately familiar.

One deputy states it all too clearly.

"Br'er Rabbit has gone back into the briar patch."*

* * *

Back in Clearwater, with the drama of the previous night behind them, residents and officials are demanding answers. The Tampa Tribune describes the feeling as "mingled fear and indignation."

Officials were already under fire for the violent Russell's ill-explained release in 1941. Now, how could a man who has escaped several facilities before, accused of such a horrific crime, be allowed to escape so easily?

Calls for a grand jury investigation are already being heard.

Sam Henderson, a Palm Harbor resident, speaks out on behalf of his frightened and angry neighbors.

"I think Russell's escape was an example of gross neglect and high inefficiency," he tells the Clearwater Sun. *"Now we're living under a dread fear and we don't like it. We feel that if somebody had exercised care, all this wouldn't have happened. Maybe we need an investigation and perhaps some overhauling."*

The guard attacked by Rastus Russell appears to reporters at the Clearwater Jail. Dressed in a white, loose-fitting shirt and trousers, Curry is a thick man. His head is wrapped in white gauze, which covers the open gashes and bruises inflicted by his prisoner's homemade club. His left eye puffed and purple/black, Curry tells his side of the story through swollen lips.

The jailer is amazingly candid in his public comments, explaining the story in a way that does not attempt to cover his obvious mistake.

---

* *Clearwater Sun, August 30, 1949*

"I was the only one on duty," he explains, *"when someone up on the cellblock called for an aspirin. I don't know who called for it. Usually Mitchell* (William Gordon Mitchell, confessed arsonist), *took care of dishing out the aspirin, but apparently, he had run out. So I cracked open the cell door and started to toss the box in to them. But three of them shoved the door back on me and the next thing I knew, I was fighting all of them."*

At the time, Curry is not aware that James Porter, the third inmate in the melee, was trying to help stem the attack by Russell and McClaury. Curry claims that if McClaury had not intervened, he would have subdued Russell and thwarted the escape attempt.

"Frankly, I don't remember exactly what all happened; it took place so suddenly," Curry continues. *"But we fought all the way down the steps. Then Russell broke into the clear and ran through the door.* *

A photo of the beaten jailer taken immediately after his attack appears in the St. Petersburg Times the same day his comments appear in the Clearwater Sun. In the photo, Curry is bare-chested, head bandaged, a puzzled stare on his face as he examines the metal blackjack Russell used to beat him about the head.

The next day, Curry poses for a photo outside of the jail, pointing to the section of fence Russell jumped to escape from his facility. There is no table visible in the photo, and no mention of it in Curry's comments.

Yet, reporters go easy on Curry, perhaps giving some leeway to the battered guard.

Todd Tucker is faced with tougher scrutiny. In addition to engineering the search for Rastus Russell, the Sheriff has a second investigation running back at the jail.

Residents and media alike want to know how this could happen and who was involved.

Tucker would like to know the same thing.

Giving an impromptu press conference from his makeshift "field headquarters," which consists of his personal patrol car near the Curlew Creek Swamp, the Sheriff does his best to tell what he knows.

"The iron concrete reinforcing rod," says the Sheriff, *"undoubtedly was smuggled into the jail by another prisoner. It was an old rod. That*

---

* *Clearwater Sun, August 29, 1949.*

267

eliminates the theory that it came from the new jail construction. But our jail has been badly overcrowded, and it is entirely possible that the ten-inch section of iron was brought into the jail by some prisoner."

Tucker is clear. Rastus Russell had outside help. The question is, from who?

When the conversation turns to the mysterious, dark-haired stranger with the Hillsborough license plate that visited Russell the morning of his escape, the Sheriff announces that the person in question has been cleared.

"We have checked him," Tucker explains, "But the visitor has been given a clean bill of health."

He does not elaborate further.

This is odd. Rastus Russell is jailed for three weeks and receives absolutely no visitors. Then, on the day of his escape, he is visited by a strange man. The man, like Russell, is described as dark-haired, with a dark complexion, and possibly of Greek descent. Less than twelve hours later, Russell escapes with the help of a weapon smuggled in from the outside. Why does Tucker not tell reporters who this man is and why he was visiting Rastus Russell? Was he a friend? A family member? Given the circumstances, it would seem appropriate to do so.

Tucker instead speculates that the smuggler might have been one of the jail's "regular customers," i.e., drunks and vagrants, who regularly spend a night or two at the facility before being released. Did Russell bribe one of them?

There will be time to seek answers later. Right now, the Sheriff has a fugitive to catch.

But these answers, like so many things Rastus Russell, will never come. To this day, it is not known, at least publicly, how Russell acquired the iron rod used in his escape or who helped him get it.

* * *

During this incredibly busy morning, Tucker has also had time to question fifteen-year-old Ray McClaury. McClaury, realizing his charge of breaking and entering will now be greatly expanded, is quick to cooperate and eager to spill his beans.

"He told me, if I would help him slug the jailer and break out," he tells Tucker, *"that we could lay low for a few days and then beat it out of the country."*

The teenager claims he has no idea where Russell acquired the blackjack the convict used as a weapon to escape. He does, however, exonerate fellow inmate James Porter, telling Tucker that Porter tried to help Jailer Bryan Curry.

Asked why he helped Russell, McClaury claims Russell threatened to kill him if he refused.

By early afternoon, the search party for the escaped Russell has ballooned to over 1,000 searchers, including more than 200 law enforcement personnel, 150 national guardsmen and the rest armed citizens.

Officers, deputies, and patrolmen from around West Central Florida are not only searching the swamps but also combing towns, streets, and neighborhoods in the surrounding areas. Through Pinellas and Hillsborough Counties, roadblocks manned by lawmen armed with shotguns and teargas check every vehicle that passes through, causing traffic jams and frustrated travelers on this sweaty Monday.

On the chance his quarry may have escaped the county under the Sheriff's nose, Tucker issues a statewide alert to all law enforcement agencies in Florida. He also announces the printing of 10,000 to 20,000 circulars featuring Russell's photo and description to be mailed to law enforcement agencies around the country.

With the sensational news coverage, calls and leads begin to pour into every police department in the area. "Sightings" of Russell begin coming from all corners of west central Florida. While most turn out to be fruitless, officers must still be dispatched to investigate each one.

At 11:30 a.m., a report is phoned in from Faith Mission on Crystal Beach. A person there claims they heard a swimmer at the end of the Crystal Beach Pier between 3:30 and 4:30 a.m. last night.

"It sounded as if the swimmer were tired," the witness tells the officer.

He also claims he then saw a figure come out of the water and walk along the shore.

*   The Evening Independent, August 29, 1949.*

269

With Crystal Beach suspected as one place Russell may return for revenge, officers race to Faith Mission. After a commotion with police cars, reporters, and curious onlookers, the report is dismissed.

* * *

Thirty-eight-year-old Edward Denzil Pulley has been in his office since early this morning. The General Manager and part owner of radio station WTAN in Clearwater has been broadcasting Rastus Russell's description to its listeners since the infamous convict's escape last night.

At approximately 1:00 p.m., Pulley takes a call in his office.

He is stunned at the raspy voice on the other end.

"This is Russell," the voice claims. "You lay off broadcasting my description or I'm coming there for you."*

The phone clicks dead.

Shaken, Pulley immediately dials Clearwater Police.

But he leaves the broadcasts running.

There is little, however, police can do. In 1949, there is no technology available to trace phone calls after they are completed. While some dismiss the call as the work of a crank, Tucker and his team take the call seriously.**

In five days, Edward Denzil Pulley will be dead.

* * *

The call to WTAN will not be the only riveting development today.

Sometime in the early afternoon, another call comes into the Sheriff's office from Crystal Beach.

---

*   *This is not an exact quote but paraphrased from the description given by Pulley.*

** *In the "old days," the only reliable way to trace a call was to wiretap the line before the call. Call tracing would take a leap forward in the 1970s but still required working through a switchboard. It wasn't until 1992 that Malicious Caller Identification, also known as *57, was offered as a subscription service to the general public. If dialed immediately after a malicious call, the service provider could record metadata that could be available to law enforcement later.*

Someone, presumed to be Russell, had been to the Browne residence and ransacked the place.

The report sets off an all-out alarm. Tucker, apparently, takes the report seriously. The Sherrif does, after all, have the Browne home on his list as one potential place a vengeful Russell could attempt to revisit. However, unlike the Sam Crain home, he has not posted officers there. This is likely because, at the time, no one is living there.

Police vehicles from around the county, some diverting from the search on Curlew Creek Road, swarm to the now infamous home in Crystal Beach.

As word gets out to the public that police are swarming back to the house in which Rastus Russell allegedly committed his bloody acts, sightseers from Pinellas County and beyond flock toward Crystal Beach.

Who would not want to witness the capture of an escaped murderer taking place back at the macabre location of his heinous crime? What a photo op it would be – officers hauling a captured Russell out of the very house where blood still stained the wooden floors where his spree of violence exploded.

For the second time in just over three weeks, a convoy of law enforcement vehicles surround the two-story home on Rattlesnake Road. A report comes in that a suspicious man was seen walking along the shore of the nearby bayou. Another meticulous search of the wooded area in South Crystal Beach begins.

Again, like three weeks earlier, an eager contingent of armed volunteers pour into the woods along with officers and deputies, like a tribe of hunters hoping to flush a grouse.

The little community and the roads leading into it soon evolves into a circus-like environment. Inside the stone pillars marking the entrance to Crystal Beach, cars sit motionless in gridlock, hoping to get further in, to see something, to hear something.

On Old US 19 leading up to Crystal Beach, a traffic jam of over 1,000 vehicles lines the road, leading all the way back through Palm Harbor and beyond. The excited sightseers, many women and girls, call out from slowly moving or even roadside parked cars.[*]

---

[*]   *Clearwater Sun, August 30, 1949.*

Completing the event-like atmosphere, the Coast Guard helicopter searching the swamps five miles to the southwest, diverts to
Crystal Beach and joins the search there.

Rastus Russell may be a feared criminal and murderer. But he is
also a local sensation.

* * *

54

August 29ᵗʰ, 1949
Crystal Beach, FL
Afternoon

*J*ust prior to the report of Rastus Russell back in Crystal Beach, Sheriff Tucker makes two key decisions.

First, he dismisses the National Guard.

Secondly, he lifts all roadblocks in the area.

The Sheriff believes that as long as roadblocks remain in place, Russell may remain hidden. If they are lifted, he may come out in the open, where someone might see him.

Tucker knows the killer will be desperate. Living on the run is hard, especially in the hot, dirty, insect and reptile infested swamps of Pinellas County in August. Even for a seasoned local like Russell, lack of adequate food, shelter, and drink can break a man down quickly – and push him to desperate or careless acts.

Tucker knows that if he can prevent Russell from escaping the area, it will only be a matter of time before his fugitive surfaces.

But the Sheriff is losing patience with Rastus Russell. In addition to taxing and embarrassing his deputies and the entire law enforcement staff of two counties, this man has terrorized his community for nearly a month. Tucker has had enough. It's time to take the gloves off.

Tucker offers a $500 reward for the capture of Russell, "dead or alive." In doing so, he sends an implied but clear message to his officers and the general public: "If you see him, shoot him."

* * *

It is just after 12:00 noon when a small contingent of officers, including J.E. Holder of the Dunedin Police Department, enter the former home of Norman Y. Browne. The scene inside is eerie, having been little disturbed since police closed up the crime scene nearly three weeks earlier.

The home is still very much in disarray. While the bloody gore that lay on the floor and bedroom has been cleaned, the stain it left behind still lingers on the floorboards and bare mattresses. The section of barbed wire fence backed over by a fleeing Miles Crum still lies pressed into the high grass, exactly where Crum's back tires left it.

Officers and deputies meticulously comb through the house. Outside, dozens more search the outside of the property, the garage where Norman and Anne Browne were tied, and the perimeter of the yard. They also filter into the surrounding woods, supported by hordes of citizen volunteers.

Each hopes to catch a glimpse, trail or clue of Rastus Russell.

But by late afternoon, despite the exhaustive search, none is found.

Officer Holder reports that some men's clothing is missing, and a freshly smoked cigarette is found. How he would know men's clothing is missing is questionable. A smoked cigarette could be from nearly anyone. The observations prove little.

However, two "newspapermen" who had been in the house recently with Mr. Browne's attorney in an effort to retrieve personal papers, arrive to examine the home. These are men with every incentive to find any clue of a second Rastus Russell home invasion. They report no evidence that anything had been disturbed since their last visit with the attorney.*

In addition, while the media whips up speculation that Russell is bent on taking vengeance, he is a cunning escapee. While the convict may have a score to settle, he is being hunted like an animal and running for his life. He is likely looking for a place to hide and a route out of town, not making a bee-line to a witness to settle a score. There would be little incentive to return to the Browne home. Surely he knows that is one place his pursuers would wait for him.

---

*   *Clearwater Sun, August 30, 1949.*

As the hours pass by, the hopes of the officers and enthusiastic public has faded. Despite the frenzy, the Browne home rumor has indeed turned out to be just that.

It is interesting to note that at the very time swarms of armed men are scouring the woods around the Browne home for Russell, he is possibly, if not likely, still hunkered down in the basement of the burned out Junior High School, only a few blocks east of Crystal Beach.

* * *

Tucker's men are growing tired. In a day that has included slogging through some of the county's most unpleasant terrain in the brutal heat, chasing down dozens of empty leads, and the drama of phone calls and murder houses, the determined officers and deputies need a break. Many have not slept since Saturday night – now nearly forty eight hours. The Sheriff himself is suffering from lack of sleep. With nightfall only hours away, the all-out blitz to find the escapee may need to pause. A smaller force of fresher officers will continue to patrol for Russell through the night.

For citizens of Pinellas County, especially those in Palm Harbor and Crystal Beach, sleep will be hard to find. The boogie man they thought safely locked away is now outside their door again. In their minds, he is hungry and wants to feed. Russell's dramatic escape has elevated him from brutal murderer to near-mythic status. Across the county and beyond, fathers, mothers, and children have huddled around their radios, waiting for the next update on the search for the killer. Now, with doors and windows tightly locked, some sleep with loaded weapons while others take turns keeping watch.

"(You would) have to close all windows when you went to sleep at night," says Linda Henry. "...Every household slept with a gun nearby because that is when Rastus would get out and roam."

No one feels safe.

No one.

* * *

55

In 1949, Citrus Park is a tiny farming community about seventeen miles Northwest of Tampa. As its name implies, it consists mostly of orange groves. Like Palm Harbor, it also has its share of cattle ranches, given its abundance of fertile, flat land.

At the northern end of Citrus Park is an African American farming community.

It is here at the corner of Gunn Highway and Tampashores Road* that Raleigh Allen has established his small grocery and filling station to serve his neighbors, many of whom are family.

It is late on Monday Night, August 29th, when an intruder slinks around to the front window of the little grocery store.

Fifteen miles to the west in Palm Harbor, a night shift of lawmen continues to patrol city streets and isolated country roads for Rastus Russell. Even at this hour, they continue to field tips from rattled citizens who cannot sleep.

But here in the country, it's dead still. The only sounds are the steady shrill of a chorus of crickets, accompanied by a falsetto of bullfrogs, chirping tree frogs, Great Horned owls, Whippoorwills, and katydids. The grocer has long since gone home. Like most of his community who work hard during the day, he is sound asleep.

How Rastus Russell arrived here is a mystery. Sheriff Todd Tucker will later speculate that the fugitive may have hitchhiked. But

---

*   *Tampashores Road is now called Racetrack Road.*

given the news sensation Russell has become, it seems unlikely he would risk hitching a ride.

Russell has spent the day resting and hiding out in the basement of Palm Harbor Junior High. But with night falling around 8:30 p.m., he not only needs to move, he needs to eat. And if he is going to make a break for the state line, as he told Ray McClaury, he will need money.

Gathering such resources will be safer and easier in the areas between Palm Harbor and Tampa, areas in which Russell is intimately familiar. Here, he knows not only backroads and escape routes but establishments most likely to provide easy targets. Hitting the road and hoping to accumulate resources in unfamiliar territory would be infinitely more fraught with risk.

Russell knows Raleigh's store. He has passed it countless times on his commutes between Palm Harbor and Tampa. He rarely takes main roads, preferring the barely traveled country roads of north Pinellas and Hillsborough counties. That he would travel fifteen miles out of Palm Harbor to resupply himself seems questionable. Then again, it makes sense in a roundabout kind of way: Palm Harbor is simply too "hot" with law enforcement and an armed citizenry swarming around town like angry hornets. To hit one of his old haunts would be asking for trouble, especially if he plans to stay in Palm Harbor.

Instead, this quiet little corner of Citrus Park might do just fine tonight.

Creeping around the front of the store, the lock pick uses some type of winch to pry open the front shutters. Once open, he rips away the plastic screening from the window and climbs through the window.

The burglar leaves blood on the window and sill where he enters. Either he cuts himself in breaking through the window, or he is still bleeding from an old wound. If the latter is the case, it suggests a serious laceration, likely involving an artery or vein.

Parched, the intruder first bounds to the red and white Coca-Cola cooler in front of the counter. Reaching inside, he pulls out a cold bottle of orange drink, pops the cap on the opener on the front of the machine, and partially chugs the contents. He plops the half-empty bottle down on the counter, stamping another splotch of blood on the wooden surface as he does.

Refreshed, the thief can now go to work. Shifting attention to the "jook organ," he jimmies open the cover, revealing the coin box inside.

Leaving more blood on the music box, he pockets the coins. Owner Raleigh Allen reports the theft yielded approximately $20 in nickels; it is later speculated that the burglar's take consisted only of pennies.[*]

The robber then grabs a box of peanut butter crackers, a box of cookies, and a carton of cigarettes. Downing the rest of the orange drink, he sets the empty bottle atop the cooler from which he took it.[*]

Cradling the stolen booty in one arm, the bleeding robber crawls back through the same window from which he entered and vanishes into the singing darkness.

* * *

It is approximately 7:00 a.m. on Tuesday morning when Raleigh Allen hears a knock on his front door. Allen is just sitting down to breakfast before leaving to open his store.

His visitor is a friend. The friend tells him that he had just passed by Raleigh's store and noticed the front window to his store was wide open.

Allen is a slightly heavy-set, middle-aged African American man. He is known to be good-natured, quick with a joke, and quicker to laugh. Already dressed in his work attire, a thigh-length white grocer jacket, and a white cap worn by meat cutters or fry cooks at a hamburger stand, Allen rushes to his store.

Discovering the opened bloody window, damaged jukebox, and empty soda bottle, Raleigh hops back in his car and drives to the nearest payphone to call the police.

While he is gone, Hillsborough County Deputy Sheriff Bill Brooker pulls up to the front of the store. Brooker has been on alert since yesterday for any signs of Clearwater's violent prison escapee. In fact, it's weighed on his mind to the point he couldn't sleep last night. When first light arrives, Brooker is out the door. He has a hunch.

---

[*]   *Clearwater Sun, August 31, 1949.*

"...This morning, I set out for town with my wife and checked several houses to see if anybody might have seen him," Brooker explains. *"I stopped at Allen's place and found the window shutter jimmied open. Then I radioed the office for help. Pretty soon Allen came in. He had been out calling officers when I got here."*

Within the hour, more than twenty law enforcement vehicles are parked in the lot and along the road outside of Allen's country store. Among them are Sheriff Todd Tucker and Constable/Detective Walter Carey.

Over the last several weeks, Carey has become somewhat of a Rastus Russell expert. And although it is Tucker who is directing the investigation since the escape (and commanding the media spotlight,) it is Carey who is doing much of the behind-the-scenes detective work.

Carey is convinced the break-in is the work of Russell. The blood is a telling clue. But there is another reason Carey believes Russell is responsible.

"Whenever he stole cars in Tampa, he never traveled the same highways," Carey says. *"He always drove in these back roads where he has been going for years and knows every inch of them. That's why I think he's traveling around here now, because he knows this section."*

Carey believes Russell must be traveling in a stolen car. Earlier in the month, Russell boasted to Carey about his car-stealing prowess.

"I asked him where he'd get the wire to fix the car so it would start without a key," the constable remembers. *"He told me he didn't need a wire. He could take the little metal tips of his shoe laces and have a car ready to go in two minutes."*[**]

Again, all of the major players in yesterday's chase drama are summoned, this time to Citrus Park. Forensic expert J.F. Peacock arrives with his fingerprinting kit. And from Plant City, one of the busiest men in Central Florida over the last forty-eight hours, officer Harvey Frazier, is on scene with his reliable hound, Flip.

Flip, used to Russell's scent by now, darts feverously through the woods. Off goes a team of officers behind him, into the brush.

---

[*]   *Tampa Tribune, August 31, 1949.*
[**]   *Tampa Tribune, August 31, 1949.*

* * *

Fear can drive people to fast action. Back in Palm Harbor, jumpy citizens are growing restless.

Telephone switchboards and police departments in Tarpon Springs, Clearwater, and Dunedin are overwhelmed with calls asking for updates on Russell's chase. Russell has been "spotted" as far north as Anclote Key (north of Tarpon Springs), as far south as St. Petersburg, and just about everywhere in between.

In Clearwater, an ice delivery man complains it is taking him twice as long to cover his route. Telling a reporter that all the women have their doors and windows locked, he says they will not let him deliver his ice without close inspection, even though they know him.

One woman spreads the word that she is an excellent shot, hoping to dissuade any potential intruder from selecting her house.

With a large percentage of the population armed and getting twitchy, Tucker and other officers sense the growing risk of an accidental shooting. The Sheriff's office warns residents to refrain from making unnecessary trips at night in order to prevent such an event.

Tucker is also hampered by a posse of vehicles following his car every time he goes somewhere. He orders the public and media to stop following his car, feeling it is hampering the investigation.

While public participation in the hunt was both understandable and appreciated in the early part of the hunt for Russell, the Sheriff and his deputies realize the situation is getting out of hand.

Tucker issues a warning to those cruising the highways armed with weapons. Stressing that while he appreciates the cooperation from citizens, it is becoming counterproductive.

"It's a dangerous practice," Tucker barks, "and I won't tolerate it."

"If we need the citizens and their guns," he adds, "we'll let them know."[*]

The public may be scared, but they are also angry.

In Pinellas County, a group of prominent citizens draft a written appeal to Florida Governor Fuller Warren. The document demands an immediate and sweeping investigation into two subjects:

---

[*]   *Clearwater Sun, August 31, 1949.*

- The lack of punishment for Russell's long series of crimes in Pinellas County
- Russell's escape from the county jail on Sunday night

The document shows that suspicions about Russell's lifetime of incredulous "good luck" in regard to his criminal activities existed even in 1949.

The document's drafters will be happy to learn that a grand jury is convening the very next day to begin investigating the jailbreak in Clearwater only three days earlier.

Jailer Bryon Curry will not fare well.

As news that the burglary of Raleigh Allen's store might be the work of the dastardly Rastus Russell, the sleepy community of Citrus Park springs into high alert.

Like in Palm Harbor, Clearwater, and Crystal Beach, the residents of Citrus Park and nearby Keystone Lake arrive to assist in the search. As cars and pickup trucks begin convalescing around the tiny store, men and boys carrying rifles and strapped with sidearms emerge from vehicles. By midday, they number in the hundreds.

Keystone and other small lakes in the area are populated with splatters of vacation cottages and cabins, popular in both winter and summer. The news sends a chill through the out-of-town visitors, who are here for the sunny days and quiet nights. Those who travel with guns make them visible. Campers carrying shotguns or holstered pistols became a common sight in the little villages.

Their hosts are no less disquieted.

At El Rancharo Ranch on nearby Echo Lake, electricity is still out from Saturday's hurricane. This means the water pump does not work in the cottage community. Owners Mr. and Mrs. J.E. McGlamery must travel to a nearby waterworks to fetch water for their guests.

As Mr. McGlamery carries jugs to his vehicle by the camp, Mrs. McGlamery follows, an automatic shotgun propped defiantly on her shoulder. McGlamery's militant pose is featured in the Tampa Tribune.

* * *

It is not long before a slow-walking Officer Frazier returns from the line of towering Florida Pines behind the Raleigh Allen store. Flip has sniffed valiantly through the dense brush. But his efforts are of no avail. By the time Frazier arrives, both deputies and well-meaning citizens have already tracked around the store and through the woods so many times, too many new trails have been laid down for poor Flip to find Russell's.

As the deflated officers process the news, a new alarm sounds.

A breathless citizen volunteer bursts into Tucker's makeshift command center. He has just come from the church across the street. He has found footprints leading around the building.

The Mount Pleasant AME Church is a tiny, one-room church with an abbreviated steeple. The building sits adjacent to a small schoolhouse that the church has recently purchased. The church is nestled in a cozy thicket of bushy oak and poplar trees adjacent to a citrus grove. Sitting about 100 yards off the road with a long driveway, it is a center for the local African American community.

Frazier, Flip, and the team of pursuers, resting outside Allen's store from their jaunt through the woods, leap back into action. They rush across the street to find, sure enough, footprints leading all the way around the windowed structure.

Is Russell holed up inside?

Surrounding the building, officers burst through the chapel's front double doors, shotguns and pistols pointed inward, fingers curled tightly around triggers.

But the church is empty.

Again, men and dog scour the land around the building, the adjacent schoolhouse, the bordering citrus grove, even the on-property outhouse.

Again, Flip can't find a scent.

As officers scrape through the woodlands, a black and beige Ford with a Florida Highway Patrol logo on the door ambles up the church driveway. Two highway patrolmen step out.

"What's the all the excitement about?" one asks a deputy.

The deputy explained that footprints had been found.

The two patrolmen break into laughter.

"Those are our footprints!" the patrolman chuckles. "We went all around the church this morning looking for signs of Russell."[*]

The search comes to a grinding halt.

* * *

Despite the robbery the night before, Raleigh Allen is having a good day. While he lost about $20 in nickels (or $1.00 in pennies, no one knows for sure) and a few boxes of snacks, he is more than making up for it with the landslide business at his store. Between hungry, thirsty lawmen and citizen volunteers, Allen is selling out of supplies. His drink box empties so quickly that he has to suspend sales until a new load of drinks can be cooled.[*]

As evening descends and Pinellas lawmen return to their own county, Hillsborough officers and citizen volunteers regroup and launch an all-night search, hoping to catch the elusive Russell on the move.

But it will be fruitless.

By the time the first officer arrived on scene early this morning, Rastus Russell is already back in Palm Harbor.

If and how he committed the Citrus Park robbery will remain a mystery for the ages.

---

[*]   *Tampa Tribune, August 31, 1949.*

56

I n 1949, Avon Park is an isolated outpost in the deeply wooded
swamplands of central Florida. It is approximately eighty miles
southeast of St. Petersburg and over an hour's drive from Tampa.

It is well after midnight when Highway Patrolmen Gracy and
Hicks are traveling on Highway 98 about a mile north of town. There
is a light rain falling as they cruise up the dark, remote section of
highway leading through one of the many nearby swamps. A light fog
drifts above the surface of the pavement, adding to the isolated feeling
of the night.

Suddenly, the lawmen catch a glimpse of two men in the headlights. Sitting on a log just off the road, the men are eating food from
a sack.

Despite being an hour and a half drive from Clearwater, the
officers are aware of the statewide alert for Rastus Russell sent out by
Tucker's office the day before.

Seeing the approaching patrol car, the men drop the sack and flee
towards the woods.

In addition to the suspicious behavior, Gracy and Hicks believe
one of the men looks like the man in Tucker's photo.

The black and cream-colored Mercury Eight cruiser darts to
the side of the road and halts. Whereas modern-day patrolmen have
a carnival of red and blue lights to ignite while on an active call, Gracy
and Hicks have only a single red light mounted on top of their depart-
ment-issued vehicle. It is not the familiar rotating flash that we know

today. It is a solid red light that shines straight ahead, fading on and off. A siren is also mounted on the vehicle.

The patrolmen leap from the car and give chase, rumbling through the high grass. Through the shaky streams of their flashlights, they watch the suspicious men bound through the field and vanish into the tree line.

Gracy and Hicks call in the suspicious men before heading back towards the woods. Deputies from Sebring, the nearest law enforcement station, rush to the scene. The Highway Patrol, well aware of the Russell manhunt, is taking no chances. They request bloodhounds from both Lakeland and Plant City.

Whether the Plant City dogs are Frazier's is unknown. While Frazier is one of the few officers with trained dogs in the region, the Plant City officer has been in the swamps of Pinellas County all day and might still be there.

It is early morning on Tuesday, August 30, when Todd Tucker is awakened by a phone call. The bleary-eyed sheriff spent the night in his office, sleeping only a couple of hours.

Who called Tucker has been lost to history. But the man's message is clear.

Get in touch with Highway Patrol in Bartow. They might have your boy cornered in Avon Park.

* * *

It is well after sunrise when Pinellas County Deputies Carl McMullen and Parker Jackson arrive at an isolated, wooded area outside of Avon Park. They pull their personal car alongside the road with other cars from the Highway Patrol, Sebring Police, and Plant City Police. A team of bloodhounds has tracked the suspects through the woods and officers have apprehended the two men near a lake about a mile into the woods.

If Jackson and McMullen can confirm they have Rastus Russell in custody, they will make their boss, Todd Tucker, a happy man. This is likely their hope as they weave through the tall grass and into the woods where their suspects are confined.

Meeting the other officers, the Pinellas County Deputies join the other lawmen in questioning the men.

The two quickly realize that neither suspect is Russell. The haggard-looking men are hikers from Georgia. Why they ran from the patrol car the night before is unknown.

With nothing on which to hold them, the officers release the men.

Disappointed, Jackson and McMullen start back to Clearwater.

57

By the time dawn arrives on Tuesday morning, August 30th, Rastus Russell has possibly traveled fifteen miles to Citrus Park and fifteen miles back to Palm Harbor. He has presumably secured a little change and enough food to satisfy his ravenous hunger, at least for today. Running through swamps in 94-degree heat burns mountains of calories, especially for the thick-bodied Russell.

His risky supply run is no small feat.

Russell's ability to slip in and out of Palm Harbor without being detected by hoards of eager lawmen is impressive.

The escapee almost certainly didn't travel the fifteen miles to Citrus Park by foot. Therefore, he either stole a car to drive there and back, had help, or never went at all.

If the convict had help, one would think he would not need to steal a handful of pennies and return to Palm Harbor. He could instead hide out at a pal's home or even catch a ride out of town.

Thus, it seems likely that if Russell did commit the Citrus Park robbery, he stole a car to drive there and back. The fact that Russell only takes a handful of goods indicates that he had to park the vehicle far away and walk to the store, taking only what he could carry.

Walter Carey, in fact, suspects just this scenario. But no vehicle is reported stolen.

It is possible its owners were away, or he stole a car no one would know was missing. But criminals tend to repeat the same modus operandi. For the murder in Crystal Beach, Russell stole a Ford in Tampa, used it to commit his crime, and then returned it to the same spot in which he found it. It seems reasonable to suspect that Russell could have used this same strategy for a quick jaunt over to Citrus Park and back to Palm Harbor. If this is the case, the owner may never have known it was "borrowed," at least not for a while.

Another possibility is Russell destroys the car. Is the car with skis and northern license plates that Wilburn Crain remembers burning in the woods near the Crain home the same car Russell used to travel to Citrus Park? Crain couldn't remember the time frame, only that it was "around the time" when the Russell story was unfolding.

Being this is the only crime in which the car used was not accounted for, it is certainly a possibility. This is especially true given Rastus Russell's whereabouts that Tuesday morning.

For it is daylight again and time to lay low. Smart enough not to spend two days in the same place, Russell does not return to his school building sanctuary. Instead, he is back on Curlew Creek Road and frightfully close to the Sam Crain house, the place where he spent so many quiet days and felt the first pangs of attraction for young Dorothy Jean.

Surely, he knows, or at least suspects, that if he comes within viewing distance of Crain's home, he will be shot on sight. Yet, one has to wonder how deep the bitter pull of revenge is tugging on the disturbed Russell. These are people Russell considered family. He lived with them, ate with them, fished with them, and presumably, drank with them. He considers Dorothy Jean his "wife" and the Crain family his "in-laws." And now they have committed this most treacherous act against him, betrayal.

There are no direct quotes on record of Russell swearing vengeance against the Crains, only Tucker's comment that Russell made them from the jailhouse. We'll never know how deeply Russell was committed to getting revenge. But given his proximity to the Crain home on this morning, we must at least consider that Russell is pondering it, even if it means risking his life.

Or, it could simply be that Russell is familiar with this area and knows a safe place to hide. For it is here, he finds one.

Slipping amongst the sparse farmhouses and sprawling woods along Curlew Creek Road, the fugitive finds an unlocked outbuilding near the edge of the woods. Ducking inside before daybreak, Russell, safely out of sight again, beds down for the day.

It should be noted that the outbuilding where Russell is thought to have slept on Tuesday morning is less than a mile from the Crain's home – the vague but exact description given by Wilburn Crain as to the location where the burned car was found.

It would make sense that if Russell dumped the car near Curlew Creek Road and continued on foot, he would likely be seeking shelter in that area.

Thus it is at least a possibility that the car Wilburn Crain remembers burned in the woods was the car Russell used to drive to Citrus Park and back on Monday night.

* * *

It has been a tumultuous month for Dorothy Jean Crain. Not only does she find out the man living with her is a murderer, but she has also gone through the trauma of helping police trap and arrest him, and then herself spent nearly three weeks locked in a jail cell across from the very cellblock where the man is incarcerated.

She has endured the pressure and embarrassment of becoming a local celebrity, albeit for all the wrong reasons.

She then witnesses a brutal assault on a prison guard and watches the man who calls her his "wife" escape the jail before her very eyes. She knows her family is in danger and has gone into hiding. All of this is on top of the daily grind of spending life locked inside a hot, sweaty prison cell with women who have committed crimes.

It is more than a sixteen-year-old country girl can be expected to handle.

And yet, she seems to handle it with poise. When *True Experiences* magazine called her at the Pinellas County Jail two weeks ago, they offered her $75 for her exclusive story. Perhaps for the money, perhaps for the celebrity and validation any sixteen-year-old craves, or perhaps simply out of a need to tell her side of the story, young Dorothy agrees.

On Tuesday, August 30th, with Rastus Russell still on the loose and the Crain family in hiding, a writer and photographer from *True Experiences* arrive at the Pinellas County Jail. At the time she agreed to the interview, Russell was safely locked behind bars, and Dorothy expected to be released any day. Although the situation has changed drastically, she proceeds with the interview. The magazine spends half of a day interviewing the girl and taking photographs.

Bob Prichard's 1955 article appearing in *For Men Only* features a photograph of a smiling Dorothy Jean Crain talking on the telephone. This photograph is believed to have been taken at the Pinellas County Jail by the photographer that day.

The feature article in *True Experiences*, "He Held Me Prisoner – Dorothy Jean Crain's harrowing Story of Escape from a Killer's Love," appears in the February 1950 issue of the magazine. Dorothy Jean, wearing a red dress with black polka dots and sporting pigtails tied in black ribbons, graces the cover.*

The glamour shot, showing the girl's perfectly styled, sandy brown hair and brown eyes looking to the left corner of the cover, was almost certainly taken inside the walls of the jailhouse. Three months later, in the May issue of the same magazine, Marilyn Monroe graces the cover.

Dorothy Jean is in good company.

When the magazine appears on newsstands four months later, Dorothy Jean Crain receives fan mail and love letters from around the country.

* * *

Back in Clearwater early Tuesday morning, Sheriff Todd Tucker is once again at a dead end.

As the Sheriff stews in his jailhouse office, the city of Clearwater wakes up around him. By 8:00 a.m., the sun is already baking the asphalt streets and concrete sidewalks. Soon, they will be sticky, blazing skillets. There may be a killer on the loose, but the people of Clearwater still have to go to work. While it's the offseason for tourists, a handful of hearty vacationers still pack picnic baskets in their

---

* *Despite an exhaustive effort, we were unable to secure a copy of this article to review for this book. However, in Prichard's 1955 piece in For Men Only, he is believed to have used the True Experiences interview to tell Dorothy's version of events. Thus, the story itself is covered in this book. The cover of this magazine is displayed in the photo section of this book. Anyone in possession of this magazine or the article itself, please contact the author of this book.*

trunks and cheerfully head for the white sands of Clearwater Beach, killer be damned.

Tucker himself would no doubt rather be enjoying a morning cup of coffee looking over his cattle ranch.

Not this morning. Rastus Russell has seen to that.

The Sheriff has spent the night tromping through the woods around Citrus Park with a weary band of Pinellas and Hillsborough County Deputies. Searching for any sign of their fleeing prisoner with a fresh team of dogs, they have again come up empty-handed. Tucker, has spent almost all of the last forty-eight hours awake. Blue rings have swollen beneath his sagging eyes.

While the scope of the Russell search has now expanded to Hillsborough County, Tucker, his men, nor anyone else has any idea where the fugitive is.

The Sheriff now must rely on catching a lucky break. But Tucker believes Russell is still in the area. The food he stole won't last long. The experienced lawman knows his fugitive will have to surface again soon.

.

58

August 30, 1949
Ozona, FL
Evening

It's well after dark on Tuesday night, August 30th, when Rastus Russell once again walks up the front steps of Willa Mae Skinner's home. Her Ozona house is about three miles from where Russell left his daytime hideout near Curlew Creek Road.

The fugitive has wisely elected to skip visiting Sam Crain's home and walked the three miles through back roads and wilderness trails to reach Ozona once again.

While Willa Mae claims to be afraid of Russell, the fugitive obviously trusts her, else he wouldn't be visiting again. After all, she gave him food once and will likely, at least Russell believes, provide it again.

Willa Mae answers the door, and again, a conversation ensues. We do not know what is said. However, Russell makes an "appointment" to see her on Thursday at 8 a.m. While we cannot know what the arrangement was, it is presumed that Russell asks the woman for food and/or supplies.

Despite her prior relationship with Russell's mother, Willa Mae cannot bring herself to continue to help the fugitive. Sometime between the time Russell leaves and the following evening, she contacts the Pinellas County Sheriff's Office.

Responding deputies are at first skeptical of Willa Mae's intriguing story. However, they decide it would be a serious error to neglect any possible lead. One must imagine the conversation between the deputies, one painting the verbal picture of the two standing before a furious Todd Tucker after Rastus Russell escapes again in Ozona.

The deputies agree to set a trap for Russell. They will wait in the weeds around the Skinner house on Thursday morning and see who shows up.*

But by Thursday morning, the playing field will have shifted dramatically. The events of the next several hours will overshadow the encounter with Willa Mae on Tuesday night.

It is not known how Rastus Russell spends the rest of his night after visiting her.

His whereabouts are unknown until exactly 4:20 a.m. Wednesday morning.

---

* *St. Petersburg Times, September 2, 1949. The article reports that Russell set the appointment with Willa Mae on Wednesday night but also says she spoke to reporters Wednesday night. It seems unlikely these two things happened on the same night. Given that Russell is thought to have been in Tampa or even Thonotosassa on Wednesday night, it is likely that the newspaper simply misstated the night of Russell's visit. It is also possible that Willa Mae is confused and/or the deputy's skepticism is warranted. However, this version of events – that Russell visited on Tuesday - seems most feasible given the other pieces to the puzzle.*

59

August 31, 1949
Palm Harbor, FL
4:20 a.m.

D.B. Fowler is awake.

Fowler is not accustomed to hearing many noises at this hour, at least not on this quiet western edge of Palm Harbor. That is why the car engine cranking outside his bedroom window summoned him from sleep.

Fowler turns to look at the alarm clock beside his bed. It's 4:20 a.m.

The engine fails to turn over, then begins cranking again.

Curious, Fowler climbs out of bed and shuffles to his window. Everything looks dark and quiet. On his secluded Palm Harbor street off of Old US 19, homeowners typically turn out their lights at night, even porch lights, to save electricity. He notes lights at his neighbor's house a few doors up and across the street. Fowler knows this man drives a taxi.

Fowler then watches a car drift slowly past his house. Its headlights are off, making the vehicle hard for Fowler to identify in the dark. As the car reaches the highway, the lights switch on. The car lazily pulls onto Old US 19 and turns south towards Dunedin.

It must be his taxi-driving neighbor leaving early for work, Fowler reasons.

Satisfied, he crawls back under his covers and fades back to sleep.

* * *

Cruising down Old US Highway 19, John Calvin Russell has a fresh set of wheels. For now, he does not change the license plate,

Florida 4-4423, Pinellas County. The bluish-gray Ford Sedan is a fairly new 1948 model. For some reason, its paint has a pink tint, a detail its new driver will not notice until daylight. Regardless, it is the perfect vehicle for a long trip.

Throughout his crime spree of 1949, Russell shows a preference for stealing V-8 Fords, the same car favored by Clyde Barrow fifteen years earlier. Barrow liked the cars for their big engines and fast speeds – enabling him to outrun most police cars. Russell may have preferred them for the same reason, especially if he is considering a run for the state line.

But traveling requires money and supplies, things of which Rastus Russell is presently short. Not to mention, his new cruiser is low on gas.

Not to worry. Russell has another stop in mind.

Only three blocks from where he used a metal wire to pry the ignition switch and start his new vehicle, Russell turns right onto Pennsylvania Avenue. Less than a block from the highway sits Lipsey's Shell Station.*

J.R. "Roscoe" Lipsey has run the service station for only six weeks, taking over from the former owners. Located in a strategic location across the railroad tracks from the Palm Harbor Train Station, Lipsey hopes to benefit from selling fuel and snacks to those traveling to and from the train.

Rastus Russell is taking a risk operating in Palm Harbor, where the search for him is more aggressive than almost anywhere else. But the fugitive has a plan.

Besides, Lipsey's station is out of view from the heavily patrolled main highway, likely a reason Russell chose it over downtown Palm Harbor landmarks such as Barlow's or "Pop" Stansel's station.

Russell brazenly rolls his new Ford to a halt at the front door of Lipsey's, right beside the gas pumps. He kills the headlights. Closing his driver's side door gently so as not to make a sound, the experienced burglar tiptoes to the office door of the filling station.

Although he can pick almost any lock, Russell chooses to bypass solving the Yale lock on the door in favor of a more direct mode of

---

* *The building housing Lipsey's Shell Station is still standing. Today it is known as McBee's Garage.*

entry. He punches a hole through the small glass window adjacent the door. He reaches through and turns the door lock.

Roscoe Lipsey carries a fair amount of groceries at his filling station, a fact of which Russell is aware and likely a reason for targeting the business. Unlike his venture in Citrus Park, Russell has a car parked outside. This time, he can stock up.

He does.

The fugitive methodically begins hauling out merchandise and loading it into the trunk of the sedan.

His haul includes two cases of Coca-Cola, two cases of Pepsi, eight open cartons of cigarettes, including Herbert Tareyton's,[*] (Russell is a heavy smoker and tobacco user. Running from the law is a stressful business, meaning his appetite for tobacco is likely as strong or stronger than his desire for food,) two boxes of cigars, several cans of tobacco, six packages of matches, two boxes of candy bars, eight to ten loaves of bread (all of the bread in the store,) along with miscellaneous cookies and cakes. He also grabs three glass jars of peanuts, of which Russell, strangely, leaves the lids inside the filling station.

With his vehicle loaded with tobacco, food, and drink, Russell moves to the cash register. Here, like in Citrus Park, he again strikes out. Before leaving his shop on Tuesday evening, Roscoe Lipsey removed the cash from his register. All that remains is a slot full of pennies, about $1.00 worth. Russell scoops them out and shovels them into his pants pocket.

Considering Russell's most pressing needs—food, drink, tobacco, cash, and gas—Lipsey's would seem to be an efficient place to rob.

There is just one more commodity to secure. A full tank of gas and Russell will be ready for a long trip.

While we cannot know what is bouncing through Rastus Russell's mind, it seems a good bet he is preparing to make a run for the state

---

[*] *In 1949, Tareyton's were branded as an upscale cigarette with a slogan of "Discriminating people prefer Herbert Tareyton." The ad campaign features prominent people in society giving testimonials. The campaign is apparently successful as newspaper reports specifically mention Tareyton cigarettes being stolen, as though this is a greater crime than merely stealing "regular" cigarettes. Source: www.tobacco.img. standord.edu)*

line. He knows he cannot live under this kind of heat forever. If he stays in Palm Harbor or even in the Tampa Bay area, he is almost certain to be apprehended sooner or later. He's already told Ralph McClaury his plan: lay low for a while and then make a run "out of the country." To get out of the country, he must first get out of Florida.

In 1949, crossing a state line led to wider jurisdictional issues than it does today. Coordination between law enforcement was not nearly as efficient. Often, simply leaving a state was enough to set a criminal free of pursuit from the law.

Russell spent the last seven years, though some of it incarcerated, in the wide-open Midwest. If he is nothing else, he is a creature of habit. He knows that area and doubtlessly has contacts there. His 1943 draft registration card lists him as being married and living in Gary, Indiana. There is every reason to believe he plans to head back to the nation's breadbasket and not out of the country.

But there is a problem. Whether Lipsey has locked the gas pump or Russell cannot figure out how to work the pump mechanism, the convict cannot force any gasoline out. The fugitive tries desperately to make it work. He begins pounding, scraping, and grinding on the nozzle, handle, and pump itself in a vain effort to draw the liquid fuel.

It is of no avail.

He has made enough noise. It is time to go. Russell climbs back into the Ford and quietly cruises into the night. Lipsey's has been a limited success. But the fugitive cannot run without gas. His mission this early morning is still incomplete.

It's nearly 5:30 a.m. when D.B. Fowler wakes again. His sleep has been restless. Something about that car is bothering him. Like everyone else in Palm Harbor, Fowler has heard and read the news reports. He has watched as officers from around the region converged on his normally quiet little town in search of a desperate fugitive. Perhaps this puts him in a heightened state of suspicion. Fowler decides to investigate.

Stepping outside his front door in the emerging twilight of dawn, Fowler notices that the car of his next-door neighbors, James and Ruth Smith, is not in the driveway. Fowler knows what time Smith goes to work at a lumber yard, and it's not 5:30 a.m. It is then that Fowler notices that his own vehicle, a pickup truck parked beside Smith's in the adjacent driveway, has been left with the driver's side door open. It appears someone has tried to siphon gas.

Fowler rushes to his neighbor's house and begins yelling outside the home. When there is no answer, Fowler runs up the front steps and pounds on the door, finally awakening the Smiths.

It is close to 5:45 a.m. when Ruth Smith calls the police to report her car stolen.

* * *

Less than an hour later and only three blocks away, a bakery delivery man is making his regular stop at Lipsey's filling station. The delivery man typically leaves bread at the door for Lipsey to collect when he opens his shop.

Immediately seeing the broken glass, the man calls police.

Lipsey arrives shortly afterward, unaware of the break-in, only to find police cars surrounding his business.

* * *

Todd Tucker is just waking up to the news of two thefts in Palm Harbor, the calls coming in almost simultaneously. While the investigations are barely underway, Tucker already suspects Russell.

The sheriff's strategy of lifting roadblocks has worked. Tucker's rabbit has come out of its hole.

Tucker's first order is to immediately reestablish roadblocks along all major and minor roads. The prey is vulnerable in the open. That's where Tucker will have his best chance of taking him.

But Rastus Russell is already out of Pinellas County.

Tucker is just beginning to process the news of his two Palm Harbor crime scenes when he gets his third riveting call of the morning. It's the Hillsborough County Sheriff's Department. A man just bought gas in a gas can at a Tampa filling station. The man paid with pennies, had a cut on his left hand, and was on foot. The station attendants believe it was Russell.

Tucker's rabbit is back in Tampa.

60

As sheriff deputies interview James Smith, the Palm Harbor resident gives police two key pieces of information.

First, he and his wife had just returned from a trip to Georgia. Traveling the backroads of the southern state had kicked up plenty of red clay dust, coating the car's blue-gray paint and giving it a pinkish hue.

Secondly, Smith estimates there were only about four gallons of gas in the tank. This is enough to get the thief a fair distance but not too far.

In fact, it is enough to get to the corner of Nebraska Avenue and North Bay Street in the Sulphur Springs area of Tampa. This is where Rastus Russell's stolen Ford sedan runs out of gas. This is also the general area where the car used in the Browne murder is found, where W.J. Graham is robbed and given a fatal beating, and where Russell's part-time home, that of Maud McCord, is located.

W.L. Pritchett, 53, and Ellwood Shealy, 33, are working at the filling station on the crossroad at 6:30 a.m. Shealy worked the overnight shift, and the older Pritchett has just arrived to work the daytime shift.

With Russell's known home in the neighborhood, Pritchett and Shealy, like most of their north Tampa neighbors, are following the Russell story. As twenty-four-hour filling station attendants, the two are not unaccustomed to interacting with odd characters.

Thus, when they note a haggard-looking man approaching the store on foot, the men are not overly suspicious.

"He had a couple days growth of beard and looked exhausted," notes Pritchett.

The clerks describe the man as 30 to 35 years old with black hair and brown eyes. They later tell police he was wearing dirty khaki trousers and a red shirt.

The stranger walks to the counter where Pritchett meets him.

"He asked me if I had an extra gasoline can," explains Pritchett, "and when I said I did, he said he wanted two gallons in it."

Pritchett fills the can with the requested amount and hands it to the man.

"This is regular gas, isn't it?" asks the man. "I don't want high test. I want to use it to mix some paint."

When Pritchett confirms it is, the stranger pulls out a handful of pennies and counts out 53 cents. As he does, the clerk notices a large cut on the stranger's left hand, between the thumb and forefinger.

"He seemed nervous counting them," adds Prichett. "Then he walked out fast, going west on North Bay, looking back over his shoulder a few times."

As the stranger walks off with the filled gas can, Pritchett has no idea it is John Calvin "Rastus" Russell, accused murderer, escapee, and infamous fugitive. But he has an odd feeling. The man acted strange… and that cut. Didn't they say Russell had cut his hand? Shealy, finishing up his end-of-shift duties, does not pay much attention to the interaction, only getting a cursory look at the strange customer.

When Pritchett suggests to Shealy that the man might have been Rastus Russell, Shealy scoffs.

"Oh no," he tells Pritchett, "That's not Russell. I know Russell!"

Shealy is referring to knowing *of* Russell, having seen him several times from living in the Sulphur Springs neighborhood near the home of Maud McCord.

Shealy goes home, and Pritchett continues his shift, nearly forgetting his early morning encounter.

* * *

Back in Clearwater, the public is just reading about the Citrus Park robbery in the newspaper. But that is not the only story of the day.

Sheriff Todd Tucker is in damage control mode. And Dorothy Jean Crain is becoming a local celebrity.

True Experiences Magazine reps were not the only visitors the teenager hosted yesterday. Hearing of the publication's visit, local reporters showed up to report on the national magazine's visit. St.

Petersburg Times photographer Al Hackett, the same photographer to snap Rastus Russell's photo at the jail, is among those present to photograph Dorothy Jean.

Given the present situation, not to mention her experience of the last thirty days, the sixteen-year-old displays remarkable poise.

Charming the crowd, Dorothy jokes with jailers, reporters, and the other women prisoners.

She says that with John (Rastus) Russell on the loose, jail might not be such a bad place to be. However, she adds that if Russell is caught, she would like to go home. She says she would be glad if he is caught and that she fears for her family's safety.

Personal trauma notwithstanding, the teenager has shown hints of embracing the notoriety. As Bob Prichard notes in his 1955 piece, as he and others stood on the shore watching the girl and her brothers wade in from the flats of Dunedin with Russell still fleeing police, she initially hid her face from photographers. However, when prodded, young Dorothy removed her hat and sunglasses, fluffed her wet hair, and crowed, "Shoot!"

One can sense the image transition of Dorothy Jean Crain, or as Tucker refers to her, "the Crain girl," from potential suspect and girlfriend of a killer to media darling. The media, now seeming to be on Dorothy's side, wants to know why she is still in jail. Why is Tucker still holding her?

Responding to questions about Dorothy's continued incarceration, Tucker attempts to share some of the decisions to keep the girl confined with State Attorney Chester McMullen. Tucker states that he met with McMullen yesterday and that the two agree she should be held because her family is "the floating type" and probably would leave town if she were not held. In other words, she is still being held as a material witness.

But the Sheriff has bigger fish to fry today than questions about Dorothy Jean Crain. In addition to the chase for Rastus Russell, the heat for Sunday's prison escape keeps getting hotter. With citizens drafting letters to the governor, media asking questions, a grand jury investigation, and Russell still on the loose, the escape is not reflecting well on the Pinellas County Sheriff's office. And that means it's not reflecting well on the Pinellas County Sheriff.

Should Russell disappear and never be recaptured, it will not play well in the next election and would leave a permanent stain on Tucker's law enforcement legacy. Tucker now has skin in the game. Catching Rastus Russell is not only what is best for the community, but it will also go a long way toward alleviating Tucker's political headaches, which seem to be growing more acute by the day.

To complicate matters, residents of Crystal Beach are complaining that the National Guardsman posted to guard Thelma Crum and her little store have disappeared, leaving the victim and witness unprotected. The same complaint is made about the Crain home on Curlew Creek Road, where deputies are no longer present. Apparently, the men were redeployed to Citrus Park on Tuesday morning to help in the search for Russell.

And so, it is little surprise that Tucker has had only three hours sleep in the last seventy-two hours. Now, on this Wednesday morning, with two fresh strikes from Tucker's fugitive, the sheriff must address questions that are piling up.

First, he advises John Chestnut, chairman of the Pinellas County Commission, that he has redeployed guards to the homes of Sam Crain, Thelma Crum, and the secret location of Anne Browne.

Tucker then addresses the media's questions about Russell's escape.

The sheriff blames both the jail and the jailer.

He states that the jail is overcrowded and obsolete, forcing jailers to house dangerous criminals like Russell with small-time offenders like McClaury.

He then torches Jailer Bryan Curry, stating Curry was negligent in forgetting to lock the downstairs door and forgetting to take the proper keys with him upstairs.

Lastly, Tucker blames the fact that there was only one jailer on duty, the second deputy still out on a call when Russell made his play.

Tucker states the truth in all three cases. But it does not erase the fact that, much like today, the person at the top must accept the ultimate blame.

Yes, it sure would help to catch Rastus Russell.

But there is likely a third motivator in play now, aside from public duty and career politics.

Pride.

The convict escaped from Tucker's jail, embarrassing the Sheriff and bringing a wave of pressure down on his head. Tucker takes personal pride in being good at his job. There is no way he's going to let some wily little weasel like Rastus Russell make him look the fool.

It's personal now.

*   *   *

Despite W.L. Prichett's suspicion that the man who purchased gas from him early this morning was Rastus Russell, Pritchett takes Shealy's opinion that it's not the fugitive. He doesn't call police.

But somebody else does.

Sometime shortly after the strange man buys two gallons of gas from Pritchett, a call comes into the Hillsborough County Sheriff's office. There is a suspicious individual walking along a road near Nebraska Avenue. The caller thinks it might be Russell.

Virtually every law enforcement agency in West Florida has been fielding a slew of nonstop "Russell tips" for the past forty-eight hours. Thus, when this one comes to the Sheriff's office, nobody gets too excited. Two deputies are sent to investigate.

Canvassing the neighborhood, the deputies flash Russell's photo to residents, asking if they've seen him. They have little luck until they reach the filling station at the corner of Nebraska and North Bay. It is there that W.L. Pritchett sees the photo and tells deputies that it is the man who came to his station early this morning. When Prichett tells the lawmen his story, the clothes, the cut on the hand, the deputies immediately call headquarters.

When Shealy is called back to the station to talk to deputies, he initially doesn't believe the man was Russell.

"I had seen Russell several times when he lived over here," Shealy tells a reporter, "and, although I didn't get a close look at this fellow this morning, I didn't think it was Russell…his hair looked different than I remembered it."

But after reviewing a recent photo presented by the deputies, Shealy changes his mind.

"...when a detective came around and showed me a new picture of Russell, I felt pretty sure he was the man I saw this morning," adds the night clerk.

As Hillsborough Deputies and Tampa Police officers flock to the scene, tracking dogs are once again summoned.

When Tucker gets the late morning call, he leads a sizable contingent of his twenty-five deputies racing to Sulphur Springs.

Not only does Tucker assume command of the search, the newly energized Sheriff, rifle propped on shoulder, personally joins the tracking team in combing the surrounding woods and neighborhoods.

The dogs aren't the only ones smelling Rastus Russell's proximity.

* * *

It's early afternoon on Wednesday when Maud McCord hears car engines outside.

Looking out the front window, McCord watches a total of eight police cruisers, some personal vehicles, some marked cars, halt abruptly on the street outside her home. As armed officers pour out of vehicles, the aging McCord sees them surrounding her house. Several approach the front door.

When McCord lets them in, the officers fan out through the home. Others comb around the outside of the house, garage, and yard. Having been here before, the officers know where to look. There is no record of what conversation took place between McCord and the officers.

After a thorough search, they do not find Russell. The only potential clue is a fresh set of tire tracks in the driveway.

* * *

Back in Palm Harbor, Crystal Beach developer Fred Sage is reviewing the building remains of the Palm Harbor High School.* After discovering footprints leading down to the basement, Sage discovers what appears to be a place by the boiler where someone slept. Sage notifies deputies.

---

* *Why Sage was there is unknown. It may be he is involved in the rebuilding plan.*

Investigators note the approximate shoe size of the footprints. They are size ten, the size Russell wears.

On Curlew Creek Road, a resident discovers that someone has been inside an outbuilding of his property. When deputies arrive, they find 51 pennies on the floor where the person appears to have stayed.

* * *

The information dump of the past twenty-four hours has police, reporters, amateur sleuths, and everyday citizens trying to guess where Rastus Russell might be and where he might show up next.

At this point, no one knows for certain if the robberies in Citrus Park or Palm Harbor are actually Russell. When forensic officer J.F. Peacock announces that no prints found at either site match Russell's, speculation grows even further. However, Peacock is quick to point out that there were many prints inside both crime scenes, and not finding one of Russell's is inconclusive either way.

He also notes that the jukebox inside Raleigh Allen's store had the top skillfully removed, indicating the work of an experienced thief. The only prints found, however, are those of some of the store's regular customers.

Some speculate that Russell has already left the area. Others question why Russell would go to Tampa and then double back all the way to Palm Harbor, where a virtual armed camp is looking for him.

In addition, outside of the Tampa filling station attendants, no one has actually seen Rastus Russell since his escape Sunday night.

But the news of Russell's sighting this morning has awakened the city of Tampa. They are now part of the sensational story from across the bay and the biggest manhunt in Bay Area history.

The grapevine begins running wild. As the massive manhunt is still unfolding in Sulphur Springs, calls flood the switchboards of the Sheriff's Office, Highway Patrol, and Tampa Tribune. Russell has been captured. Russell is cornered. Russell is sighted in North, South, East, and West Tampa. Russell has been shot at the Farmer's Market. He abandoned his car in Lowry Park. He was hiding in the swamps at Six Mile Creek. He is at Waring's Fishing Camp near the Gandy

Bridge. Was parked along the road between Hillsborough State Park and Thonotosassa.

While it is impossible to know which, if any, of these reports is valid, the last one, knowing what we know now, is intriguing.

The only thing for certain is where Rastus Russell is not. That is, the woods and neighborhoods around the filling station in Sulphur Springs, where he was at 6:30 this morning. Although Todd Tucker, his deputies, tracking dogs, and another army of police and armed citizens will search well into the night, they will once again come up empty.

Two gallons of gas will be enough to keep this fugitive out of harm's way for another night.

61

August 31, 1949
Thonotosassa, FL
Approximate 10:00 p.m.

I f Crystal Beach and Palm Harbor are small, rural beach communities, Thonotosassa is absolute wilderness.

Located about thirteen miles northeast of Tampa, the tiny community's centerpiece is Lake Thonotosassa, a picturesque freshwater lake that is the largest in Hillsborough County. While city dwellers from Tampa are known to visit the lake on weekends, the hidden treasure is primarily enjoyed by the locals.

1949 Thonotosassa, outside of the tiny town and occasional country home, is almost entirely made up of citrus groves. In fact, the citrus industry is the largest employer in the area. Outside of the lake and groves, there are only dirt roads and swamps. The area is sparsely populated and strikingly beautiful.

It is here that John Calvin Russell was born and lived to the age of ten. It is here that his grandfather, Dr. Thomas Baker, a pioneer resident, drove a horse and buggy in the 1880s, settled with his grandmother, Mary Eliza Rigby (Baker,) and raised eight children. It is here, in Thonotosassa Cemetery on the northeast corner of the little town, where Claude Estelle Baker McCoy, Russell's mother, is buried.

And it is to here, chased to the point of near exhaustion, that Rastus Russell comes home. While we can't know the exact reasons Russell chooses to retreat here, they seem semi-obvious.

For one, while Palm Harbor is his adopted home, Thonotosassa is the home of his early childhood. It is here that Russell was surrounded by family, living in a large household with his grandmother and several aunts and uncles. As an illegitimate child, it is unknown how he is treated by the family or how he feels about them later. But he may feel more comfortable in an area where he has relatives and/or old friends, perhaps willing to provide shelter or assistance.

Secondly, he may have wished to visit his mother's grave before leaving town. Locals in Palm Harbor who know Russell believe this is the entire reason he went to Thonotosassa. While this is possible, Russell has been in the area for nearly six months. It is likely he has already visited his mother's grave. Perhaps he wishes to visit one more time before leaving the state permanently. However, it seems unlikely this would be the only reason the fugitive retreats to the small town.

Lastly, and most importantly, Thonotosassa is a great place to hide. Its sprawling swamps and orange groves provide ample places to stay out of sight, especially for someone who knows them in and out. It is likely that Russell plans to regroup here for a few days, perhaps collect more gas, money, and/or supplies before making a break for the state line.

He knows the places to start looking for those things.

It is nearly 10 p.m. on this muggy Wednesday evening when Rosa O'Brien is preparing to turn in for the night. The full moon lights up her spacious property on Seffner Road that backs up to Lake Thonotosassa. Surrounded by orange groves, the elderly O'Brien lives in the massive Victorian home that she once shared with her husband William, her son Bill, and an adopted son. But that was before her sons moved out and her husband passed away. Now she occupies the long, isolated home alone, her nearest neighbor nearly a half mile away.

Despite the scenic, moonlit night, the tall, kindly O'Brien is on edge. There was a time when her sister, Mary Baker, lived nearby. But that was before Mary passed back in 1928. Rosa reads the papers. She knows her great nephew, John Calvin Russell, is on the run from the law. Many suspect he will return to his roots.

Rosa O'Brien hopes he won't. For although he is family, she fears the troubled young man.

Since his birth, the young Russell has been a source of embarrassment for the proud Baker family. Although he is brought up a Baker, the fatherless boy goes by the name of Russell, a name his mother adopted in the late 1920s for only a few years. Claude Estelle claims it came from her "late" husband, but no marriage record exists. To this day, the origin of the name Russell is a mystery.

Rastus Russell's life of crime has brought a further distancing from most family members, Maud McCord's hospitality notwithstanding. The Baker family is likely grateful the troubled Rastus has kept the Russell name, although he occasionally uses John Baker as an alias.

Unfortunately for Mrs. O'Brien, her great-nephew has decided to pay a visit tonight. And he's not coming for tea and biscuits. As O'Brien prepares for bed, she hears noises on her back porch facing the lake. Somebody is trying to break in.

The noises are loud, banging, and violent, making no attempt to disguise a forced entry. She has no doubt who it is.

Terrified, O'Brien pulls on a robe and bolts out the door. Running to her car in the detached garage, O'Brien struggles to start the engine. But like a scene from a B-grade horror movie, the car will not start.

The frightened old woman does not stick around to figure out why. She scurries out of the garage, across the yard, and out onto the pressed dirt of Seffner Road.

One-half mile south of Rosa O'Brien's house on Seffner Road, Noma Justa kneels in her bathroom, giving her four-year-old daughter, Virginia, a bath. Noma's husband, Herbert, sits in the living room, reading a newspaper.

Pausing her washing, Mrs. Justa hears a noise outside. Not certain if it is a humming or buzzing noise, she calls out to her husband to go outside and check out the sound. She thinks one of the family cats may be injured or perhaps caught an animal.

Herbert Justa folds his newspaper and rises to his feet, then shuffles out the door to investigate. When he rounds the corner of the house to the bathroom window, what he finds stuns him.

A disheveled, confused Rosa O'Brien stands at the window, trying to draw the attention of Mrs. Justa. Her hearing aid is ringing loudly, the noise ultimately drawing the attention of Mrs. Justa.

The eighty-two-year-old woman has made the half-mile trip down Seffner Road, on foot, in the virtual middle of a dark orange grove at night. She is terrified.

After Justa leads the shaking woman inside the house, she tells the younger couple that her great nephew, John "Rastus" Russell, the man from the newspapers, is at her house.

Virginia Zagar (Justa), the four-year-old in the tub, tells the story as she remembers it that night:

I only lived at the time, about a half a mile from the house of his aunt Rosa O'Brien. And that's where he was. I don't know how she knew he was on his way, but she must have known. I remember her well as being an elderly woman, kind of on the tall side, I guess. Very, very sweet lady.

Back in those days there were very few that lived on this road. I mean all the houses were at least a half a mile or more away from each other. And I can only think about four or five neighbors at that time.

But anyway, he got out to her house and I guess she heard him trying to break in. You got to remember the house, her house was very long. I do remember that she had a real long hallway inside and I guess she heard him trying to get in the door, on the porch that faces the lake, and it scared her. And bless her heart, she went out, got into her car and the car wouldn't start. So she walked in the dark all the way up to our house.

My mom was giving me a bath at that time. She heard a noise outside. She thought it was one of our kitties. She didn't know what was going on. She hollered at my dad to go out and look and he found Mrs. O'Brien standing at the window trying to get my mother's attention.

And evidently what my mother heard was her hearing aid buzzing. But after that, I don't remember what happened with Mrs. O'Brien, what she did that night. I just remember that my dad went down to a couple of the other neighbor's houses to warn them what had happened. And it was kind of a scary night.

And that's my account that actually happened. I have kept that in my mind all the time. It was a full moon that night that I can remember too. So the crazies come out on the full moon and this guy was definitely a lunatic. He was crazy.

But it was so traumatic that I remember those details to it. And I don't know whether I slept that night or not. I was probably terrified, but I was so young. But that's what I remember about it. Yes, he was within a half a mile of where I lived and he probably would've killed his aunt. She was his aunt and I don't know whether he wanted to rob her, if he wanted to kill her. There's no telling. I don't know the details of that. I just know that he wound up out here.

Yes sir, he did.[*]

While Mrs. Zagat's story is riveting, it does not make the newspapers the next day. This is because reporters that day will have a much bigger story to report. One report does mention, however, Mrs. O'Brien as Russell's aunt living in the area.

It is not known whether Justa or any of his neighbors called the police, if they investigated O'Brien's home, or if anything was taken. There are no reports we could find.

What is strange is not that John Russell would go to his great aunt's house, but why the elderly O'Brien would fear him so much. While he has certainly committed crimes and assaulted strangers, there is no record of him ever attacking anyone in his own family. However, one would think that if Russell expected a warm or at least sympathetic reception, he simply would have knocked at the front door, much like he did with Willa Mae Skinner.

At the same time, if Justa believed Mrs. O'Brien's story, why would he not call police? If he did call the police, reporting that a relative of Russell had just had a break-in from a man she believed to be Russell, would it not have brought a massive response from law enforcement on Wednesday night?

---

[*]   *From interview with Mrs. Virginia Zagat, August 2, 2024.*

Yet, Rastus Russell is almost certainly in Thonotosassa that Wednesday night. And as we will find out the next day, he is almost certainly in the area of Mrs. O'Brien's and the Justa's homes. The break into his aunt's house is likely to gather supplies for his long trip.

Todd Tucker, Walter Carey, and the rest of the law enforcement community of West Central Florida will get few more chances to nab him before he's gone. If they are going to get him, they better get him soon.

62

S heriff Todd Tucker has another long, nearly sleepless night. Returning to Clearwater after another fruitless evening of man-hunting through thick grass and soupy air, he managed to grab about an hour's sleep at the jail before rising to begin the search again. If he dreamed at all, he likely saw Rastus Russell in his visions.

While reports continue to pour in from both sides of Tampa Bay, there have been no confirmed sightings or actions by Rastus Russell in the last twenty-four hours. Tucker is not surprised. His fugitive secured enough supplies at the Palm Harbor robbery to hole up for a few days. All he needs is a safe place to hide. The Sheriff knows his time is limited. When Russell has enough gas, supplies, and money, he will make a run for the state line. But he'll almost certainly need to surface again before making his final break.

Today, however, Tucker will have to take time out from the pursuit. He is scheduled to appear before the grand jury at the Pinellas County Courthouse this afternoon.

The eighteen-man jury convened yesterday to begin the pre-scheduled investigation of the Norman Y. Browne murder, in addition to two other unrelated murders in the county. However, after addressing the body yesterday, Judge Bird adds a fourth assignment to the jury.

After listing the three original crimes to be investigated, Bird states:

317

"One of the men charged with one of these crimes has escaped from the county jail (referring to Russell.) *I don't know whether there has been any negligence or not. There are things the public wants to know about it."*

Bird continues:

"If anything is to be found anywhere about it, you gentlemen are to investigate it and report it. Or, if no negligence is found and it was one of those things in human affairs, then of course, you shall report that also."*

The eighteen men spent yesterday afternoon touring the jail and interviewing witnesses.

Today, Tucker will get to sit and answer questions from the investigating body. He is no doubt *overjoyed* at the prospect.

While lawmen on both sides of the bay continue to investigate tips, the trail of Rastus Russell has largely gone cold again.

* * *

At 7:00 a.m., a team of officers from Dunedin Police and Pinellas County Sheriff's Office hide in the tall grass and shrubs surrounding the Ozona home of Willa Mae Skinner.

Russell has made an "appointment" with the elderly woman to come to her house at 8 a.m., presumably for food and supplies.

Officers are skeptical that Russell will show, or if he was ever there in the first place. Nonetheless, they wait in the wet, insect-infested shrubbery for four hours.

Russell doesn't show.

At 11:00 a.m., they load their weapons back into patrol cars and depart.

* * *

---

*   *The Tampa Tribune, September 1, 1949.*

The midmorning sun is already searing through his open windows when Denzil Pulley, general manager of radio station WTAN, sits down in his Clearwater office to open the station's mail.

Pulley was personally threatened by a man believed to be Rastus Russell three days earlier. Pulley ignored the demand of the unsettling phone voice but called police.

As he sorts through the daily correspondence, he comes across a white envelope, personally addressed to him. The envelope has a Tampa postmark from 11 a.m. yesterday (Wednesday, August 31).

When Pulley opens the envelope and unfolds the white piece of paper inside, a chill must shoot down from the top of his head to the curled toes inside his wingtips.

The handwritten words are scrawled in pencil. They read:

> *"I told you once to lay off that broadcasting my description.*
> *Tucker and that James guy better watch out two.* (misspelled)
> *I mean just that.*
> *If not now, later for sure."*

By "James," the writer is presumably referring to Pinellas County Deputy Sheriff Wilmer James, who has played an integral role in the manhunt for John Calvin Russell. When Pulley flips the paper over, he sees several sets of figures and notations for building materials and the words scrolled over top of them

> *"The Clearwater police are dopes."*[*]

It appears as though whoever wrote the note, used a piece of scrap paper taken from an office or a trash can.

There is no signature.

Pulley immediately dials Sheriff Tucker.

Tucker asks Pulley to bring him the note. Pulley says he will.

Then Pulley, perhaps displaying courage or perhaps sensing an acute opportunity for self and station promotion, reads the letter over the air. He then defiantly blasts out the detailed description of Russell again.

---

[*]   *The Evening Independent, September 1, 1949.*

Then he heads to the courthouse.

Upon examining the letter, opinion is split between the deputies on duty. Some believe the note is the work of a hack.

Tucker does not.

The Sheriff orders it checked for fingerprints, then summons a handwriting expert to compare the writing with Russell's boyish penmanship.[*]

But Tucker knows who wrote the note. And it has not gone unnoticed that the long-time lawman is singled out in its text.

The Sheriff may have let this rabbit get under his skin. Now he knows he is under the rabbit's skin as well.

* * *

Sitting in his office, Tucker finally allows entry to the reporters clamoring outside his door. There has been a deluge of new developments in the last forty-eight hours. They include:

- The Citrus Park robbery of Raleigh Allen's Store Monday night
- The vehicle stolen in Palm Harbor early Wednesday morning
- The burglary of Lipsey's service station on Wednesday morning
- The presumed sighting of Rastus Russell at a Sulphur Springs filling station on Wednesday morning
- The threatening letter sent to WTAN this morning

The breathless reporters want Tucker's take on all the happenings. Are they all related? Are they all the work of Russell? How do you know?

When asked if he is taking the note to WTAN seriously, the Sheriff allows himself a moment of gratuitous bravado but also shows his rising frustration with the bold criminal:

"Of course I am taking the note seriously," Tucker barks.

---

[*] *The Evening Independent, September 1, 1949.*

"And for Russell's information," he snarls in his slow, southern drawl, "I accept his challenge. I'll meet him anywhere, any time."

Tucker then takes the opportunity to pontificate, bringing the media and public up to date on his thinking about the latest developments.

Despite a lack of conclusive evidence, Tucker is convinced that Russell is behind all five of the new incidents he is suspected of.

The Sheriff explains:

> *"Here's why I am sure that the job was pulled by Russell* (referring to the Lipsey Filling Station Robbery.) *First, let's consider the evidence found at the station. There were the usual stocks of auto tires and accessories lying around. These things are convertible into cash. If the filling station had been broken into by an ordinary thief, those tires and accessories would have been stolen. But what was taken? Just crackers, soft drinks, bread, and other food."*

Tucker continues:

> *"So the man who broke into that station was in search of food and drink and nothing else. Of course, he was after gasoline for the stolen car and would have gotten some too, if he had located the switch operating the electric fuel pump."*

The Sheriff refers to the fugitive's style of burglary as "the Russell technique."

When asked about the Citrus Park robbery, Tucker is no less certain.

"That was Russell too," he states. "Because we find in that robbery the same passion for food and drink."

Forensic expert J.F. Peacock, despite a lack of confirming fingerprints, is quick to back the Sheriff's analysis.

"...whoever robbed the juke organ cash box did so by carefully removing the entire box with a rod... (it) shows Russell's handiwork."

Peacock seconds the notion that the Citrus Park store was raided by a "hunger-crazed" Russell.

---

*   *The Evening Independent, September 1, 1949.*

Tucker and his men believe Russell has enough supplies to sustain him for at least thirty-six hours. They are also onto his pattern of resting during the day and moving at night. The Sheriff reiterates his belief that the convict will have to surface again to replenish his supplies and that it is only a matter of time before he is killed or captured.

But privately, he cannot be so sure.

In somewhat of an acknowledging nod to his adversary, the Sheriff offers Russell some backhanded praise.

"Russell is one of the craftiest individuals I've ever come in contact with," says Tucker. "He banks on the element of surprise and pulling the unexpected. In fact, Russell told a fellow prisoner in jail that he had always been able to outsmart the law by doing things the law never figured he would do. And that has marked his every move since the jailbreak."

Indeed, Russell's improbable four-day flight through Pinellas and Hillsborough Counties has been nothing short of amazing. Tucker must be utterly flabbergasted at the incredible streak of luck or divine intervention the escapee has experienced since his violent escape.

The weary Sheriff, surrounded by a team of equally exhausted deputies, then offers a self-revelatory note of frustration.

"I guess I should have taken instructions in the art of trapping rattlesnakes," he laments.[*]

---

[*] *The Evening Independent, September 1, 1949.*

63

astus Russell must be feeling confident today.
Safely out of the treacherous streets of Pinellas County and the populated suburbs of Tampa, the fugitive is back on his home turf. More importantly, he is deep in the country, in a sprawling ocean of endless orange groves and dense woods.

Finding anyone out here would be difficult, especially someone as familiar with the territory as Russell.

The convict knows this. For the first time, he can relax a bit. He is almost free. One or two more scores, and he can be on his way. He might literally get away with murder.

So confident is he, in fact, he does something he has not done since his escape nearly four days earlier.

He goes out during the daytime.

While it is not known fact, Russell likely spends Wednesday night camped in an orange grove in Thonotosassa. In fact, he likely spends it in a grove owned by his own family, the Bakers. Today, however, he has decided to drive Jim Smith's 1948 blue-gray Ford, covered in Georgia clay dust, to Dover.

Dover is a tiny village about ten miles southeast of Thonotosassa and nineteen miles east of Tampa. Why he risks the long drive is unknown. Perhaps he thinks he may be recognized in Thonotosassa.

It is early afternoon when he pulls into the Dover Cash Store. Inside, he shops, buying crackers and cold drinks. How he pays is unknown.

On his way out of the store, Russell stops and picks up a copy of the Tampa Tribune, featuring his picture on the front page. It is here that Russell learns, if he didn't already know, that the station attendants at the gas station in Sulphur Springs had identified him yesterday. He learns that his actions have brought more drama to his Aunt Maud in Tampa. And he discovers that the thefts in Palm Harbor have been attributed to him.

The store clerk, noticing Russell's haggard appearance, believes Russell pays an inordinate amount of attention to the front page before replacing the paper on the rack.

The man in the red shirt and dirty khaki pants slides back into the Ford and drives north on Thonotosassa Road.

After Russell drives away, the clerk, Percy Wheeler, puts two and two together. He phones Plant City Police.

It's nearly 4:00 p.m. when Thonotosassa grove worker Frank Edwards turns off of Seffner Road down a dirt path leading deep into an orange grove. Edwards is inspecting the groves for storm damage from the hurricane that blew past Tampa Bay last weekend.

About half a mile from Seffner Road, the path reaches the edge of the grove. Edwards' pickup truck continues another quarter mile into the thick grove, where it dead ends close to the edge of Lake Thonotosassa. At the spot where the road stops, the trees are so thick that one cannot see what is 100 yards ahead.

It is here that Edwards, described as a "nervous type," discovers something that shouldn't be here.

A blue-gray Ford sedan is parked under the sprawling lower branches of a large orange tree, just beyond the road's end. It sports a Pinellas County license plate. Edwards, who has not kept up with the news cycle, is unaware that police are searching for Russell in the area.

However, he works these groves every day. He knows that regardless of time, a vehicle parked this deep in the grove, especially with a Pinellas County plate, is suspicious.

Upon inspecting the surrounding area, Edwards notices the fresh ashes of a campfire and several empty soda bottles sitting around.

Unsettled, the citrus worker retreats to his truck and steers it back out of the windy, dusty road. Turning north on Seffner Road, Edwards drives towards Thonotosassa, past the homes of Virginia Zagat and Rosa O'Brien.

Closer to town, he arrives at the country store of Ben Turner. From there, he calls the Hillsborough County Sheriff's office to report a suspicious vehicle "stuck in the sand."

Hearing news of a suspicious Ford sedan found near the birth-place of Rastus Russell, Hillsborough County Sheriff Hugh Culbreath is quick to respond, scrambling a contingent of deputies to the area. What Culbreath does not know at the time is that there is one more fact about the location of the vehicle that might intrigue him.

It is parked in a grove owned by members of the prestigious Baker family.

Russell's kin.

* * *

Deputies report back to Culbreath that the car matches the description of the one stolen by Russell. Preliminary evidence at the scene suggests as much, too.

Culbreath wastes no time. In addition to summoning more deputies to the scene, he calls in Harvey Frazier and his team of bloodhounds.

Culbreath then phones his top homicide detective, Bob Spooner.

The thirty-seven-year-old Spooner is a tall, quiet man who carries a big stick. Originally pursuing a career as a prize fighter, he spent time in New York City. However, he returned to Tampa after discovering the industry's corruption. With the Depression in full swing and a family to support, Spooner took a job as a Hillsborough County Deputy.

During his time on the job, Spooner becomes known as a no-nonsense, hard-nosed cop with a penchant for getting to the bot-tom of things. Having risen through the ranks, Spooner has estab-lished himself as a man as tough as the job, thriving in the rough, tumble, and sometimes violent Tampa underworld.

Spooner is one of the last to argue against putting cages in police cars to separate the prisoners in the back seat from the officers in the front. Spooner's argument is simple. With a cage, a prisoner can swear, spit, kick, and otherwise cause a ruckus in the back seat, with the officer in the front unable to take any corrective action. Without the cage, Spooner has the ability to "keep things peaceful."

With an imposing 6'4" frame and a deep, slow voice, most prisoners are unwilling to try him.

He is described by a relative as "the closest, living thing to a real-life John Wayne there was."

Most importantly, Sheriff Culbreath knows he can count on Spooner to get tough jobs done.

It is for this reason he calls the detective on this late Thursday afternoon and asks him to go to Thonotosassa.

"I want you to work the dogs with Frazier," he tells Spooner. "You know the area and you know Frazier."[*]

Indeed, if there is anyone who knows the groves and swamps of Thonotosassa as well as Rastus Russell, it is Bob Spooner.

Like Russell, Spooner grew up running barefoot through the mossy oak woods of the rural area, swimming in the lake, and eating oranges off the trees.

There is no evidence that Spooner knows Russell personally. But he most certainly knows members of the Baker family, given the tiny population of the farming community.

Spooner makes his home with his wife, Anna, and two children in Plant City, sixteen miles from Thonotosassa. He is quite familiar with Plant City PD and Officer Frazier.

The deputy has just returned from vacation with his family, this being his first day back on the job.

Spooner accepts the assignment with his usual nonchalance. With the Dover store clerk identifying Russell in a photo and the discovery of the Ford Sedan in Thonotosassa, the detective knows there is a good chance he may run into the state's most infamous fugitive today. Then again, false alarms have run rampant the last four days.

---

[*] *From interview with Spooner family member, asking to remain anonymous.*

Nonetheless, the detective loads his .12 gauge, pump action shot-gun with .00 buckshot and heads out the door.[*]

* * *

When Spooner arrives at the scene, a Plant City squad car guards the entrance to the dirt road leading to the grove. Spooner passes the officer and guides his patrol car back to the sandy path. When he reaches the end, he sees a bevy of Plant City Police and Hillsborough County Deputies milling around the abandoned Ford. Frazier is already on sight with his trusty hound, Flip.

Frazier chose seventeen-month-old Flip because the black, mid-sized female K-9 had tracked Russell in Clearwater and knew his scent well.

As Deputy Spooner joins the officers, he sees the same thing the other lawmen are seeing. Whoever parked this blue-grey V-8 Ford, covered in pink dust and with a Pinellas license plate, has set up a makeshift camp.

In addition to the empty drink bottles lying about the camp, candy and snack wrappers litter the ground and interior of the vehicle. Cigarette butts are scattered about the ground. The ashes of a campfire suggest someone spent at least one night here.

Nearby on the ground lies the vehicle's air filter, likely removed by the mechanic Russell for cleaning. Pages of newspaper also lie hap-hazardly around the site, some folded, some crumpled into balls.

When officers pop the trunk, they find a treasure trove of food-stuffs and other supplies. These include two cases of soda, boxes of cookies, and four cartons of candy. In the backseat of the vehicle are twenty packages of assorted cigarettes, two boxes of cigars, a jar with 49 pennies, an empty gas can, and a maroon shirt stained with dried blood.

---

[*]   *.00 or "double-aught" buckshot is a shotgun shell filled with eight or twelve pellets that are one-third inch in diameter each (the size of a small marble.) Used for hunting big game at close range, the shell carries a massive wallop with tremendous stopping power and can do devastating damage. One description of getting shot with a dou-ble-aught buck shell is like getting shot with a .38 bullet twelve times, all at once. Source: Ammo.com)*

In the front, there is no ignition key. Instead, wires have been pulled out of the ignition switch and twisted together.

Across a branch of a nearby orange tree, a pair of swimming trunks hang drying benignly in the breeze, appearing oddly normal in the abnormally surreal scene.

Spooner knows this is no false alarm.

A deputy relays the news back to Sheriff Culbreath at headquarters. The car is indeed Russell's. And he must be very, very close.

* * *

Back in Clearwater, Sheriff Todd Tucker is sitting before the Pinellas County grand jury on the second floor of the Courthouse when a deputy brings him an urgent message. Hillsborough County Deputies have found Jim Smith's stolen Ford in a Thonotosassa orange grove. They think Russell is in the grove.

Tucker must be bleeding from the eyes. He wants nothing more than to jump into his patrol car and speed to Tampa. But he is obligated to the grand jury. Instead, he dispatches several deputies to join the search, telling them he will join them as soon as he is finished. Tucker returns to the grand jury room.

* * *

As dozens of deputies and officers fan out into the woods, with more arriving by the minute, Flip has worked herself into an agitated state. She has already caught a strong "spore" of her quarry and is pulling Frazier to go. The other officers will head in every direction, hoping to beat the fleeing Russell out of the bushes.

Frazier and Spooner will follow Flip in a more targeted approach.

* * *

Rastus Russell is the most comfortable he's been all week. He has a full belly, his fill of cigarettes, a quiet, hidden place outdoors, and a lake. It is the same lake, incidentally, at which he spent many days of his childhood swimming and exploring. Earlier, he bathed for the first time since his escape, washing off layers of sweat, grime, and blood from his four-day flight from the law. For some reason, he took the trouble to change into a swimsuit before doing so – the origins of its acquisition unknown.

When finished, he changes back into his dirty prison pants.

In 1949, the spring-fed Lake Thonotosassa water was relatively clean. Russell has found if he fills empty whiskey bottles with lake water and lets the sediment settle to the bottom, the water on top is pure enough to drink.

It is about 4:00 p.m. on Thursday afternoon. The fugitive is on his way back from filling a bottle at the lake, walking the approximate 100 yards to his campsite, when through the orange trees, he sees police cars surrounding his parked vehicle.

Shirtless, wearing only his bloody, brown khaki's, a dark belt to hold them up, and the blue-black, unlaced sneakers with white soles he wore in his escape, Russell drops the bottle and bolts back into the grove.

The fugitive must be perplexed as to how the law found him so fast, hidden so deep in the dark green canopy of the orange grove that seems to stretch from horizon to horizon.

He knows the dogs will come next. He also must know he's in a bad spot. If he is to get away this time, he will have to pull the craftiest escape he has ever made.

* * *

Spooner and Frazier follow the enthused Flip in a westerly direction. The terrain is rough, out of the grove and into an oak scrub, then a second grove. Their progress is slow. But Flip persists, tracking the scent patiently, without noise.

Spooner explains what happens next:

"We trailed almost a mile that way when suddenly Flip doubled back. We followed her three-quarters of a mile back toward the car before she cut away to the north."

Russell knows he is being tracked, doubling back to throw the dog off the scent. He has been successful in accomplishing this in the past. He's counting on the same trick to save him today.

---

*   *St. Petersburg Times, September 2, 1949.*

"We must have tracked that guy three miles or more, in and out of the grove, through the wet, mushy ground around the edge of the lake, and through the high palmetto growth," Frazier explains.[*]

The trio track the fugitive for nearly an hour, traveling in a crazed quilt pattern, indicating Russell was desperately trying to confuse the dog.

Entering into another swampy thicket, the patient Flip suddenly becomes excited, straining on her harness, the hair on her back standing up.

"She pulled along steady through the grass," Frazier explains, "then she got 'wind.' She sort of lunged forward and strained toward her man".[*]

"She headed into the heart of a swamp and the way she was acting, Frazier knew something was up," says Spooner. "He had been with the dog with me behind, but he stopped there until I caught up."[*]

"I could tell from the way Flip was acting up," says Frazier, "that she was really getting close. So I stopped and held her in check."[***]

The two men scan the landscape and don't see anything. But Flip remains insistent.

"Then we saw a man peep from behind a large tree," explains Spooner. "He saw we had spotted him and jumped back behind the tree. We knew it was Russell."[****]

Frazier, in full police uniform and cap, draws his .38 service revolver from its holster. Spooner jumps into a crouch, leveling his shotgun at the tree. The two advance to within fifteen yards of the tree.

"Come out with your hands up!" shouts Frazier.

There is no movement.

"Come out now, or we'll kill you!" Spooner commands.

A bare-chested, muscular figure steps from behind the tree, a smoking cigarette dangling between two fingers of his left hand. He remains partially obscured by the tree; his hands are not raised.

The two lawmen know immediately they are facing Rastus Russell, in the flesh. It appears as though he is weighing the odds of fighting vs. surrendering.

But Frazier has orders: Shoot to kill. And he has a clear shot.

---

[*]   *Clearwater Sun, September 2, 1949.*

[**]   *The Evening Independent, September 2, 1949.*

[***] *The Evening Independent, September 2, 1949.*

Still holding Flip's leash with his left hand, Frazier fires three rounds from his .38, at least two piercing Russell's torso.

Russell twists slightly, absorbing the blows.

Then, with a voracious scream, Russell raises a hidden switchblade knife over his head, steps from behind the tree, and bullrushes the men in furious charge.

"He come out of there like a wild man," notes a Spooner relative, relaying Bob Spooner's personal version of the story to his family.[*]

For the first time, Spooner sees the raised knife in the fugitive's right hand.

Frazier fires again.

Spooner lets go with a blast from his .12 gauge, the cannon-like boom echoing throughout the grove. The charge stops Russell's forward momentum, spinning him sideways.

"I hit him with a load of buckshot," Spooner explains, "It spun him around."

But Russell remains on his feet.

Spooner pumps the shotgun and fires another blast into Russell, then pumps and fires a third time, both charges tearing into Russell's upper body.[**]

(At least one account states that Spooner carried an automatic shotgun, meaning no pump would be necessary. However, in Spooner's personal account later, he states he "reloaded" between shots, meaning he would have pumped the gun to load another shell into the chamber.)

Spooner describes the exchange in his own words:

"Frazier fired first with his .38 caliber service revolver. Russell sort of spun around. Then I cut loose with a full load of buckshot from my shotgun and that spun Russell completely around. I reloaded and fired two more barrels."

Rastus Russell spins, falls, and lands face down in the muddy, leafy soil.

---

[*] *From personal interview with Spooner family member, May, 2024.*
[**] *The Evening Independent, September 2, 1949.*

As Spooner and Frazier run up to the mortally wounded convict, he flips over on his back, his hips arching up in agony, straining so forcefully it pops his belt buckle and tears his pants open.[*]

Spooner's shotgun blasts have ripped open Russell's left side, one wound in the hip, one in the side, and one on and underneath the left arm. Russell's left arm is folded over his chest, revealing a massive hole near his armpit. His left arm is almost completely severed at the tricep.

The officers lean over Russell, who looks back into their faces with pained, squinted eyes.

"Well," he gasps, "You fellows killed me. And I'm glad you did it."[**]

Rastus Russell's body then goes limp, his open eyes still staring up at the blue sky of the late afternoon.

The "Mad Killer" of Crystal Beach is dead.

---

[*] *This is the official version of how Russell's pants got opened. However, several interviewees for this book, including Rick Cary, grandson of Walter Carey, repeat the rumor that Russell was in the act of defecating at the time he was shot. While it seems odd that Russell would take the time to relieve himself when being chased by a posse, it also seems odd to imagine a belt being broken simply by a man writhing. Only Spooner and Frazier know what actually happened that day. Russell's death photos show his pants and belt clearly open.*

[**] *From the testimony of Bob Spooner to the St. Petersburg Times, September 2, 1949.*

64

I t's approximately 5:05 p.m. when the crackle of Frazier's .38 and the thunder of Spooner's .12 gauge rivet the officers and citizen posse, combing the nearby groves.

It has been just over an hour since Spooner and Frazier set off from the stolen car with Flip.

Within minutes, nearly 100 lawmen and local volunteers surround the muddy oak grove where Rastus Russell's lifeless body lay.

For what seems like a long time, the men crowd around the body, somberly assessing the dead outlaw. They take turns getting close, rotating out when they are satisfied with the viewing.

Russell's dark brown eyes remain open, staring skyward. His mouth is half open, never having closed since uttering his final words. His hair is slicked back, freshly combed from his recent dip in the lake. His left arm lays folded across his shirtless chest, the arm's upper half splayed open, exposing the larger, fatal wound under his left arm. Ironically, this is the same spot on the torso in which Norman Browne was fatally stabbed.

An autopsy will later find twenty-one individual slugs in Russell's body, including Frazier's bullets and Spooner's pellets, indicating neither lawman missed their shots.

Still clasped in Russell's right hand is the switchblade knife he used as the only weapon in his final charge. Beside his body in the mucky soil lies the half-smoked cigarette still held between his fingers when the fatal shots rang out. The only other items found in his possession are a comb, a cheap pocket watch, and a handkerchief. No money is found on his person.[*]

---

[*]   *St. Petersburg Times, September 2, 1949.*

One officer notes that Russell's dark hair seems markedly grayer than it was three weeks earlier. Another comments that the body looks remarkably well for a man who has been on the run, outdoors for four days and nights – leading to speculation that the fugitive had help or shelter in his flight from the law. He has only a two-day stubble of beard, indicating he has shaved at least once since his escape. There is a noticeable lack of cuts, scratches, and bites on the body, the multiple cuts on his hands notwithstanding.*

But Russell's run has not been a cakewalk. After four days of little food, little drink, and constant movement through the sweltering days and steamy nights of Tampa Bay August, the fugitive has lost nearly twenty pounds from his 180-pound frame.

He is killed less than a mile from the site of his mother's grave, further fueling speculation that he had gone home to Thonotosassa to say goodbye to his mother before fleeing.

Less than a mile away, with the burnt smell of gunpower still lingering in the soupy air, a children's softball game is underway, the sounds of laughing and cheering faintly perceptible in the distance.

One wonders if they heard the gunshots, perhaps dismissing them as a farmer shooting a snake or a coyote.

Life in Thonotosassa goes on.

* * *

It is nearly an hour before Justice of the Peace and Coroner Ward Holloway arrives from Plant City. Holloway must examine the body and make a pronouncement of death before police can remove it.

By now, reporters have arrived, and photographers, having trekked through the three-quarter-mile stretch of swamp and grove to reach the body, are liberally snapping photographs. Officers, eager to have pictures taken next to the infamous outlaw, crowd in for the camera. The shots will doubtlessly grace office and den walls for decades to come.

---

*   *Police discover that Russell had several cuts on both hands likely resulting from the prison break in Clearwater. However, the large gash on his left hand was probably responsible for the majority of the bloodshed.*

Holloway arrives on scene shortly after 6:00 p.m. Wearing cotton slacks and a white, short-sleeved shirt buttoned over top, a tank top t-shirt, the coroner's neatly slicked, blackish-gray hair, formal white wing tips, and fedora seem oddly out of place in the bloody mud surrounding the body.

Holloway dutifully poses for photographers, lifting Russell's left wrist as though checking for a pulse and striking a serious look. The cameras explode with flashes.

The justice of the peace then removes the fedora, slips on his round-rimmed spectacles, and begins his examination in earnest. With help from Deputy K.C. Meyers, Holloway scans the body from top to bottom, observing the wounds, turning the body on its side, and looking for other marks on the back and sides.

Holloway proclaims the body is that of Russell, pronounces him dead, and issues a preliminary verdict that the shooting was "justifiable homicide," a conclusion that will be upheld days later.

Ironically, across the bay in Clearwater, the Pinellas County Grand Jury has just returned five indictments. They are first-degree murder in the death of Norman Browne, assault with intent to murder for Miles and Thelma Crum, assault with intent to murder for Anne Browne, and assault with intent to murder for Lester Lambert.

All indictments are against the same defendant: John Calvin Russell.

Sheriff Todd Tucker is just getting ready for a recess when a deputy brings him a message.

John Calvin Russell has been shot dead in Thonotosassa.

Tucker receives the news expressionless. The sheriff must certainly feel relief, but a hint of disappointment must also taint the news. Human nature is human nature. The near-obsessed Tucker has spent only five and a half of the last 91 hours sleeping. It is not difficult to imagine the Sheriff wishing he had been there.

When Tucker announces the news to the grand jury, the panel erupts with chatter and utterances of approval.

* * *

65

As lawmen linger around the kill site, a discussion begins as to where the body of Rastus Russell should be transported. From the crowd steps one Bill O'Brien, a second cousin of Russell. O'Brien, ironically, is the son of Rosa O'Brien, whose home was terrorized by Russell the prior evening.

O'Brien tells the officers that Russell has several aunts and uncles in the area, and that the family will make arrangements.

The Wells Funeral Home in Plant City is contacted to come out to Thonotosassa and collect the body. Reporters from newspapers and radio stations across the Bay Area are electrified, calling every police headquarters, local tipster, friend, or family member near Tampa for information. Thonotosassa is a remote location and the news dripping out is sparse. The only word they have is that Rastus Russell has been shot dead. The who, how, and exactly where are still unknown.

Reporters race to the tiny village, not knowing where they will go when they arrive. But word is spreading fast around the town. Before Russell's body is even removed, a crowd has gathered around the head of the dirt road leading back to the kill site. Cars are not allowed back, but pedestrians willing to make the three-quarter mile trek are permitted to view the campsite from a distance. The site where Russell is killed is far into the swamp, and police try to keep onlookers out. But some try to find it anyway.

Arriving on scene are two workers from the Wells Funeral Home. Their job is to retrieve the body of John Calvin Russell.

A member of the Spooner family describes this first-hand account from one of the men:

"As a kid I'd heard how big this guy was, Rastus Russell. And I thought maybe they were exaggerating a little bit.

And so when I was a teenager, I knew this guy who was on the police force that had been working at the funeral home at the time. They recovered the body. So I went to him one time and I said, 'I understand you saw the body.'

He said, 'Well I did a little more than saw the body.'

He said, 'I was working part-time at the funeral home when they said they'd shot Russell and they needed a couple of guys to go out there with the ambulance and a stretcher and bring the body in.'

So he said, 'This other guy and I went out there.'

One of the things in the newspaper said he was in an orange grove. He started in an orange grove, but he left the orange grove, climbed a fence and was in the swamp. Now, if you've ever been around Lake Thonotosassa, there's still some swampy areas around out there.

And so when they were tracking this guy, they had left the orange grove and like I say, he went over a fence and was in the deep woods. And so when Gerald, that was the guy that was working at the funeral home, went in to get him, he said they got to the body and they put the stretcher on the ground and rolled him over on the stretcher and they started back to the ambulance. When they got to the fence, they had to pick this stretcher up, just these two guys. He said when they were about halfway over the fence, Russell's body rolled off the stretcher on top of him. He said it was heavy, but when he landed on top of him, it flattened him out. I thought, 'Well that's one memory you'll never forget.'"*

A Clearwater Sun Reporter, one of the first on the scene, as able to capture some of the initial reaction from the officers involved.

As the reporter watches, an unidentified deputy is pacing off the several hundred yards that separate Russell's body from the stolen car.

"That fellow," comments the deputy, "wasn't smart. He was crafty and cunning, like an animal. But he wasn't smart."

A woman standing along the road near the Russell kill site shouts at passing police cars, "I hope this means you've got that Russell so that we can have some peace around here!"

Deputy Wilmer James, looking over Russell's bloody body, remarks, "Well, I guess we can catch up on our sleep now."

---

*   *From 2024 Interview with Bob Spooner Family member.*

James, no doubt, will. He was singled out in Russell's threatening letter to WTAN.

Back at Hillsborough County Sheriff's headquarters in Tampa, a deputy replacing a riot gun in a weapons rack remarks, "I feel like we've just won an election!"*

The men pulling the triggers, however, are a bit more subdued.

Deputy Spooner, one of the hardest of hard men, reflects on the event in the immediate aftermath:

"I have been a police officer for eleven years. This is not the first time I've fired at a criminal. But it's the first time I've killed, or helped kill a man."

Officer Frazier reflects Spooner's sentiment. While there is no direct quote available, Frazier comments that he was sorry that he had been forced to shoot Russell, but had done so because he had been warned the hunted man was armed and "would take desperate chances to escape."

While most are relieved Russell is dead, there will be a controversy later as to whether police used extreme force in shooting Russell. Some believe Russell was not given a fair chance to surrender before being gunned down. Others question how big a threat a pocket knife really was to officers, some even questioning whether Russell actually had a knife, or whether it was placed in his hand after the fact.

While Spooner and Frazier both state that they fired after Russell charged with a knife, they were the only ones to witness the event. And while this will become the story in the official record, the event will be a source of quiet mumbles for decades.

However, in a bombshell revelation in my interview with a close family member of Bob Spooner who chose to remain anonymous, I was told that Spooner himself told a slightly different version to his family years afterward.

Spooner told the family member that he had wanted to take Russell alive. He stated that when Russell peaked out from behind the tree, he thought the ragged fugitive was going to surrender. Then Frazier opened up, sending Russell into a rage and causing him to "come out of there like a wild man."

---

* *Clearwater Sun, September 2, 1949.*

Thus, according to this account, Russell was not charging when Frazier initially fired his weapon.

On the other hand, while Russell may not have made an aggressive move, he did not comply with Frazier and Spooner's order either.

The coroner issued a preliminary finding of a justified shooting even before Russell's body was cold. He states later there will be no inquest unless the State Attorney's office orders one.

They do not.

In 1949, there was still a bit of the Old West left in the Florida legal system.

The good guys killed the bad guy. Everyone was safe again. It was that simple. There wasn't any great appetite for questions.

As nightfall approaches, deputies start the stolen Ford belonging to Jim Smith of Palm Harbor. The car still has two gallons of gas in the tank. The men will need to fill it with gas before the drive back to Palm Harbor. They do. But after a stop at the Sheriff's Headquarters in Tampa, they encounter the owner, Jim Smith, awaiting the return of his vehicle. Aside from a small dent on the front fender and the pulled ignition switch, the car is in good shape. In fact, it even has a cleaned air filter, thanks to its temporary driver.

Sheriff Tucker plans to return the stolen merchandise found inside to its rightful owners.[*]

While the groceries found in the vehicle can mostly be traced to Lipsey's Shell Station in Palm Harbor, there is nothing found that conclusively ties the thief to the robbery in Citrus Park.

---

[*] *In 1949, laws and procedures for evidence collection on dead criminals were a bit grayer than today. After Frank Hamer led the ambush that killed Bonnie and Clyde fifteen years earlier, it was said he handed out the weapons found in the car as souvenirs to those officers who had participated. While there is no record of it, it seems reasonable to assume, given the notoriety of Russell, that some of Russell's small personal belongings could have been kept as souvenirs, possibly still sitting in a family collection somewhere.*

In fact, some officers even question if Russell was responsible for the Citrus Park robbery. They point to the fact that Raleigh Allen claims there were $20 in nickels stolen from his jukebox. Yet, only 31 pennies are found in a peanut jar taken from Lipsey's. No trace of a single nickel is found, nor are there any reports of anyone matching Russell's description paying for a purchase with nickels.

With dusk falling upon Thonotosassa, Frank Edwards, the grove tender who first reported the stolen vehicle, looks over the swampy tracks and trails winding throughout his workplace. Most of the lawmen, along with Russell's body and car, have departed.

Edwards, lingering at the site, watches a steady stream of curious onlookers hiking into the muddy swamp, seeking the death site and possible souvenirs. When they arrive, they are rewarded with a body imprint in the mud, dark blood still staining the leaves surrounding it.

In less than twenty-four hours, rain will wash it all away, erasing any trace of the violent encounter that happened here.

* * *

While curiosity about Russell's death would produce yarns, rumors, and legends for years, there is one obvious conclusion one could draw, given the nature of Russell's final, desperate charge.

While it had no name at the time, today's term for such an action might be "suicide by cop."

In my interview with the Spooner family member, I was told that Spooner himself had such suspicions.

Why would a man armed only with a small knife, charge two heavily armed officers of the law?

Either he was crazy, or he wanted to die.

His final words seem to confirm his intentions.

"You fellows killed me….and I'm glad you did."

And these are not the first suicidal words the violent criminal has uttered. Before and throughout his violent summer of 1949, Russell made several references to suicide and his own death.

"I tried to drown myself but didn't have the guts."

"If I ever get in a corner, I'll kill myself."

"I'd rather die in the electric chair than go back to Chattahoochee."

"If I'm so bad like they say, just put me to sleep."

Russell may have tried to drown himself in the Dunedin Flats. But he couldn't bring himself to do it. In Thonotosassa, he wouldn't have to. There were two souls willing to do it for him.

When looking out from behind the tree, Russell was likely weighing the realities of going back to prison or Chattahoochee against death.

If Frazier did indeed fire first, he made the decision easy for Russell.

Either way, in the end, Russell made the decision to charge, almost certainly knowing he was charging into oblivion.

One St. Petersburg woman, interviewed later, shared her take on Russell's final words:

"After all he had been through, perhaps God gave him a final flash of understanding in that moment."

Perhaps.

Or perhaps Rastus Russell was simply glad he was not going back to Chattahoochee.

---

*   *Clearwater Sun, September 2, 1949.*

66

While Sheriff Todd Tucker wasn't the one pulling the trigger on Rastus Russell, he is certainly vindicated in the aftermath. After all, it was Tucker's relentless pursuit that led Russell to the grove in Thonotosassa, where he was discovered. It was Tucker's strategy to bring Russell into the open that eventually led to the convict making a mistake.

An editorial in the St. Petersburg Times surmises as much:

*"Sheriff Todd Tucker... certainly atoned for the momentary lapse on the part of one his jailer, which led to Russell's escape."** *

Tucker has just enjoyed his first full night's sleep in five nights. *The Evening Independent* notes the improvement in Tucker's appearance and disposition:

*"The Sheriff was a completely different man today. Gone where the deep furrows that lined his face yesterday, gone the circles beneath his eyes and back once more the gentle disposition that has made the Sheriff one of the county's most popular officials.** *"*

Indeed, the morning of September 2nd is a bright one for Sheriff Todd Tucker.

In his first full address to the press since Russell's death, the Sheriff takes a few moments for some lighthearted banter:

"It took me quite a spell to go to sleep even last night when I knew it was all over," Tucker cheekily tells reporters. *"I rolled and tossed for a couple of hours. But when sleep finally came, I don't think an earthquake would have awakened me."*

---

*   *St. Petersburg Times, September 3, 1949.*

**   *The Evening Independent, September 2, 1949.*

The Sheriff then acknowledges his disappointment, which must be acute, for not being at the final scene of the Russell chase:

"I was sorry I could not have been at the scene of the shooting," says Tucker, *"but the grand jury is in session and I could not leave the courthouse."*

Tucker states that both Pinellas and Hillsborough officers have concluded that it was Russell who robbed Lipsey's Service Station, stole Jim Smith's 1948 Ford, and robbed Raleigh Allen's Grocery Store in Citrus Park.[*]

Police also believe Russell "could have been" the one who called WTAN and mailed a threatening letter to the station.

Tucker is quick to praise his law enforcement colleagues for the teamwork it took to bring Russell down.

"I want to express my sincere thanks particularly to the Clearwater, St. Petersburg, Largo, Dunedin, Tarpon Springs, and Bellair Police Departments," says Tucker. "The constables, especially Walter Carey of Tarpon Springs, have been very helpful."

The Sheriff goes on to praise the Highway Patrol, the Coast Guard, the Border Patrol, State Game Wardens, the Hillsborough County Sheriff's Office, Tampa, Lakeland, and Plant City Police. He also singles out Harvey Frazier for praise.

"Credit for the ending of the job must go to Sheriff Culbreath's fine organization," Tucker adds.

Tucker sums up the ordeal: "Together, we want to make this section a tough place for the lawbreaker, and we want everyone to know it."

"I hope Russell's death will calm the fear of all Pinellas County citizens and they all will enjoy a good night's sleep tonight."

---

[*] *Despite a lack of evidence, police close the case of Raleigh Allen's store, attributing it to Russell. There is still some question as to whether Russell actually committed the robbery. Nickels supposedly stolen from the juke box are never recovered, and when Russell bought gas the next day, he counted out pennies, not nickels. No fingerprints found match Russell's. In addition, it seems nonsensical for Russell, who was known to be in Palm Harbor at the time, to steal a car, drive fifteen miles to Tampa to rob a store, then drive fifteen miles back. No one knows how he got there. No car theft for that night is ever attributed to Russell. While we discuss how this could have occurred in a previous chapter, the Citrus Park robbery remains questionable in regard to the actual culprit.*

* * *

With the killing of Russell, Spooner and Frazier become semi-celebrities with both the law enforcement community and the media. But it is Flip who steals the heart of the public.

After giving his prize pup a well-deserved rest back at the Plant City Kennels with her counterpart, Flop, Frazier gives his K-9 all of the credit for the success.

"…the dog has to have the credit, not the officers," says Frazier. "If we hadn't had the dog, we never would have found the man."

* * *

After being informed of Russell's death the evening prior, Sheriff Tucker released Dorothy Jean Crain from her cell at the County Jail. Having no further need for material witnesses, there is no reason to hold the girl.

Walking with her father to the family's car outside the jail, Dorothy gives a quick comment to an inquiring reporter in regard to Russell's death:

"I'm glad to hear it," the teenager responds, "Now I can go home. I was worried more about what Russell would do to my family."

The Crain's are certainly glad as well. They can now return to their home on Curlew Creek Road and sleep soundly.

* * *

67

A t 3:00 p.m. on Friday, September 3rd, it is quiet inside the viewing room of F.T. Blount Funeral Home.

At the front of the room is a simple wooden casket containing the body of John Calvin Russell.

Earlier in the day, a reporter allowed inside the mortuary room where the corpse lay on a metal table comments that Russell looked "calm" in death. Noting that Russell's face and upper body showed little evidence of spending four days in swamp and thicket, the man speculates Russell could have carried on in the wild for an indefinite period.

Other than the funeral director and a pastor, there is only one person in attendance at the private ceremony.

Maud McCord stands solemnly in front of the body. McCord has requested her nephew's body be transferred from Wells Funeral Home in Plant City to this one, on Nebraska Avenue, near her Tampa home.

Outside, throngs of people wind around the building, hoping to get a glimpse of the body of the most notorious monster ever loosed on their hometown. But it is not to be. Despite the outcry, the mangled body of Rastus Russell will not be open to public viewing.

After the quick service, McCord exits the funeral home from a private doorway. Shortly thereafter, the body of Rastus Russell is slid into a cremation oven.

68

September 3, 1949
Valdosta, GA
Evening

I t is just after dark, and Edward Denzil Pulley, general manager of radio station WTAN in Clearwater, is making good time.

More than just a general manager, Pulley built WTAN only two years earlier. He has also built ten other radio stations throughout the south, including cities such as Nashville, TN, and Macon, GA.

Forty-eight hours after the death of Rastus Russell, the radio engineer is on his way to Macon, GA. He is not going to visit the station he built there. He is driving up to retrieve his wife and two children. Pulley's family is there visiting relatives.

Only five days earlier, Pulley received a threatening letter demanding he stop broadcasting Russell's description on the air. The letter ended with the cryptic words, "If not now, later for sure." It was presumably from Rastus Russell himself. Pulley did not heed the warning.

But Russell is dead now. Whether Pulley's family was sent away to escape Rastus Russell, or simply on a coincidental visit, is irrelevant now. It is safe to come home.

As Pulley passes north of Valdosta, GA, on US Highway 41, a flatbed truck driven by Charlie Jordon of Valdosta crosses the center line. It slams head-on into Pulley's car.

The station manager is killed instantly.

Jordan is later arrested for driving while intoxicated.

Some sources note the eerie coincidence of Russell's threat and the timing of Pulley's death, as though the criminal had made good on it from the grave. At the very least, if Pulley's family was indeed sent to Macon in response to Russell's note, his death can be at least partially attributed to Rastus Russell.

69

March 1950
Sam Crain Home
Curlew Creek Road, Palm Harbor

It has been over a month since the Rastus Russell story appeared in *Uncensored Detective* and *Official Detective* Magazines. It has also been that time since Dorothy Jean Crain's personal interview with *True Experiences* Magazine appeared on newsstands.

The girl has returned home and tried to pick up a normal life again, tending house and watching her younger siblings, including Wilburn Crain, while her mother, father, and older brothers work.

But the magazine coverage, along with the teen's cover girl looks, has made Dorothy somewhat of a celebrity.

When she was released from Todd Tucker's Jail, she told the media she was "glad" John Russell was dead.

But out of the public eye, it is a different story. Around the Crain house, Dorothy is morose, and sulks for days.

"She couldn't understand why they had to kill him," says Wilburn Crain, referring to Russell.*

We may never know the true nature of the relationship between John Russell and Dorothy Jean Crain. Whether it was a real love affair plastered over and hidden from the media, a case of a star-struck teenager who simply got in over her head, or a kidnapping with a dose of Stockholm Syndrome, there were almost undoubtedly some feelings between the two.

---

*   *From personal interview with Wilburn Crain, May 2024.*

Dorothy maintains that the couple was never married, never traveled out of state, and that after promising to take her to California where they could become movie stars, Russell instead gave her a cold night sleeping in his stolen Ford, then two months living with his Aunt Maud. She claims all were done unwillingly, that she did not dare escape for fear Russell would kill her and/or her family.

Despite the girl insisting the couple never fulfilled their plan to go to California (as Russell claimed they did), Wilburn Crain relayed a strange story that occurred after Russell's death that sheds some suspicion on Dorothy's version of events.

In March of 1950, Dorothy receives a letter from a man named James Blue. It is not known if or how Dorothy knows Blue.

But Dorothy writes back, encouraging Blue to visit.

A few weeks later, Blue arrives at the Crain home, where he is welcomed as a guest. He carries a guitar. He plays and sings with the Crains and stays for a short time. Dorothy and Blue seem familiar, as though they know each other from somewhere.

When he leaves, Dorothy leaves with him.

They return to Blue's home.

He lives in Visa, California.

70

I t is a somber day inside the home of Miles and Thelma Crum. Their seven-year-old daughter, Judy Louise Crum, lies gravely ill in her bed inside the single-story stone house across the alley from their store. The Crum's moved into the adjacent home a few years ago, moving out of the apartment above the store and converting it to storage.

Little Judy never quite recovered from the family's fateful encounter with Rastus Russell six and a half years earlier.

After initially showing signs of recovery, Judy wanes. Thelma notices that Judy never smiles or laughs. Then, after the baby takes another turn for the worse six weeks after the attack, doctors discover that Judy has been suffering from a skull fracture the entire time. They also realize that Judy has suffered a spine injury that likely damaged her brain.

She undergoes several surgeries to repair the damage, each one filling the Crum's with hope, each one with only marginal success. Doctors are never able to completely solve the problem. Eventually, the child develops cerebral palsy related to the spine injury.

Despite the Crum's unwavering dedication to her recovery, she will never laugh, never learn to speak, and never be able to walk on her own. She will suffer a series of never-ending health problems as a result of her condition.

On Saturday morning, January 28th, 1956, 7-year-old Judy Crum dies from bronchial pneumonia related to her cerebral palsy.

Six and one-half years after his death, Rastus Russell claims his final victim.

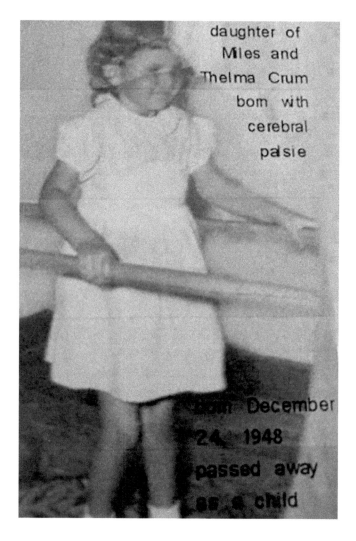

daughter of
Miles and
Thelma Crum
born with
cerebral
palsie

Born December
24, 1948
passed away
as a child

Judy Crum shortly before her death. The picture erroneously states
she was born with cerebral palsy. The child's illness developed
as a result of her injury at the hands of Rastus Russell.

1951 Photo of Orange Grove By Lake Thonotosasa near where Rastus Russell was killed. Courtesy Virginia Zagut

1951 Photo of Sefner Road Looking South. Russell was killed just over the hill from here. Courtesy Virginia Zagut

1951 Photo of Virginia Zaguts Childhood Home. Rastus Russell's Aunt Fled here on the night of August 31, 1949. Courtesy of Virginia Zagut

Contents of Russell's Trunk Found at Kill Site

Coroner Holloway Counting Bullet Wounds on Russell's Body

Coroner Ward Holloway Takes the Pulse of Rastus Russell

Deputy Sheriff Bob Spooner The Closest Thing to a Real Life John Wayne

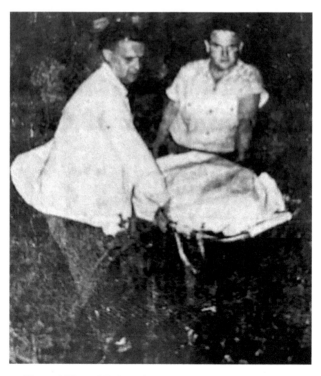

Funeral Home Workers Carry the Body of Rastus Russell

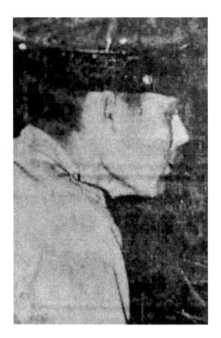

Officer Harvey Frazier

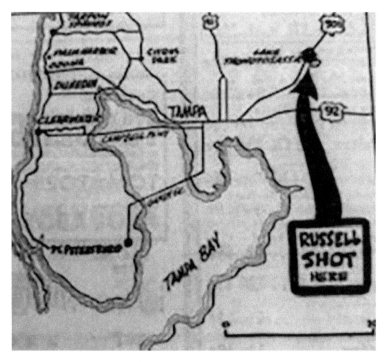

Period Map Showing Location of Russell's Death

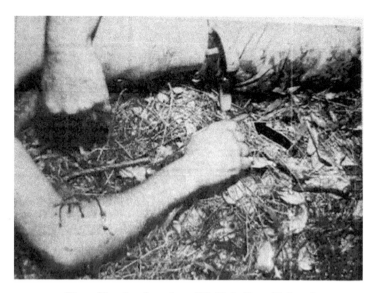

Photo Showing Location of Knife in Russell's hand

Russell Death Photo

Russell's Body

The Image of Rastus Russell will live on for years as
illustrated in this 1955 Newspaper Article

The Russell Case Dominated Local Headlines in August 1949

Epilogue

The case of Rastus Russell will go down as the most sensational manhunt in the history of Pinellas County, Florida through 1949, and possibly even to date.

Several of the old-time residents interviewed for this book reiterated the same refrain, "that is when we started locking our doors at night."

Russell will remain a reference point for future crimes and criminals for years after his sensational crime and manhunt. For years and even decades afterward, parents in Crystal Beach, Pinellas, and Hillsborough Counties coax their children into the house at dusk by warning, "Night is when Rastus comes out."

With the death of Rastus Russell, many of the questions about his case, his whereabouts during the chase, his reason for believing the Browne's had money, his reason for robbing the Brownes, his relationship with Dorothy Jean Crain and the Crain family, his mysterious cycle of arrests and freedom, all seem to die with the man himself. It's as though the law, the media, and the community just wanted to forget it ever happened.

It would seem a cliché to say the case of Russell was an end of innocence. But the people of Pinellas County, Florida, will rapidly lose touch with the "old" Florida so many cherish. Within five years of the murder, Crystal Beach grows from forty-five homes to over 200 homes. Pinellas County shoots into an age of explosive growth. Today, Pinellas County is one of the most densely populated counties per square mile in the United States.

The legend of Rastus Russell grows over time. A local movie theatre, looking to capitalize on the criminal's notoriety, runs an ad for a new suspense movie with a headline beginning, "If you thought Rastus Russell was Scary…"

But time has a way of smoothing over harsh memories. In 1959, the murder of the Clutter family in Holcomb, Kansas is brought chillingly to life by Truman Capote in "In Cold Blood," riveting the nation.

On August 8, 1969, exactly twenty years and one day after Rastus Russell butchers Norman Browne in Crystal Beach, the Manson gang commits the most infamous murders in the history of the United States at a chateau in Los Angeles, California.

The case of Rastus Russell fades as other modern murders grab the headlines. Serial killers and mass shooters dominate the terror headlines in the new era: Gacey, Bundy, Dahmer, Columbine, Sandy Hook.

In 2005, 56 years after the murder, Adrienne Young and Little Sadie released the album *The Art of Virtue*. On it is the folk song *Rastus Russell*, an ominous ode to Russell's crime and manhunt that occurred in 1949. It seems Ms. Young had a relative in Pinellas County law enforcement that was involved in the Russell investigation and/or manhunt. Hearing the story passed down, Young became mesmerized by it, much like myself. Inspired, she penned the song. While Young takes artistic liberties with the facts, the haunting tune will forever immortalize Russell and rekindle interest in the crime more than half a century later. The song is available for free play on YouTube.[*]

It is my hope that this book will introduce this sad, frightening, and fascinating story to a new generation, much like Ms. Young did in 2005.

But for those that remember, for those that were there, they will never forget Rastus Russell.

---

[*] *We attempted to contact Adrienne Young (Ramsey) to interview for this book but were unsuccessful.*

Thelma Crum: Thelma Crum recovers from her head wound. She spends the next six and a half years helping her husband run the grocery in Crystal Beach and tending to her now-handicapped daughter, Judy. When Judy dies in 1956 as a result of her injuries sustained in the Russell attack, Thelma Crum is devasted. An interview with Michael Rodriguez, a close family friend still living in Crystal Beach (2024), reveals that Thelma was "never the same" after the death of baby Judy. Miles Crum told Mr. Rodriguez that Thelma blamed herself for Judy's injuries and spent the remainder of her days wracked with guilt. She suffered psychological issues and strange quirks, such as being radically opposed to having her photo taken. She never spoke of the attack. She was described as nice but distant. She never had another child. After moving south of Tampa Bay with Miles around 1990, she died in 2001 at age 81. She is buried alongside her husband, Miles, at Sylvan Abbey Memorial Park in Clearwater, Florida.

Miles Crum: Miles Crum, miraculously after several months, recovered from being shot point-blank in the stomach with a shotgun. The charity fund set up for him and his wife paid all of his hospital bills. He lived with a large, grotesque scar on his lower abdomen and a colostomy bag for the rest of his life. But Crum, despite his family's experience and the death of his daughter, remained defiantly cheerful. He ran the store in Crystal Beach for many years, his store becoming a landmark and fond memory of children growing up in the 1950s. He would often walk and work around the store without a shirt, given the hot climate. Children remember seeing the large scar on his belly. But they also remember the kind man who was eager to provide a popsicle and a joke. He sold the store in the 1970s but remained in the home next door, investing in rental property. In 1953, he was declared (by a group of his Crystal Beach buddies) the unofficial mayor of Crystal Beach. Crum occasionally gave interviews to the local papers in the years that follow but avoided telling his story again. In later life, he became a devout Jehovah's Witness, as did his wife. In about 1990, the Crum's sold their home and moved to Wimauma, Florida, southeast of Tampa. He died in 1999 at the age of 81. He is buried at Sylvan Abbey Memorial Park in Clearwater, Florida.

Pinellas County Jailers: After the death of Rastus Russell, the Pinellas County Grand Jury issued a scathing report in regard to the County Jail, its jailors, and the escape of its most infamous guest. The jury blasted the jail, determining the facility was overcrowded, unsanitary, filled with insects, mixed juvenile offenders with hardened criminals, and offered food that did not provide minimum nutritional needs. Citing jail personnel with "gross negligence" and being "stupid and disinterested," the body recommended the dismissal of head jailor Nash and assistant jailor Brian Curry. While the Grand Jury obliterated the jail staff, it praised Tucker. Citing the Sheriff's cooperation with the Grand Jury, it stated that Tucker's instructions for the jail were "sufficient for adequate and proper administration of the jail," but "these instructions had been generally ignored or loosely executed."

Tucker came to Nash's (who was on vacation at the time) defense, but the pressure grew too strong. Tucker relieved Nash of his duties at the jail but was quick to point out that the former head jailor was "still in the sheriff's department." Assistant Jailor Jack Townsend, who was off the night of the escape, leaving the newest jailor to work alone, resigned the next day. A few days later, Curry, on duty the night of Russell's escape, resigned as well. Nash made no bones about who he blamed for the escape. When asked if he had any comment to make about Townsend, he said, "No, because it would be unprintable." A new staff replaced the old in the days and weeks that followed.

Crum's Grocery: Closed in the 1970s. The Crums sold the building but remained living next door. The store became a multi-family residence, renting rooms and apartments to residents. Today, it is a single-family residence beside the post office in Crystal Beach. While the paint and windows are modern, and the front awning long gone, the building retains its original structure. In the front parking lot, one can still see the oval hole in the concrete where Crum's gas pumps once stood. The stone house beside it, where the Crums made their home, is also still standing, looking much the same as it did in 1949.*

---

* *Photo of Crum's store in early 1950s courtesy of Palm Harbor Historical Society. Photo on the right taken by author in 2024.*

The Browne (Murder) House: After the murder of Norman Browne, Anne Browne moved out of the house and never returned. She relisted the house for sale, attempting to sell the property. Ownership records are sparse, but the home was boarded up, fell into disrepair, and sat vacant for many years. Children growing up in the 1950s recall the spooky old Browne house sitting back in the woods off of Rattlesnake Road with weeds and brush growing up around it. Everyone knew what took place there. It was the kind of place teenagers dare each other to visit at night.

Wesley Henry, old-time Crystal Beach resident, describes what it was like passing the house as a boy growing up in Crystal Beach.

"Have you ever heard the saying 'Whistling past the graveyard?'" he asks jokingly.

At some point, possibly in the late 1960s, the home was purchased and renovated. The house was lifted off its foundation and turned so that the front door faced a different direction (possibly to give the larger windowed side the best view of the water.) The new owners gave the house a new outer shell, pasting over the old chipped white paint with pink asbestos tile. They demolished the old garage. It is unknown how long they remained in the house.

In 1988, after a developer bought the property and surrounding land, the house was demolished to make room for a new development. Today, a modern-looking single-story home with a swimming pool sits on the former site of the Browne's home.

The Robert Cotton House: Robert Cotton's house, where Thelma and Miles Crum fled after being attacked, remains on Vincent Street on Crystal Beach. It remains much the way it looked in 1949. It has been well cared for and is a magnificent example of the typical house in Crystal Beach in the 1940s.[*]

Lipsey's Shell Station: Robbed by Rastus Russell in the early morning of August 31, 1949, the Palm Harbor building remains today, operating as McBee's Garage. The building is located just east of the Pinellas Trail on Pennsylvania Avenue.

Raleigh Allen's Grocery Store: It is no longer in existence. However, the church across the street where deputies searched in vain for Rastus Russell is still there, much the way it looked in 1949. It sits

---

[*]   *2024 Photo.*

about 100 yards off the road near the intersection of Gunn Highway and Racetrack Road in Citrus Park, Florida.

Blue Sink: This hundreds-foot-deep natural spring, which was a favorite swimming hole for decades and where Rastus Russell supposedly sunk a stolen car, is still present in Palm Harbor. But its glory days are long over. The water hole is now on private property, fenced off from the public, and overgrown with brush and moss. Public swimmers are a liability for its owners.

The Old Clearwater Jail: Was closed in the Spring of 1950 when the new jail opened across the street. Construction of the new jail was accelerated as a result of Rastus Russell's escape, with new escape-proof features added after the high-profile incident. The "new" jail was used until 1979 when today's modern Pinellas County Jail was opened on 49th Street in Clearwater. The jail built in 1949/50 became an administrative building for the courthouse and remains in use today. The "old" jail from which Rastus Russell escaped was used for archive storage for a while until it was demolished. Today, a "Rebel" Gas Station sits on the corner lot where Russell's jail cell once stood. *(Photo courtesy of Tampa-Hillsborough Public County Library System.)*

The Old Pinellas County Courthouse: Where Rastus Russell was ordered out of the state by Judge Bird, where the Crain's were interrogated, and where Todd Tucker appeared before the grand jury, remains in service today. Built in 1917, the downtown Clearwater building is a remarkable example of early 20th-century architecture. The massive, dark wood courtroom inside is breathtaking. The building offers tours to those who arrange one ahead of time.

The Sam Crain Home: Formerly located on Curlew Creek Road (Now Curlew Road) in Palm Harbor, the house was demolished in the 1960s. Today, a modern housing development sits on the spot. However, Curlew Creek, where Rastus Russell taught Wilburn Crain to swim, remains on the South Side of Curlew Road.*

Maude McCord's Home: Formerly located at 914 Louisiana Avenue in Tampa, the home no longer stands. It was replaced by a new home in the 1990s when a new development was built.

---

*   *Photo courtesy Crain Family.*

Rastus Russell Kill Site: The site where Rastus Russell was killed was an orange grove and swamp in 1949, the grove owned by Russell's own Baker family. Today, the site is in the middle of a massive strawberry field held by private owners. Seffner Road is now called Kingsway Road. The kill site is about three-quarter mile west of Kingsway Road. Thonotosassa is still very much a rural community, the vibe of "Old Florida" still present in its pleasant country roads. The Baker family legacy remains as well, with both a Baker Creek and Baker Boat Launch near the lake.

Mrs. Anne Browne: Browne spent some time living with her daughter at an apartment in Dunedin in 1949. She also spent some time living with the Crum family after the murder of her husband, helping Thelma Crum run the store. The Browne's daughter, Elizabeth (aka "Betty,") was a model in New York City at the time of the murder.

It is unknown where Mrs. Browne spent the immediate years after the murder, but she never returned to the house on Rattlesnake Road. She did, however, visit Crystal Beach, returning to visit the Crums. In an interview given several weeks after the murder of her husband, Mrs. Browne gives her philosophy on life:

"I am not a pessimist. I realize I may live for many years. My mother died at 84 and I have a strong constitution, similar to hers. She always looked on the bright side of life and if a person broke an arm she would say, 'it might have well been a neck.' I want to make the most of the years left by being a Christian and doing what is right."

But she also adds, *"The memory of that horrible Sunday cannot ever be erased."**

Linda Henry, a long-time Crystal Beach resident and a child at the time of the murder, remembers Anne Brown visiting in the years following the crime. She remembers seeing the deep scar still visible on Mrs. Browne's left wrist. Eventually, Anne Browne moved to Rutland, Vermont, to live with her daughter. Elizabeth Browne died at the age of 44, presumably of a barbiturate overdose. Anne Browne lived out her years in Vermont, dying in 1985 at the age of 97. She is buried in Vermont.

Norman Young Browne, is buried in the Dunedin Cemetery on August 11, 1949. His headstone remains there today, with the words "REST IN PEACE UNCLE." Despite a search, we were unable to determine the niece or nephew who posted the eternal epitaph.

---

* *Clearwater Sun, September 9, 1949.*

Walter H. Carey, Sr: The Pinellas County Constable who relent-lessly pursued Russell until his capture on the Dunedin Flats and then helped track the fugitive after his escape from jail, remained a constable until 1965, when he retired. The constable's office was phased out a few years later and absorbed by the Pinellas County Sheriff's Office. Carey was a popular constable, having been reelected five times. He worked many cases with friend Todd Tucker after the Rastus Russell event, including a fatal shooting that took place at the home of Furrell Crain (Dorothy Crain's brother) in 1961 (Crain was not home at the time.) Carey received two letters of commendation from FBI Director J. Edgar Hoover, one commending the constable for his apprehension of a fugitive (I was unable to confirm if this was Russell) and another upon his retirement. In 1964, he received the Outstanding Citizen of the Year award from the Tarpon Springs Moose Lodge for public ser-vice rendered to the community. After retiring, Carey spent his summers at a second property he owned with his wife near Franklin, NC. Carey passed away on December 12, 1988, at the age of 86, in Tarpon Springs. He is buried at Cycadia Cemetery in Tarpon Springs, FL, alongside his wife, Isadora.

Sam Crain: After Rastus Russell was killed, police discovered more stolen articles in Russell's "room" at the Crain home. Sheriff Tucker was meticulous in returning the items, most minor, to their owners. The Crains moved back into the house. One month later, Flora Crain gave birth to the couple's eighth child, Gary. The family moved out sometime in 1951/52 when Sam Crain bought a house on Oak Street in Clearwater. There, Crain enjoyed woodworking in his spare time but remained feisty. One day, becoming angry at someone or something, Crain stormed out his front door with a shotgun and shot a limb off the tree in his yard. In 1956, Dorothy built a house on the same street. Sam remained a citrus worker but took a new job with Hood's Packing Plant in Dunedin, FL, likely coinciding with his move to Clearwater (the Pasco Packing Plant provided the house on Curlew Creek Road.) In 1964, Sam and Flora Crain, both 57, divorced. In my 2024 interview with Gary Crain, he said Sam "left" his mother. Sam moved to Trinity, Texas, where he would live for the rest of his life. However, he would remain close to his family. Staying true to his nature, Crain got in a bar fight in Texas at the age of 91. When asked who won, he replied, "Well, I did."

"He was a little guy," said son Gary, "But no one could push him around.""

When Sam Crain died in 2002 at the age of 94, his body was returned to Florida. He is laid to rest next to his ex-wife, Flora, who died in 1991 at the age of 85. Both are buried at Serenity Gardens Memorial Park in Largo. **

---

*   *From 2024 Interview with Gary Crain.*
**   *Photos courtesy of Crain family.*

Dorothy Jean Crain: According to Wilburn Crain, after spending several weeks in California with James Blue, Dorothy decided that she "didn't want to be with him" and returned home to Florida in late 1949. She then began dating James Ross Milner of Tulare, California. On August 15, 1950, Dorothy and Milner were married in Pittsburg County, Oklahoma. It is unclear of how or where she met Milner or how they came to be married in Oklahoma. On March 17, 1951, Dorothy gave birth to her first and only child, a daughter. Despite her brush with darkness and notoriety, Dorothy went on to live a mostly normal life, making every effort to put the entire event behind her. In fact, when I interviewed her youngest brother, Gary, he had never heard of Rastus Russell or anything having to do with this story. Dorothy, Sam, Flora, nor any of the elder siblings, had ever mentioned it to the younger ones – ever. When I requested an interview with Dorothy's daughter, she declined, pointing out that this was a painful event in her mother's life, and she did not wish it to be dragged up again. She herself was only made aware of it in the mid-1990s when the St. Petersburg Times published a retrospective piece about the story.

Dorothy divorced James Milner in 1952. Sometime around 1955, Dorothy married George White. White adopted Dorothy's daughter. In 1956, Dorothy and White built a house on Oak Street in Clearwater, just a few doors down from her parents. It is here she would spend the rest of her life. Siblings remember Dorothy visiting often and many family gatherings. Like many in her family, she was a music lover. Her favorite was country. Her brothers, Gary and Wilburn, played guitar. Dorothy invited them often to play at her house, the girl joining in on the impromptu concerts.

Sometime after 1962, Dorothy and White divorced.

In 1968, Dorothy marries Robert "Bobby" McCorcle, whom she described as "the love of her life." In 1981, they, too, divorced, but Dorothy kept his last name. There is evidence that McCorcle continued to play a role in her life afterward.

In the 1970s, Dorothy took up painting. Watching Bob Ross became one of her favorite pastimes. She turned out to be a gifted artist. Later, she expanded to different crafts, including making cards, dolls, and doll's clothes and some even sold online. Her later years appear to be well spent, surrounded by family, friends, and grandchildren. One of her favorite foods was peanut butter and honey on toast.

On March 15, 2023, Dorothy Jean (Crain) McCorcle passed away at the age of 91. Her remains are cremated.

Gary and Diane Crain are fortunate enough to inherit some of Dorothy's belongings. With boxes of old photographs, household items, arts and craft supplies, and keepsakes, they found not a hint of their relative's wild encounter in the Spring and Summer of 1949 – as though she had, understandably, completely erased it from her life's record.

And then, at the bottom of a box, still in a glass picture frame, they found one single item.

The February 1950 cover of *True Experiences* magazine is inside, preserved in time, 16-year-old Dorothy's face gracing the cover. It includes the article teaser "*HE HELD ME PRISONER – Dorothy Jean Crain's harrowing story of escape from a killer's love.*" (*Photos courtesy of the Crain family*)

Sheriff Walter Todd Tucker: In addition to being the lead figure in the pursuit of Rastus Russell, Todd Tucker's legacy as Sheriff would be "modernizing" the agency. Tucker is credited with adding a Central Records and Identification Bureau, the building of the new jail, and starting the department's first in-car radio system (a tool they did not possess during the hunt for Russell.) The pursuit of Russell, with its ultimate outcome, elevated Tucker's profile in the law enforcement community (this despite Tucker running the jail from which Russell escaped.) In 1951, he was elected president of the Florida Sheriff's Association. He also served as vice president of the National Sheriff's Association. In early 1952, presumably at the top of his game, Tucker announced he would not seek reelection as Sheriff. Only a few days later, on January 10, 1952, his wife, Nellie May Tucker, died of natural causes at the couple's Largo home. It is unclear as to whether the Sheriff's career announcement was related to the health of his wife. Four months later, in May of 1952, Tucker married his second wife, Pura, in Valdosta, GA. Shortly afterward, he hired his new stepson, Thomas Adcock, as a deputy sheriff. Adcock goes on to a successful career in law enforcement. Tucker's 27-year career in Pinellas County Law Enforcement came to an end in 1953 with his retirement. He was 54 years old.

Tucker and his new wife spent the next several years at their ranch in Largo, where the former Sheriff raised cattle. Both Tucker and Pura brought children and grandchildren to the marriage. In 1960/61, the couple moved to a waterfront home on Lake Tarpon in Tarpon Springs, Florida. Here, Tucker enjoyed spending time with his grandchildren, fishing, and sipping a cold beer and/or cigar when the situation warranted.

But the good times were short-lived. In September of 1961, Pura Tucker died at the age of 63. Sometime afterward, Tucker moved back to St. Petersburg, the town where he grew up. The former Sheriff remained active in civic organizations, becoming a 32nd-degree Mason and serving as a member of the Elks, Shriners, and American Legion, amongst many others. In 1969, Todd Tucker died in St. Petersburg at the age of 70.

Maude Baker McCord: After taking in her troubled nephew and dealing with the traumatic aftermath of his death, the widow continued to work into her late 60s. She worked as a stenographer and book-keeper at a small general store in Tampa. McCord died in Tampa on December 27, 1963, at the age of 81. She is buried at the Thonotosassa Cemetery, close to her sister, Claude Estelle Baker McCoy.

Paul O'Brien Baker died in Chicago on the 28th of February, 1958. He was 63 years old. Little more could be found on Mr. Baker for this book. For now, his relationship with his nephew, any contact they had in Chicago, or his appearance on a 1920 Census as Rastus Russell's "father" remains a mystery.

Claude Estelle Baker McCoy: Claude Estelle's tombstone in the Thonotosassa Cemetery is shared with her sister, Celestia, who died the same year, 1942. The stone is prominent in the old and tiny graveyard, bordered by an iron fence. The grave is surrounded by several members of the Baker family. One can almost picture a dirty and bloodied Rastus Russell standing in front of it, bidding her farewell before he makes his run for the state line.

Hillsborough County Sheriff's Deputy Bob Spooner: A dedicated student to his craft, Spooner was fascinated with criminal psychology and interrogation techniques. He attended a school in Chicago to learn how to operate a lie detector test. When he returned, he was promoted to first assistant criminal deputy to Tampa's Sheriff Culbreath. In December of 1950, barely a year after felling Rastus Russell in a Thonotosassa orange grove, Spooner was offered the job of Police Chief in nearby Plant City. It was a natural fit for Spooner. Plant City was not only where he made his home, it was also where he began his career in law enforcement. The job would also reunite him with his colleague and the only other officer to participate in the Russell shooting, Harvey Frazier. Spooner enthusiastically accepted. He began the job on January 1, 1951, and immediately went to work in upgrading the department of twelve officers. With Spooner's accounting training at the FBI Academy, he overhauled the department's finances, which were in a sorry state when he assumed command. He reduced officer hours to eight-hour shifts, gave them one day off per week, and ordered summer clothes to "get them out of those fourteen-ounce serge pants." Spooner proved to be a popular chief in and out of the department. He went on to serve 22 years, longer than any other chief since the department received its charter in 1927. When asked about Spooner later, former Plant City Police Captain James Watsun, sums it up as "He was just an all-around good man."*

Spooner retired in 1973 and enjoyed a long retirement. He helps organize Plant City's Little League program and becomes active in organizing American Legion Baseball. He is a passionate outdoorsman and spends much of his time hunting and fishing. In 1995, Spooner

---

*   *Photos courtesy Plant City Photo Archives.*

and his wife, Anna, moved to Anderson, SC. Spooner passed away there on April 21, 1998, at the age of 86.

In his later years, a family member asked him if he'd ever regretted shooting Rastus Russell in 1949.

"No," Spooner answered. He said he never had a second thought about it.

"There wasn't any debate in his mind about whether he did the right thing," said a family member.

Officer Harvard M. "Harvey" Frazier: Nine months after his colleague Bob Spooner was hired as his boss, Harvey Frazier left the department and became a Hillsborough County Sheriff's Deputy. It is unclear when or why he left the Plant City Police. His relationship with Spooner is also unclear. In my interview with a Spooner family member, he hinted (although did not overtly state) that Spooner felt Frazier fired too soon on Russell. Within ten weeks of the Russell shooting, Officer Frazier would be involved in two more shootings. The first took place on October 19, 1949, and was eerily similar to the Russell shooting. An ex-convict accused of shooting a policeman was on the run through the swamps and scrubs east of Tampa. A posse of over 200 armed officers and citizens chased him for three days. Frazier was on the case, and so was Flip. They tracked the alleged shooter to an orange grove near Bartow, Florida. Frazier and Lakeland Officer Carl Purvis shot the suspect as he charged from behind a tree with an open knife.

Less than three weeks later, Frazier and fellow Plant City Officer William Meredith returned fire at a robbery suspect that shot through the windshield of their cruiser.

After Frazier's hiring at the Sheriff's Department, he seemed to disappear from public view. It is unknown how long he remained a deputy, but there are no further mentions of him in the records that I could find. All we have that I am hesitant to present here is an unsubstantiated claim by an old-time resident of Palm Harbor, Mr. Ralph Jones.

Mr. Jones was a teenager at the time of the Russell case and participated in one of the posse's hunting the fugitive. Jones told me that an extended relative of his was married to "one of the officers that shot Russell." He told me that this officer had struggled with the memory of the shooting and had a "really hard time." He said this officer eventually spent time in a mental institution because of it. Because we know Spooner spent the next 22 years as Plant City Police Chief, it leaves only the possibility that, if true, the officer would have been Frazier. Given Frazier seems to have dropped out of sight after 1951, the window of speculation can remain open. But it is an admittedly big window. The only other clue we have to Frazier's life after 1949 is his obituary. Frazier died on May 23, 1994, at the age of 73. His obituary listed him as "self-employed in the citrus and nursery business." It also listed his Army service in World War II. Curiously, it makes no mention of his career in law enforcement.*

Dunedin Flats: The Dunedin Flats were dredged in the early 1950s. While this provided a deep-water channel for larger-keeled boats, the silt it produced virtually destroyed the flats for scalloping. With the sand and silt scooped from the bottom, dredgers created a series of equally spaced artificial islands between the Flats and Honeymoon Island. If Rastus Russell were to attempt to swim away today, he would

---

* *From 2024 Interview with Ralph Jones.*

have a much closer island in which to swim – not that it would do him much good. The islands are tiny and consist mainly of thick mangroves. For a good view of the area in which Russell was captured, visit the current location of Ozona Blue, a bar and restaurant that overlooks the former Dunedin Flats in Ozona, Florida. Today, this water body is known as Smith Bayou. George's Marina, where Rastus Russell was brought ashore for his famous photograph exiting the water, is still in operation today as a private marina.*

Barlow's Filling Station: The building where officers and armed citizens from around Tampa Bay swarmed before setting off to capture Rastus Russell was for many years known as Marvin's Garage, a car repair service. Today, the building houses Big Time Carts, a Golf Cart sales and service business. In Palm Harbor, Crystal Beach, and Ozona, golf carts are one method residents use to travel about, ensuring plenty of business for the current occupants. The building sits on US Alternate 19 North (known as "Old" US 19 in 1949) and Florida Avenue in Palm Harbor. Across Florida Avenue sits a Mobil gas station, the building that was once Pop Stansel's service station. It was here that a teenaged Rastus Russell was known to steal bottles of Yoo Hoo from the drink machine. He likely pilfered from Barlow's as well.**

---

*   *2024 Photographs.*
**   *2024 Photo.*

Crystal Beach: Today, Crystal Beach remains a thriving community. The hidden seaside treasure offers a mix of modern, high-end homes with enough of the old-time buildings and cottages to retain its historic character. Sadly, in September of 2024, just as this book was going to publication, Hurricane Helene blew past Pinellas County, driving an eight-foot storm surge onto its shores. Crystal Beach is devastated with many of its historic homes virtually destroyed by the floodwaters. The area will eventually rebuild and recover. But many of the homes and buildings that would be recognized by Anne Browne, Miles Crum, or Rastus Russell, will likely be gone.

John Calvin "Rastus" Russell: The mysteries of Rastus Russell's journey from maladjusted boy to mischievous teen to murderous criminal are many after his death. From his series of escapes from punishment, his relationship with the Browne's, the mystery of his true father, his "lost" years spent in the Midwest, his other "wife" in Indiana, his relationship with the Crain family and his two-month disappearance with Dorothy Jean Crain, some questions about the infamous criminal may never be answered. Most who knew the answers took them to their graves.

In the weeks following Russell's death, Pat Murphy of the St. Petersburg Times interviewed Dr. Herbert D. Williams, a clinical psychologist. While Williams had never met Russell, he believed Russell was a psychopath, or as he put it, had a "psychopathic personality." But he did not believe Russell was insane.

He cited Russell's feelings of rejection stemming from early childhood. He explained that a psychopath is often one who grows up in a rejecting environment, feeling neglected and unloved. He cited Dorothy Jean Crain's claim that Russell told her his mother was "always too busy to bother with him" when he was a child.

But until he was ten, Russell grew up in a home with his mother, grandmother, and several aunts and uncles. At first, it seems strange to imagine the boy feeling rejected in such a familial environment. But when one considers the fact that Russell was possibly a child born out of wedlock and likely possessing a darker complexion than the rest of the predominantly Irish Bakers, it is possible the boy experienced disapproval from relatives. This could have either caused his early malfeasant behavior or exacerbated it.

As a single mother working to maintain a boarding house, perhaps Russell's mother did not have much time to spend with him. With the absence of a father, a mother consumed with earning a living, and a family that could have (at least some of them) scorned him and his mother, it is not difficult to imagine the boy feeling alienated.

Dr. Williams also cites Russell's glandular imbalance at a young age as contributing to his disorder.

Williams went on to explain that a psychopath has "no capacity for affection nor ability to relate himself to other people. He is incapable of feeling remorse, love, or pity. Self-centered, he is able to see no reason to deny himself anything."

Williams concluded that the best thing that could have been done with Russell would have been to lock him up for life, for the protection of society.

This is not a psychology book, and I am not a psychologist. But based on spending a year studying Rastus Russell, I believe the "Jekyll/Hyde" syndrome floated by staff doctors at Chattahoochee during Russell's stay there may better describe Russell's condition. The clinical name for this today is *disassociated identity disorder*. The condition is described as the same person having two individual personalities, one good and one evil. This diagnosis would go a long way toward explaining many of Russell's actions.

In other words, inside Russell's body, there could have been the normal and decent "John," the one who loved his mother and taught Wilburn Crain to swim, and the evil "Rastus," who bullied, robbed and beat other people and ultimately killed Norman Browne.

After Rastus Russell was cremated on September 3, 1949, his ashes were released to his Aunt Maud McCord. There is no official mention of what happens to them after that.

However, in my interview with Virginia Zagut of Thonotosassa, I was provided with excerpts from an old, since defunct blog about Thonotosassa history, maintained by several since passed old-timers. The blog cites an official Thonotosassa website (also no longer viable) stating that Rastus Russell's ashes are buried at the Thonotosassa cemetery, the same cemetery as his mother and other family members.[*]

The citation all but confirmed a suspicion I had since visiting the cemetery in June of 2024. Amongst the graves of Claude Estelle Baker McCoy, Maud McCord, Paul O'Brien Baker, and Celestia Baker are three tiny square stones. Each has only the letter "B" on top. I presumed this stood for Baker. One sits in front of the grave of Claude Estelle Baker McCoy. It is very easy to imagine Maud McCord laying her nephew's ashes next to his beloved mother, marking the spot with a simple, anonymous stone to avoid publicity or souvenir seekers (with the other stones perhaps marking the ashes of other unnamed family members.)

It seems the logical place to lay him to rest and reunite John Calvin Russell with his beloved mother.

---

[*]   *Thonotosassafla.com – This is no longer a functioning website.*

Afterword

It has been over a year since I chose to dive down the Rastus Russell rabbit hole, travel back 75 years in time, and try to unravel a story that horrified my community for a long, long time. Every old-time resident who contributed to this book seemed to know a tiny little corner of the story. None knew the whole thing. Many provided hearsay, rumor, legend, and outright falsehood. Others provided fascinating insight and memories.

Madman started out to be a straight out-of-the-box true crime action story: The crime, the bad guy, the chase, the kill.

In researching and writing this book, the story began to feel like anything but a straight-up good vs. bad story. Instead, it became more of an examination of human nature itself – with everyone and everything being called into question - nothing or no one being 100% good or bad.

In real life, everything comes in shades of gray and uncertainty.

In the Rastus Russell story, despite the local legends, songs and myths, there is a hell of a lot of unanswered questions.

One of the strangest phenomena that I experienced as an author was one of virtual time travel. In reading through mountains of newspaper articles, photos, and interviews, I began to become so familiar with the characters, it was though I was there, knowing them as they were in 1949.

It was, therefore, a strange sensation when I found 91-year-old Dorothy Jean Crain, a person I had known only as a 16-year-old, pig-tailed mystery, living in Clearwater. She died six months before I began researching this book. But seeing a photo of a 91-year-old Dorothy was a fascinating reality check of sorts. My one regret in writing this book is that I did not begin it a year earlier, before she passed away. I like to think she would have sat and talked to me, revealed her secrets, and told me what really happened. She, if anyone, likely knew the whole story. May she rest in peace.

John Calvin Russell was a criminal through and through, probably a psychopath and, ultimately, a killer. At the same time, when the monster is asleep, we see a human side to him. A friend, a son who loves his mother, a mentor, teaching a boy to swim or fix a car. As a criminal, we also see flashes of mercy in the monstrosities he commits. He allows Mrs. Browne to fetch first aid for her husband. He spares Mrs. Browne's life when he easily could have snuffed it out – the one live witness to his horrific murder. After his arrest, Russell is quick to take all the blame for his crimes (with the exception of the Browne's murder and maiming) and make clear that his "wife" Dorothy had nothing to do with them. This is not to say Russell did not deserve what he got. But even the worst human beings are still human on some level.

On the surface, the Brownes seem like innocent, helpless, retirees. Perhaps they were. And perhaps they weren't. Is Wilburn Crain's jewelry store story and the other rumors that circulated through Palm Harbor at the time true? Did Rastus Russell really just show up at their door randomly at 6:30 on a Sunday morning? And if so, why was he so convinced the Brownes had money hidden in the house?

Also intriguing is the Crain's involvement with Russell. While Sam Crain tells the media of his frightened family living in terror of Russell, Crain and his sons do not seem to be the type who were easily intimidated

Are any of the Crain's involved in any of Russell's crimes, car thefts, or robberies? On the night before Lester Lambert was kidnapped, a robbery occurs at a nearby juke joint by a man with a sawed-off shotgun. He is accompanied by two accomplices. One report says two men. Another says a man and a woman. At the time, Sheriff Tucker was extremely interested in asking Furrell and Dorothy Crain about this crime.

There is the matter of the burning car found in the woods behind the Crain's home, around the same time as the murder of Browne.

There is the two-month disappearance of Russell with Dorothy, and then the seemingly seamless reintegration of the two into the family upon their return.

Sam Crain also makes conflicting statements about the night of the murder, first saying he watched as Russell unloaded shotguns into his car in Tampa, then claiming the first time he saw the guns were in Russell's room at his house. Grove worker friends of Russell claim *they* were the ones who helped Russell unload the car the night of the murder. Yet Crain mentions no one else at the scene.

If Rastus Russell did indeed kidnap Crain's daughter, as Crain claims, why does he still have a "room" at the Crain house, eat dinner, and joke with the Crains? Why does Russell trust the Crains to take him scallop fishing the day after he commits a vicious murder?

Is it possible that the Crain family ignored or even participated in petty crime with Russell, but when it crossed the line to murder, Sam Crain had to intervene? Or, should we accept Sam and Dorothy Crain's stories at face value, that they were terrified of Russell and did everything he said? After all, there are many, including some of Russell's past co-workers, who indeed describe themselves as terrified of the convict. These are secrets that Dorothy, Sam, Ferrell, and Allan took to their graves.

This brings us to the reporters covering the stories. Reporting in the 1940s is more exciting than it is today, often infused with dramatic effect. Sometimes, facts are stretched, assumed, or inferred to better enhance the dramatic effect of the story. That being said, why were the questions asked above not asked at the time?

Once Russell was dead, everyone seemed content to let the matter rest and go back to their lives. To the extent Rastus Russell touched the lives of those involved, it could simply be a case of everyday people getting in over their heads with a person who seemed normal, charismatic, or even exciting until he turned monstrous.

An Author's Wild Theories

My primary motivations for writing this book were twofold. One was to tell this fascinating true story, not only to an older generation that may know it only in hearsay and myth, but to a new generation with a passion for historical crime stories. Secondly, and more importantly, it was to learn the truth about what really happened, not only for you, the reader, but for myself. Unfortunately, I was only partially successful in the latter.

I have, however, after nearly a year of studying Rastus Russell and the facts of the story as we know them, concocted some of my own theories.

These theories, one of which I have shared below, are based on numerous strange circumstances that continue to revolve around this historical story.

Inconsistencies and Mysteries

It is all but certain that Rastus Russell did not target the Browne's randomly on August 7, 1949. Anne Browne is the only living witness to describe the events of that day before the Crums arrived on scene. If the Browne's did owe "a debt" of some sort, especially of an illicit nature, she would likely be loath to admit it.

I wanted to give the old couple the benefit of the doubt. But in the end, there were just too many strange stories, mysteries, and inconsistencies for me to believe the story as Anne Browne told it. Taken individually, they may not amount to much. Taken together, they arouse considerable suspicion. Let's examine them.

1. The often-repeated rumor by locals that the Brownes owed a "debt" and Russell was there to collect, either for himself or on behalf of somebody else. Wilburn Crain's story learned from his father, Sam Crain, involving a jewelry store heist is particularly intriguing, especially given the detail Crain provided.

2. Russell's mysterious first visit to the Browne home three months earlier, acknowledged by both Browne and Russell. Anne Browne provides inconsistent and changing explanations for this, at first saying he was there to repair a pump, then that his car needed water, then that he was there to look at the house.

3. The timing of this first visit. This was the approximate time that Rastus Russell left with Dorothy Jean Crain, returning only a couple of weeks before the murder.

4. Russell's comments that he "knew the Brownes" and there was "a lot he could say" but would not discuss it until he secured a lawyer.

5. Russell spending three hours in the Browne's home drinking coffee and chatting, even driving Norman Browne to "get a newspaper" before pulling a shotgun on them.
6. Anne Browne's claim that despite Russell's visit three months earlier and a three-hour coffee chat at her table, she did not know his name, claiming "he didn't say."
7. Russell leaving the Browne's home for at least 90 minutes to drive to Tampa and back, with the Brownes tied in the garage.
8. Russell's utter *conviction* that there was money in the house, despite the fact that the Browne's gave every outer appearance they were people of limited means.
9. Russell's comments to the portrait sales lady on the Saturday before the murder that he would have "plenty of dough" come Monday.
10. Dorothy's comment that on Sunday night after the murder, that Russell had returned with "a lot of money."
11. Norman Y. Browne remarrying his first wife a scandalous 77 days after the death of his second.
12. Russell's supposed three-month, cross-country trip with Dorothy Crain. Such a journey, even in 1949, would require considerable capital.

How it *Could* Have Happened

The following is a piece of purely speculative fiction. But the speculation is based on assembling the known facts and making some possible, if not logical, connections between them.

The story goes like this:

The Brownes are somehow involved, whether as owners, partners, investors, or otherwise, in a jewelry store somewhere in the Midwest or Northeast. In financial straits, the two become involved, possibly with a third or more parties, in an insurance scheme to rob the store, collect the insurance money, and then sell the "stolen" jewels to a wholesaler, thereby collecting twice.

Rastus Russell, either through connections in the Midwest or Palm Harbor, is recommended as the man to do the robbery.

Russell does the job sometime in late Spring of 1949. In May, he visits the Browne's, delivering the jewels as promised.

The Brownes, or the third party, give Russell a "deposit" on his agreed-upon fee, promising to deliver the lion's share when the insurance check is issued.

Russell, flush with cash, departs on a cross-country trip with his sweetheart, Dorothy Jean Crain.

But after a couple of months, the cash is gone. Russell returns to Palm Harbor, expecting his windfall will be delivered any day.

The two return to the Crain's where Dorothy begs her father not to press charges against Russell. Russell convinces Crain that his intentions are honorable -or- that the two actually are married. Crain relents.

Russell has made the girl big promises.

Out of money and still waiting for his insurance payout from the Browne's, Russell embarks on a series of crimes for money, robbing Lester Lambert, possibly W.J. Graham, as well as other stores and "juke joints" throughout the area.

But when the Brownes keep delaying Russell's payment, legitimate reason or not, the convict is either instructed by the third party or decides himself to collect the debt.

He schedules a meeting with the Brownes for Sunday, August 7th, to negotiate a settlement. Russell is expecting the Brownes will give him what they owe, or at least enough to appease him (or his employer.)

This is not a random robbery. It is obvious Russell has that date marked on his calendar, and is expecting to have money afterwards. He tells the portrait saleslady at Maud McCord's front door he will "have plenty of dough" on Monday. Russell believes he will get his money, one way or the other. He steals a car for the visit, just in case things get rough and he needs to get away without being identified.

He arrives and the trio spends three hours discussing the situation, negotiating. Russell and Browne then leave, perhaps to retrieve some of the jewels or cash for Russell – *not* a newspaper. But it's not enough for Russell. And when Browne tells Russell that's all he gets for now, Russell pulls a shotgun on him.

Convinced there is more money or jewels hidden in the house or elsewhere, Russell ties the couple up and demands to know where it is.

When the Brownes tell Russell they don't have it, Russell threatens to reveal the whole scheme to police.

"I'll keep the Sonofabitch quiet!" screams Norman Browne.

Infuriated, Russell stabs Browne to death.

Russell turns his attention to Anne Browne. But after Browne watches her husband die and endures repeated beating and cutting and still claims she has no money, Russell believes her. No amount of money is worth dying for, he reasons. If she knew, she surely would have told *by now*. Russell gives up, spares her life, and leaves with a threat. Anne Browne knows nothing.

Or does she?

Perhaps, after watching her husband die, Anne Browne *does* tell Russell where there is at least some money or jewels in the house. Russell stops his attack, takes the jewels, and threatens to kill her if she talks.

Either way, Russell has decided not to kill Mrs. Browne by the time the Crums show up.

Now feeling threatened, Russell attacks the Crums, then escapes with some amount of cash or jewels.

It is fascinating to note that Russell tries to kill both Mr. and Mrs. Crum, apparently because he doesn't want any witnesses. Yet he allows Anne Browne to live. Why? Does he believe she won't talk?

It is not unrealistic to believe that Russell left the Brownes' home with more than the $30 reported missing by Anne Browne.

Dorothy Jean Crain says Russell returned Sunday night with "a lot" of money. He pays his aunt, Sam Crain, and other debts totaling at least $60. Yet Anne Browne claims only $30 was stolen.

If Russell does secure a windfall, where does he stash it? Likely not at his Aunt Maud's. That home was searched shortly afterward by police.

But he stored the murder weapon and bloody clothes in his "room" at Sam Crains. This is another strange situation. After the murder, Crain tries to distance himself from Russell. This man supposedly kidnapped his daughter. Crain even put a warrant out for him. And yet this man still has his own room at the Crain house?

Does Russell tell Sam Crain or the other Crains that someone owed him money and that he was getting paid on Sunday? Does he promise to use it to take care of Crain's daughter?

Perhaps Crain knows Russell has secured a windfall, even believing it was legitimately owed to him. But when Crain finds out murder is involved, it all becomes too much. He turns Russell in.

But what of the money or jewels? If there was ever any at all, it is likely at the Crain house in Russell's room. Yet despite the other items found in Russell's room, no money or jewels are ever reported found by police.

Does Sam Crain or other family members decide to keep Russell's booty as compensation for dragging them into his sordid affair?

It is a stretch but not out of the question.

Russell reportedly threatens to kill Sam Crain while in prison. He may simply feel betrayed. But if Crain took his money on top of the betrayal, the drive for revenge would be particularly acute.

Coincidentally, Sam Crain quits his job at the Pasco Packing Plant less than a year later, leaving his company-provided home and buying a new house in Clearwater. This is on a packing plant worker's salary, raising eight children.*

As the author at the end of this fascinating tale, I wish I could tell you that is how it all went down. The truth is, I don't know how it went down. The only thing I can tell you for certain is this: I am about as convinced that the above scenario is how it "really" happened, as I am that the straight story described in the newspaper is how it "really" happened.

The truth likely lies somewhere in between a million different possibilities, and probably one in which you or I never even considered.

It is not my intention to soil the character or reputation of anyone involved in this story: Not Norman or Anne Browne, not any of the Crain family, not Judge Bird, not anyone in the Baker family, not anyone in law enforcement or the jail in 1949.

Where supposed facts are involved, I have presented them to you as they were presented in 1949. Where I have made reasonable assumptions, I have indicated that.

And where I have speculated or simply "wondered out loud" what might have happened, such as the excerpt in this section, I have noted that too.

---

* *To be fair, Crain's wife and sons also work. And Crain likely quits to take a new job at Huff Packing Plant in Dunedin.*

Rumors, innuendos, and legends are just that. And just because there are holes or inconsistencies in a story, it does not mean that malfeasance is a given. Memories skew after 75 years. Reporters report stories differently, talk to different witnesses, and write and quote much from memory (reporters had no personal video cameras or hand-held voice recorders in 1949.)

I have presented you here with the facts as we know them and the story as I perceive it. I will leave it to you, the reader, to make up your own mind as to what you believe.

Should more or new information come my way, I will certainly report it in a second edition of this book.

In the meantime, if you would like to correspond with me, correct me, provide more information that you may have, cuss me out for casting doubt on your ancestor or family member, float your own theory, or have credible information that may shed light on this story, I would love to hear from you. Feel free to email me at:

MadmanAuthor@gmail.com

I hope you have enjoyed reading this book as much as I have enjoyed writing it.

-M.F. Gross

Would you like to **learn and watch more** about "Madman" and the Rastus Russell case? Visit **MFGross.com** and get access to:

- **Author Videos** from actual sites featured in the book
- Video **commentary and analysis** on "Madman" with additional insights and theories on the Rastus Russell case
- Video and audio excerpts from **witness interviews**
- **Podcast interviews** with M.F. Gross about Rastus Russell and "Madman"
- **Contact and Booking Information** for M.F. Gross
- And Much More!

Access it all now at

MFGross.com

Acknowledgments

T hank you to all the individuals who shared memories, photos, stories, insights, and other information that made this book possible:

Linda Henry
Wesley Henry
Norm Atherton
Dixie Witt Ducker
Penny Cooke
Patricia Hanson Lock (Douglas)
Lawrence Douglas
Gary and Diane Crain
Wilburn "Bill" Crain
Michael Ramirez
Ralph Jones
Wally Ericson
Phil Thomson
Patricia Mastry
Spooner Family Member
Don Balaban
Tom Folsom
Virginia Zagar
Rick Carey
Susan Ranieri
Bill Polaski
Pat Polaski
Wren Gail Williams

Special thank you to those who helped me in one way or another in researching, writing and publishing this book

The Staff and Sheriff's Deputies at the Pinellas County Courthouse
Tom Edwards, Edwards Investigative Group
Alex Casano
Krista L. Troup, Divine Intel
Linda Allison Duschl, Palm Harbor Historical Society
Phyllis Kolianos, Tarpon Springs Historical Society
Seth Strickland, Gilliam Writers Group
April Troyer and the Research Team at Clearwater Public Library
Plant City Photo Archives
Patricia Landon, Heritage Village, Pinellas County
Mindstir Media
Robin Wallace Brown
James Schnur
Vinnie Luisi, Dunedin Historical Museum
Tammie – For letting me bounce my wild theories and ideas off you, and giving me outstanding feedback

And very special thank you to:

Terry Fortner and the Palm Harbor Historical Museum – Your help, contributions, resources, and encouragement spurred me to keep digging for the truth. You are the best!

About the Author

M.F. Gross is a former financial trader, podcast host and investment author. This is his first book on historical true crime. He lives in Dunedin, Florida where he indulges his passion for the state's rich history. He can be reached by email at MadmanAuthor@gmail.com.

www.ingramcontent.com/pod-product-compliance
Lightning Source LLC
Chambersburg PA
CBHW050908060825
30611CB00003B/4